Tips and Traps
for
Entrepreneurs

Tips and Traps
for
Entrepreneurs

Real-Life Ideas and Solutions for the
Toughest Problems Facing Entrepreneurs

Courtney Price

Kathleen Allen

McGraw-Hill

New York   San Francisco   Washington, D.C.   Auckland   Bogotá
Caracas   Lisbon   London   Madrid   Mexico City   Milan
Montreal   New Delhi   San Juan   Singapore
Sydney   Tokyo   Toronto

Library of Congress Cataloging-in-Publication Data

Price, Courtney H.
    Tips & traps for entrepreneurs : real-life ideas and solutions for
the toughest problems facing entrepreneurs/Courtney Price,
Kathleen Allen.
        p.   cm.
    Includes index.
    ISBN 0-07-052676-1 (alk. paper)
    1. New business enterprises—United States.   2. Entrepreneurship—
United States.   3. Business enterprises—United States—Management.
4. Venture capital—United States.   I. Allen, Kathleen R.
II. Title.
HD62.5.P654   1998
658.4'21—dc21   97-52332
                                                                 CIP

McGraw-Hill

A Division of The McGraw-Hill Companies

1 2 3 4 5 6 7 8 9 0   FGRFGR   9 0 3 2 1 0 9 8

ISBN 0-07-052676-1

The sponsoring editor for this book was Betsy Brown, the editing supervisor
was Penny Linskey, and the production supervisor was Clare B. Stanley.
It was set in New Baskerville by Victoria Khavkina of McGraw-Hill's
Professional Book Group composition unit.

McGraw-Hill books are available at special quantity discounts to use as
premiums and sales promotions, or for use in corporate training programs. For more information, please write to the Director of Special
Sales, McGraw-Hill, 11 West 19th Street, New York, NY 10011. Or contact
your local bookstore.

This book is printed on recycled, acid-free paper containing
a minimum of 50% recycled, de-inked fiber.

To our parents, Gordon and Catherine Hart, and Joseph and Ardell Rader, for inspiring us to take charge of our lives and maintain the entrepreneurial spirit that has been part of our families for generations.

Contents

Introduction   xi
Acknowledgments   xv

1. Finding Venture Opportunities   1

Current Entrepreneurial Trends   2
"Hot" Entrepreneurial Opportunities   12
How to Recognize Opportunities   25
Business Planning—The Key to Entrepreneurial Strategy   30

2. Personal Issues First   39

Personal Strategy Issue: Why Do You Want to Start a New
Business and What Do You Want from It?   40
Personal Strategy Issue: How Will Your Business Idea Affect
Your Personal Life?   41
Business Strategy Issue: How Will Your Business Strategies
Affect Your Venture?   46
Family Issues   50
How Much Risk Can You Tolerate?   52

3. Starting a Business   55

Choosing a Legal Structure   55
Protecting Your Business Interests   62
Securing a Patent   64
Securing a Trademark   67

Securing a Copyright   69
Protecting Trade Secrets   70
Invention Marketing Companies   71
Licensing Your Invention   73
Protecting the Name of Your Business   74
Finding the Right Location for Your Business   76
Getting Advice and Help from Experts   82

4. Buying an Existing Business   **93**

Buying versus Starting a Business Dilemma   93
Advantages in Buying an Established Business   94
Disadvantages in Buying an Established Business   97
Finding the Right Business   99
Conducting the Due Diligence   102
Evaluating the Business   103
Negotiating the Deal   106

**5. The Virtual Company—How to Look Big When
   You're Not**   **107**

What Is a Virtual Company?   107
Outsourcing to Compete   112
Using Independent Contractors   114
Strategic Alliances   117
Going Virtual from Home   119

6. Start-up Resources   **123**

The Debt versus Equity Financing Dilemma   123
Debt Financing   125
Equity Financing   136
Factors Affecting Use of Debt and Equity   141

7. Growing Your Business   **147**

Factors that Affect Your Company's Ability to Grow   148
Small Business Growth Strategies   150
Growing by Buying Another Business   157
Expanding Globally   158
Using the Internet to Grow   161

8. Finding Resources for Growth   **167**

Venture Capita   lists   167

Initial Public Offerings   171
Private Placements   174
Small Corporate Offering Registration   176
Mezzanine Financing   176
Bridge Financing   178
Retained Earnings   179

9. Building Customer Relationships   **181**

Guerrilla Marke*   182
Relationship Marketing   185
Relationship Marketing Techniques   186
Why You Need a Marketing Plan   188
Promoting the Company and Its Products and Services   190
Pricing the Product or Service   193

10. Employees: Your Most Valuable Asset   **195**

Why Your Company's Culture Is Important   196
Why Your Company Needs a Vision   197
Using Total Quality Management as a Strategy to Be the Best   201
The Company Is Only as Good as Its Employees   202
You Need a Human Resource Policy   204
Recruiting and Hiring Employees   205
Using Temporary Employees   209
Protecting Your Company Against Lawsuits   210
Deciding What to Pay Employees   211

**11. Creating and Managing the Processes in Your
    Company**   **215**

Understand Process by Taking a Walking Tour of the Business   216
Learn What's New in Manufacturing   217
Strive for Continuous Improvement   221
Manage Your Inventory Processes   222
Use Inventory Turnover to Stay on Top of Inventory   225
Know Your Trade Area   226
Shrinkage: The Problem of Losing Things   227

**12. Winning the Cash-Flow Game: The Key to
    Survival**   **231**

How to Figure What You Need to Start a Business   232
Do an Analysis of Cash Needs   235

Stay on Top of Accounts Receivable   238
Credit Lines and Other Short-Term Financing   238
Collecting What's Owed to You   240
Managing Your Company's Bills   242

13. Harvesting the Wealth   **245**

Going Public   246
Selling the Business   246
Merging with Another Company   248
Selling to Your Employees   249
Liquidating the Business   252
Planning for Succession   254

14. Entrepreneurs and Their Communities   **259**

Entrepreneurs Involved in the Community   259
The Entrepreneur's Scope of Concern   261
The Company Culture   266
Environmental Restraints   266
Economic Constraints   267
Common Problems   267

Index   275

Introduction

When we got together to write this book, we knew we didn't want to do another "how to start a business" book. There are so many books out there about how to recognize venture opportunities and start and operate new businesses. We wanted *Tips and Traps* to stand out from the crowd, and it occurred to us that the best way to do that was to follow our own advice and focus on the needs of the customer—you, the reader—who is always searching for quick, proven ways to solve your most pressing business problems. We wanted you to learn from our combined 40 years of experience as entrepreneurs, and the experiences of the thousands of entrepreneurs we've worked with over the years. In addition, we wanted you to be able to find this key information easily and quickly.

The Tips and Traps you'll find in this book cover key strategies and issues that all entrepreneurs need to know to operate a profitable business. As business owners ourselves, we've learned that some of the most important and useful information has come from sharing experiences with other business owners and learning from our failures. Along the way, business owners have shared their "street smarts" with us. We've added them to our growing database of tips and traps, and now we're sharing these lessons with you.

We've designed the book in such a way that you don't have to read it cover to cover to benefit from the tips and traps in it. Besides, who has time for that! Here's a look at some of what you'll find in the chapters ahead.

What's in the Book

Chapter 1: Finding Opportunity

Here you'll learn how to become more opportunistic, where to find innovative ideas for great businesses. And you'll learn about how to test those ideas in the marketplace.

Chapter 2: Personal Issues First

In this chapter you'll explore your reasons for wanting to start and own a business. You'll also learn how your personal and business strategies direct what you do with your business.

Chapter 3: Starting a Business

Starting a business is a complex process. In this chapter you'll look at issues like protecting your idea, deciding what kind of business you want and where you want to locate it, and how to get help from experts.

Chapter 4: Buying an Existing Business

In this chapter you'll learn about the pros and cons of buying an existing business as well as due diligence and issues related to valuing the business.

Chapter 5: The Virtual Company Concept

In this chapter you'll learn about how to create a virtual company and maybe make life a little easier by outsourcing, using independent contractors, and forming strategic alliances.

Chapter 6: Start-up Resources

Money is always an issue when you start a business, and entrepreneurs never have enough of it. So, in this chapter you'll learn how to tap money resources and how to finance your business using both equity and debt.

Chapter 7: Growing Your Business

Starting a business is one thing; successfully growing it is quite another. This is a critical point in a business's life so here you'll learn key strategies you can use to grow your business and some traps to watch out for.

Chapter 8: Finding Resources for Growth

Growth funding is a whole different ball game. In this chapter you'll learn about some of the creative sources for funding growth as well as pitfalls to avoid.

Chapter 9: Building Customer Relationships

If *us, you believe that the customer is the center of your business, then this will be an important chapter for looking at ways to better reach and keep your customers for a lifetime.

Chapter 10: Employees: Your Most Valuable Asset

If you choose to have employees (remember, it's possible to do business without them—see Chapter 5), you'll encounter numerous personnel problems. In this chapter you'll find key advice on how to manage and motivate a staff. Employees are your most important asset and this chapter will help you creatively invest in that asset.

Chapter 11: Creating and Managing Processes in Your Company

The processes you create to run your company are a key part of your competitive strategy, so here you'll learn some key tips and traps for setting up effective processes and systems in your business based on the best business practices.

Chapter 12: Winning the Cash Flow Game

"Cash is king" the saying goes. In this chapter you'll learn ways to manage cash—the life blood of all businesses. You'll get tips on determining start-up requirements to staying on top of accounts receivable, how to manage payables, and collect what's owed to you.

Chapter 13: Harvesting the Wealth

At some point most entrepreneurs reap the rewards of their hard work by harvesting the wealth the business has created. This chapter discusses how to plan for the harvest and gives the options you need to be aware of to make the best choice for you and your business.

Chapter 14: Giving Something Back

Today, an increasing number of businesses are started and operated to do more than just make a profit. Entrepreneurs are looking for ways to give something back to their community and to society as a whole. In this chapter you'll learn some ways that you and your business can become more socially responsible.

Gold Medal Tips and Killer Traps!

We wanted our favorite tips and traps to really stand out, so in each chapter look for the * identifying Gold Medal Tips and Killer Traps. These tips are some of the best we've found over the years, and the Killer Traps are things business owners should avoid at all costs. We hope that the tips and traps you find in this book will make your journey as a business owner an exciting and worthwhile adventure.

Courtney Price
Kathleen Allen

Acknowledgments

This book came about from the inspiration of our editor at McGraw-Hill, Betsy Brown. Betsy is an accomplished business editor who has keen insight into the business book marketplace and a special passion for entrepreneurs. She encouraged us to share our years of owner experience with manufacturing ventures, the music industry, hotels, restaurants, real estate, publishing companies, and foundations as well as the thrill of riding the entrepreneurial roller coaster with fellow business owners. Her insights and suggestions were valuable and will contribute to the success of this book.

We would also like to thank the Editing Supervisor, Penny Linskey, who was the soul of patience and understanding, having to work with our busy schedules and a tight publishing deadline.

I would like to thank my university students and the thousands of business owners who graduated from the Premier FastTrac® entrepreneurial training programs I co-developed. They shared their entrepreneurial challenges and successes with me, which made the Tips and Traps in this book richer and leading-edge. I would also like to thank the many entrepreneurs who have read my syndicated column with Scripps-Howard for the past seven years and sent me letters asking both perplexing and penetrating questions about how to start and grow their businesses. Their inquiries sent me searching for information to learn much about the new challenges they face daily. There were several people who shared their expertise or let me bounce ideas off them, such as my longtime partner and dear friend Mack Davis, co-founder of Premier FastTrac®. A few of the experts I called on were Don Margolis, patent attorney, and Ted Rice, franchising expert.

Lastly, to my entrepreneur husband, Gordy, who continues to proofread my columns and books and always contributes his entrepreneurial wisdom and ideas for this book as well as my other writings.

C. Price

I would like to thank the many students and young entrepreneurs I work with as a professor of entrepreneurship at the Marshall School of Business, University of Southern California, for providing the inspiration for all of the books I've written on entrepreneurs and entrepreneurship. I would also like to thank my colleagues at the Entrepreneur Program—Bill Gartner, who makes sure I do my research; Bill Crookston, my mentor; Ann Ehringer, Gene Miller, Debbie Esparza, and Marianne Szymanski, for all the tips and traps they've given me over the years. And I would especially like to thank the Director of the Entrepreneur Program, Tom O'Malia, who has been a tireless supporter of everything I do, even when it's crazy.

I could not accomplish what I do without the unconditional support of my entrepreneur husband, John, who has edited and contributed to every book I've written, and who continues to be the best partner I've ever had. Thank you. And to my wonderful family—Rob, Jaime, and Greg—who have had to put up with two entrepreneurial parents and all that comes with it. And to my extended family, Jon Weisner and Jennifer Kushell, who inspired me to devote my time working with young entrepreneurs, one of the best decisions I've ever made. Thank you.

K. Allen

Tips and Traps
for
Entrepreneurs

1
Finding Venture Opportunities

There are a multitude of entrepreneurial trends sweeping our country providing fertile ground for new venture creation. Many of these ventures use state-of-the-art technology by delivering sophisticated goods and services to niche markets once dominated by *Fortune* 500 companies. For example, small companies accounted for approximately 25 percent of all high-tech jobs and created more than half of all new innovations between 1990 and 1994. A 1997 study by the Entrepreneurial Research Consortium finds that more than 35 million U.S. households—roughly one in three—are involved in a new or small business. Many argue that these are small, lifestyle ventures, but they are still revitalizing the U.S. economy, employing more than half of the working population, creating more jobs than are lost in our economy through downsizing, and producing many new venture opportunities. The major entreprencurial trends impacting our economy discussed in this chapter are:

1. Expanding home-based businesses
2. Shift to information services
3. Increased outsourcing
4. New strategic alliances
5. Going global

6. More franchises

7. Newly unemployed becoming entrepreneurs

8. Retirees and seniors starting businesses

9. Persons with disabilities starting businesses

10. More women- and minority-owned businesses

Tip

To launch a successful venture, it's critical to understand the entrepreneurial environment in your industry.

Current Entrepreneurial Trends

Home-Based Businesses

Home-based businesses continue to experience rapid growth rates. New technology and dropping prices for computing power contribute to the rise of new home-based industries and entrepreneurial ventures. In 1980, when *Business Week* magazine reported six million home offices, many felt it was a passing fad. Some writers referred to it as "the illegitimate child of the business world." Some described the phenomenon as the "invisible revolution" or "quiet revolution." By the mid-1990s, however, the fad had definitely become a major trend as the figures reported ranged from 27.1 million to 41 million individuals working from home, depending how researchers defined "working at home."

In 1993, *Entrepreneur* magazine estimated that a new home-based business is started every 11 seconds, creating 8219 new jobs daily. It was reported in 1995 that the economic impact for the U.S. home-based business industry was $427 billion, with annual gross income from a home-based business ranging from under $5000 for a part-time or seasonal business to over a six figure gross income for a full-time business. In 1996 *Money* magazine published the results of a survey by the ICR Survey Research Group showing that 20 percent of U.S. home entrepreneurs reported that their businesses grossed between $100,000 and $500,000, while 14 percent paid themselves annual salaries of $50,000 to $250,000. The average full-time home-based salary ranges between $50,000 and $60,000 annually. The Department of Labor predicts the number of people working out of their homes will double by 2005.

Information Services

With all the advances in technology, businesses struggle to keep up with the capabilities of computers, databases, and information services and analysis. New information technologies, such as the Internet, require familiarity with e-mail management, distributed data systems, videoconferencing, on-line services, and electronic publishing, creating many new opportunities.

In addition, many firms are marketing and selling their goods on the Internet by opening virtual storefronts on the World Wide Web. Others are using electronic mailings, press releases, newsletters, and catalogs. In 1996, over $2 million in sales were made over the Internet for computer-related products and services, books, music, home electronics, videos, and travel and event tickets. The Sharper Image, one of the first retailers to exploit the concept of adult toys, reported sales of about $3 million from on-line transactions in 1996.

Outsourcing

Many entrepreneurs are starting new ventures by contracting with large corporations to provide services no longer provided in-house but outsourced so that these corporations can focus their attention on their core competencies. By outsourcing to small entrepreneurial companies, large corporations can better control costs, enhance quality, improve customer service, and increase productivity to maintain their competitive advantages. Typical outsourced services include computer programming, marketing, public relations, accounting, human resource management, janitorial services, travel management, temporary help, and other professional services.

Strategic Alliances

Other hybrid forms of new ventures proliferating are variations of partnerships or joint ventures as large companies contract with smaller firms. Entrepreneurs are structuring deals with the *Fortune* 500 and 100 companies as well as with suppliers and customers to reduce their marketing and R&D expenses along with personnel and other operating costs. Large companies have learned they are better off focusing on their strengths, usually marketing and distribution while relying on small suppliers for developing and introducing new technologies.

Strategic alliances make it easier for entrepreneurial firms to compete globally using marketing, distribution channels, and capital of larger firms. New collaborative partnerships capitalize on the complementary strengths of each firm while respecting their independence. See Chapter 5 for a more detailed discussion of strategic alliances.

Tip

The benefits of strategic alliances include access to new technologies, diffusing innovations rapidly, reducing R&D risks, penetrating new markets quickly, economies of scale, developing stronger customer-supplier relationships, and increasing profitability.

Going Global

Going global is a growing trend among entrepreneurs discovering that opportunities abroad have never been greater. Many founders expand their markets by exporting since the international marketplace is more than four times larger than the U.S. market. Exporting can increase sales by adding new markets or creating new applications to existing products and services. In 1993, the Commerce Department released a study of U.S. exporters showing that 96 percent of companies that sell goods abroad are small or midsize firms.

Global expansion is occurring because of falling trade barriers, improved communications, expanding markets, and the Internet. The North American Free Trade Agreement (NAFTA) is eliminating trade barriers between the United States, Mexico, and Canada and the General Agreement on Tariffs and Trade (GATT) passed in 1995, reduces and/or eliminates tariffs among 117 countries, creating more global opportunities.

According to the U.S. Department of Commerce, the hottest products for exporting include paper products, electric and electronic equipment, chemical products, apparel, industrial machinery, computers, along with agricultural and livestock products. In addition, the United States is the world's largest exporter of merchandise and services, with exports in 1996 of $612 billion and imports of $799 billion. In 1996, Canada was the United States' leading foreign market for exports, followed by Japan, Mexico, the United Kingdom, South Korea, and Germany. Capital goods, including aircraft, are the largest category of U.S. exports, followed by industrial supplies and materials, then automotive products and other nonautomotive products and then foods, feeds, and beverages. Also in 1996, U.S. exports of services accounted for nearly 3.2 percent of the nation's gross domestic product (GDP).

Projecting into the future, the Department of Commerce selected the following top 10 countries and hot markets hungry for U.S. exports who, they forecast, will double their share of world imports by 2010.

Top 10 Countries for U.S. Exports

1. The Chinese economic areas of China, Hong Kong, and Taiwan
2. India
3. The Association for Southeast Asian Nations
4. South Korea
5. Argentina
6. Brazil
7. Mexico
8. Poland
9. Turkey
10. South Africa

The collective GDP of these top 10 countries, which is currently only 25 percent of the industrialized world's, will comprise half of the GDP by 2010. These countries will be a bigger market than the European Union and Japan combined. Already, U.S. exports to these countries comprise almost 25 percent of our total exports. The high populations of these countries mean lucrative markets for entrepreneurs.

To find new venture opportunities, contact the Trade Information Center at 800-USA-TRADE, the international clearinghouse on exporting, and ask for the desk officer who specializes in your industry. If you are considering expanding overseas, a good reference is *International Business,* a 35-page booklet published by the American Institute of CPAs (800-862-4272). It discusses payment arrangements, export issues, and techniques for managing foreign currency risk and includes a list of other free or low-cost resources.

Tip

You must be able to offer a quality product or service at a competitive price and be able to distinguish your goods in the global marketplace.

Even though exporting opportunities are great, there are also risks, and not all entrepreneurs are positioned to sell abroad. For example, usually exporting should not be considered by most start-ups since it's hard enough to get a new venture profitable in the United States without adding the problems associated with exporting, such as detailed paperwork, complex procedures, and bureaucratic barriers. The initial costs of setting up an exporting arm can be substantial. You must justify exporting costs and include additional financing costs. Currency fluctuations could ruin your company. Collections can be time-consuming and expensive. Don't let the glamour appeal of going global distract you from your core business.

Trap

Some businesses aren't suited for global expansion, and doing so could undermine the future success of your venture.

Before deciding to export, take steps to determine your "export readiness." First, look internally and evaluate your firm's commitment and ability to enter into the global marketplace. Be prepared to take a long-term view of this process. Firms can be successful in attracting some international sales and distribution the first year out. But, long-term success takes more perseverance and planning for the additional time and costs involved with international transactions. To succeed in the global marketplace it is also essential to know your competitors and their strengths and weaknesses.

Ask yourself the following questions when considering going global.

1. Do you have solutions to any global problems?

2. Can you solve potential customers' problems?
3. Do you have a new market idea?
4. Do you have a tolerance for risk and frustration?
5. Do you have any contacts in foreign countries?
6. Can you form a win-win arrangement?

Explore ways of selling your goods overseas other than global expansion. You could use an export marketing or trading company or overseas distributors who are responsible for all aspects of marketing and distributing your products in their country. Take time in selecting an international partner.

Obtain assistance from export service providers to develop an international marketing plan. Contact your local chamber of commerce, state department of commerce, and the Small Business Administration (SBA). These resources have international trade experts who can assist you in researching exporting to other countries. They have many valuable publications and hold exporting conferences and expos. For more information about expanding globally, see Chapter 7.

Franchising

As the number of new franchise operations expands, so do the number of franchising business opportunities. During the 1990s, franchises accounted for nearly one-third of all retail sales. On average, about 300 businesses are franchised annually. In 1990, there were over 3000 franchise companies representing more than 500,000 outlets doing in excess of $600 billion in sales. It has been estimated that there will be over 9000 franchise companies by the end of the century, which is a growth rate of 500 franchise start-ups per year.

Franchising is an excellent strategy for successful entrepreneurs who want to expand their markets. It offers a way to grow rapidly in several geographic regions at once without the franchisor incurring the heavy costs associated with rapid growth. Likewise, it is often used as an entry strategy by potential or mid-career entrepreneurs who consider purchasing an established, successful franchise. The reason why many franchises are more successful than new start-ups is that their concept has been

proven, their market has been verified, and an operating system
has been established. They have confirmed that there are customers who will buy their products or services at a price at which
the franchisee can earn a profit. Franchising offers an established
trade name and reputation along with instant recognition in the
market area. It also eliminates many of the headaches associated
with starting a new venture from scratch and provides an opportunity to benefit from the experience, knowledge, expertise, and
support of a franchisor and fellow franchisees who have successfully tested and proven a business concept in the marketplace.
(See Chapter 4 for more detailed information.)

Successful potential franchisees perform "due diligence" and
research the franchise opportunity on their own as if they were
going to start a new business.

Trap

**Franchises are "turn-key" operations where the owner needs to
merely pay the franchisee fee, find a location, use the operating
manuals, and open up for business, and customers automatically
appear.**

In reality, the potential franchisee must undertake much investigation and up-front work, including locating a site, negotiating a
lease, finishing the space, obtaining the equipment, hiring the
staff, just as you would if you were going to start a venture.
Remember, no matter how reputable the franchise, how sound the
operating systems are, or how comprehensive the training is, the
ultimate success of a franchise venture relies on the owner. That is
why due diligence in thoroughly investigating the opportunity and
careful planning are still necessary to launch a successful venture.

Some of the hottest franchising opportunities which capitalize
on demographic, economic, and social trends are general services, business services, health and fitness, children's businesses,
and food services.

General Services.   Because of our busy lifestyles and shrinking
leisure time, coupled with the comparatively lower cost in starting a
service business, a boom is occurring in such service franchises as
cleaning, landscaping, decorating, automobile detailing and repair-
ing, laundry, shopping, and other time-saving services.

Business Services.   Corporate downsizing, reengineering, and out-sourcing have created many franchising opportunities by companies who are purchasing services once performed in-house, such as management consulting, accounting, training and development, product design, corporate travel, legal services, data processing, voice messaging, marketing, employee leasing and temporary help to name a few.

Health and Fitness.   As people live longer and want to remain young, many franchises have sprung up in fitness products and services, exercise salons, day spas, facial and skin clinics, home health care, medically-related products, prescriptions by mail, elderly travel clubs, as well as temporary help agencies for health-care workers.

Children's Businesses.   The increasing number of new births and children living in single-parent households or in households where both parents work has created many child-related franchise opportunities, such as nanny services, day-care centers, transportation services, sports activities centers, educational programs, and help-for-learning programs.

Food Services.   As the number of working adults, teenagers, and seniors increases, there is less time for preparing meals at home. Consequently, there are many franchise restaurants and fast-food services where healthy, self-indulgent, niche food products are sold that are inexpensive or moderately priced. The double-drive-through restaurants are prospering, as well as restaurants with distinctive, clean, and festive atmospheres.

Last, many entrepreneurs are growing their ventures but franchising them across the world. For more details on franchising as a growth strategy, see Chapter 7.

Newly Unemployed Entrepreneurs.   Today, more and more workers are being squeezed from large firms because of corporate buyouts, mergers, foreign competition, and reorganizations. Job security is no longer a benefit of large corporations and layoffs are standard. Economists forecast that layoffs will continue at a higher rate and be more far-reaching in the future. Gone are life-time jobs; every worker is vulnerable and a possible candidate for a reduction in force (RIF).

Some displaced workers are turning to entrepreneurship since there are limited jobs available and competition among applicants is fierce. Today it's risky working inside a corporation, so why not take a risk outside the corporation and start a new business? Because of this constant upheaval in bigger companies, individuals want their own sense of control and security, and many start a new company.

These same downsized employees may turn around and sell their services back to their former employer. A natural move for many executives-turned-entrepreneurs, is to start a consulting business. They usually have excellent technical and/or professional skills, good banking relationships, and collateral to borrow start-up funds. Corporations are eager to contract with displaced workers because these former employees understand the nuances of the company and can work through political issues and cut through red tape. The rule of thumb is that you can earn anywhere from 20 to 50 percent more than your corporate salary by selling the same services you provided to your former employer as an independent business owner.

Trap

Many corporate employees don't operate well in an entrepreneurial environment where they perform all tasks from emptying trash to marketing a product.

Corporate backgrounds are a double-edged sword—both a help and hindrance. Because they have become accustomed to a support staff, shared decision making, and having financial resources available, many corporate employees have difficulty switching over to an environment where they perform all job tasks themselves and lack interaction with other employees.

Retirees and Senior Entrepreneurs

Retirees want meaningful work experiences which are not readily available in the corporate world. They have talent, ambition, experience, and retirement dollars to invest in new start-ups. They also have established long-term banking relationships, personal credit history, and available assets to use as collateral for loans.

Tip

Because retirees and seniors have a broader perspective of life and business, they are more likely to seek help from experts they know personally than younger know-it-all entrepreneurs.

The American Home-based Business Association reported in 1995 that 15 percent of home-based businesses are run by retirees. As the average life span in our country increases, so will the number of senior and retired entrepreneurs.

A helpful resource is Samuel Small's *Starting a Business After 50* (Pilot Books). Small provides a popular list of businesses for older entrepreneurs, such as opening gourmet food stores, travel agencies, gift shops, or various delivery services.

Disabled Entrepreneurs

Both the physically disabled and seniors are also discovering the joys of starting their own home-based business. The Disabled Businesspersons Association in San Diego reports that entrepreneurship by the disabled is the fastest-growing segment of business start-ups in the nation today. Their research shows an 88.4 percent increase in business start-ups by the disabled in the past five years.

Self-employment has become the only employment option for many individuals with disabilities. Many have discovered that launching a new venture can create opportunities in the workplace that may eventually lead to full-time employment if that is the goal. And the good news is that some studies show that the success rate for disabled entrepreneurs is slightly higher than that for other business owners.

Women- and Minority-Owned Businesses

More and more women and minorities are bypassing traditional corporate hiring opportunities and starting their own companies or joining smaller companies with greater chance for advancement and becoming an equity owner. Women and minorities are launching new enterprises four to six times faster than any other group in the United States.

Women-owned firms represent over a third of all new start-ups and the Small Business Administration estimates the women-owned firms will increase to 48 percent by the year 2000. The number of minority-owned firms have doubled during the last decade. The biggest increase occurred among Asians and Pacific Islanders.

"Hot" Entrepreneurial Opportunities

During the 1990s, innovative venture opportunities are springing up in both new and traditional industries. In our accelerated business environment, your success as an entrepreneur is related to your ability to identify fads, spot trends, and distinguish trends with staying power from flash-in-the-pan fads. It is also critical to know what is happening in your industry, look for expanding markets, and predict where trends are heading which will keep your business on track. To succeed in the entrepreneurial world, it is critically important to continually recognize, monitor, and stay abreast of trends as well as technological, social, and attitudinal changes. Entrepreneurs who will thrive in the twenty-first century will seek out new trends and build venture opportunities based on them before *everyone else jumps on the bandwagon.*

Tip
_____

The most successful venture opportunities exploit change.

Some of the most recent trends creating new venture opportunities include advances in computer technology, the Internet, a growing global marketplace, increasing life spans, aging baby boomers, and corporate downsizing. Use the following list of hot entrepreneurial opportunities to help you identify trends you might be interested in exploring, including associated products and services. Each of these venture opportunity trends is discussed in this section.

Hot Entrepreneurial Opportunities

1. Biotechnology
2. Internet

3. Training and Professional Development

4. Fitness/Health

5. Indulgence Goods

6. Child Care and Elder Care

7. Home Health Services

8. Children's Products and Services

9. Ethnic Products

10. Home Office Products and Services

11. Smart Appliances

12. Pet Pampering

13. Retail Boutiques

14. Personal Shopping and Errand Services

Biotechnology

Biotechnology is a hot growth industry as we expand our knowledge of the human body at the molecular level. In 1992, biotechnology was a $4 billion industry, but the federal government is predicting it will expand to a $50 billion industry by the end of the decade. The world population will probably double in the next 40 years, and feeding those extra people on existing land will require biotechnological innovation. There are many biotechnology venture opportunities in agriculture, environmental science, medicine, and food-related industries.

Likewise there are many new drugs and therapies focused on life extension and improving the quality of life. Recombinant DNA and genetic engineering, which can remodel the gene code to eliminate or enhance traits has great potential in the areas of preventive medicine. It will be possible to head off chronic diseases by identifying genetic propensities and take early action by making lifestyle changes. Health-care futurist, Leeland Kaiser, predicts that by the year 2000, hospitals will become body shops where people will come in for replacement parts similar to automobile repair shops. The average life span will be 130 years, creating many new markets for our aging population. There are many exciting biotechnology opportunities in both large organizations and small firms. Some innovative corporate employees are starting new ventures under the corporate umbrella utilizing the organization's support, research and development expertise, and finances to add new product lines. Some entrepreneurs are starting new biotechnology companies often with the participation of venture capitalists because of the capital needed to bring many of these inventions to market. New venture opportunities in biotechnology include:

- Blood tests to screen for genetic diseases
- Genetic engineering
- Alternative medicines
- Bionic parts and artificial organs
- Bioelectronic products
- Animal drugs
- Inoculated eggs
- Implantable animal microchips
- Grass that doesn't need cutting

Internet

Entrepreneurs are using the Internet, or Net, as an interactive communication tool to market and sell products on the World Wide Web, combining entertainment with commerce. According to Forrester Research, Inc., on-line shopping is expected to reach $6.6 billion in 2000—a substantially greater amount than the $518 million spent in 1996.

The most common use of the Web is to distribute electronic mailings, marketing materials, publicity messages, catalogs, on-line newsletters, etc. E-mail has been the biggest use of the Internet, providing increased personal communication. However, the Web's ability to expose a venture's products and services to millions of potential customers is becoming a hot marketing tool and the reason why many owners want a Web site. In 1997, over 40 percent of large companies and 25 percent of medium-sized companies have, or plan to develop, Web sites. Some electronic storefronts are busy taking orders, and ventures that serve narrow markets such as rare wine, music, china, and books are flourishing. Some companies are delivering real-time customer support on line.

To be successful, you must have customers who already use the Internet. Or, if you have customers who purchase by mail, then it may make sense for you to market on the Net. For example, most colleges and universities, governmental agencies, and some businesses, such as technical companies, the entertainment industry, publishing, booksellers, accounting firms, investment firms, petroleum-related industries, utility and travel-related businesses regularly use the Net.

✳ Trap

Avoid using the Net as your only marketing tool, especially to start a new business. Instead, integrate it with your other marketing efforts. The Net should be used to supplement your existing marketing, not as a substitute.

Like any new technology, there are unexpected pitfalls and lots of choices to make. Finding out what works best to meet your needs will take some time and effort. New venture opportunities using the Net include:

- Designing Web sites
- Internet marketing services
- Office supplies
- Small-business equipment
- Health supplements (vitamins and self-care information)
- Home-delivered meals, sports equipment, business documents
- Specialty foods
- Gaming and add-on products
- Travel and leisure products
- Videogames and multimedia programs
- Books and magazines

See Chapter 7 for more discussion about using the information highway as a growth strategy.

Training and Development

Three of the hottest training areas are in corporate, consumer, and computer training. The explosion in Internet usage, new technology, operating systems, and updated software programs have given rise to much of this training to keep computer skills current. In addition, more smaller businesses are getting computerized. The worldwide technology training and education market is predicted to exceed $27 billion in 2000, and the information technology consulting industry will reach $18.5 billion by 2000.

Another growth market is in training and developing workers' skills and retraining downsized blue- and white-collar workers. Employees are having to make changes more quickly than ever before. Learning new management and customer service techniques has created a large market for job and business coaches. As home-based businesses grow and consumers purchase computers for their home offices, their need for computer tutoring expands. Training and development venture opportunities include:

- Customized on-site computer training by computer tutors
- Computer training centers
- Skills trainers
- Image consultants and executive coaches
- Professional organizers
- On-line and multimedia content consultants
- Videoconferencing organizers
- Programming consultants
- Electronic data interchange consultants

Fitness and Health

There is a growing trend surrounding "wellness" which should extend people's years of good health. People have progressed from the "staying alive syndrome" and are now focusing on experiencing a better-quality life, shaping up and healing their minds and bodies. Day spas reminiscent of the Roman baths are finding a bubbling market as aging baby boomers focus on remaining young and healthy. From aromatherapy messages and herbal medicinal baths to facials and cosmetic makeovers, day spas are providing luxury treatments teaching self-healing techniques for everyone.

The number of health club memberships more than doubled between 1988 and 1995. Personal trainers customize workouts and target problem areas for clients who want the washboard abs that are in vogue. "Fountain of Youth" products, such as cosmetics, health, fitness, and nutrition improvement goods, that target longevity, stamina, and wellness flourish. New venture opportunities abound in the following areas:

- Healthier foods
- Door-to-door wellness services
- Low-tech healing specialists versus traditional doctors for remedies
- Holistic healing
- Ancient remedies
- Spas and cosmetic-surgery centers
- Holistic health clubs and fitness services
- Exercise machines
- Humor clubs

Indulgence Goods

At the opposite end of this wellness spectrum is an emerging indulgence trend which reflects people rewarding themselves with small affordable luxuries such as specialty chocolates, salsas, healthy Mexican products, coffee boutiques, juice bars, and natural food and healthy gourmet supermarkets. For example, the purified bottled water mania has struck, and many people of all ages are purchasing either domestic or imported types of different waters. New venture opportunities are surging in the following areas:

- Gourmet foods in small servings
- Ice cream and other sinful desserts
- Natural foods and organic produce
- Natural water products
- Healthy frozen foods
- Energy-producing products and vitamin supplements

- Specialty coffees, tea, and wine shops
- Brew pubs and customized beers
- Imported cigars, humidors, and smoking rooms
- Specialty breads, soft pretzels, and bagel outlets
- Exotic meats such as buffalo, elk, venison, ostrich
- Quaint hotels and boutiques with specialty services
- Miniature adult toys (laptops, CD players)
- Designer baby clothes
- Aromatherapy (scented candles, bath oils, and lotions)
- Flowers

Child and Elder Care

More adults with children entering the workplace have created
the need for more small, conveniently located, 24-hour day-care
centers that encourage morals, manners, good nutrition, exercise, and spirituality in kids. Much of the commercial day care is
done in people's homes, called family centers.

With Americans getting grayer and progressing into their gold-
en years, the need has grown for independent-, residential-, and
assisted-living centers that operate like hotels and provide a
homelike atmosphere. Residents have maid service, restaurants,
dry cleaning, tailors, and salon services that offer attractive alternatives to nursing facilities or living alone. Many people want
their parents living closer to them. The solution may be "Club
Meds for Seniors" that are run much like hotels. New opportunities for child- or elder-care ventures include:

- Child-care centers and camps
- Rent-a-grandmother services
- Products and services for the homebound
- Elder-care consulting services
- Elder day-care centers and activities
- Senior travel clubs
- Independent-living centers
- Assisted-living centers

Home Health Services

As hospital costs skyrocket there is a trend to discharge patients to less expensive and more comfortable surroundings. According to the National Association for Home Care (NAHC), more than 17,000 providers deliver home-care services to some 7 million individuals, with revenues of over $27 billion. They predict that home postpartum care is among the hottest home health-care opportunities.

Because delivering routine medical treatments at home can be more cost-effective than at a hospital, some entrepreneurs contract with independent home health-care providers to care for homebound people under the supervision of health professionals.

Home health-care givers are similar to temporary service agencies, involving physical therapists, occupational therapists, nursing assistants who clean the house, cook meals, take the person to doctor's appointments, and run errands. They operate out of fitness centers, homes, schools, corporations, and free-standing locations and also provide services to people with disabilities and other illnesses. Venture opportunities in the home health area include:

- Home health-care providers
- Door-to-door medical appointment transportation services
- Homemaking services
- Elderly relative services

Children's Products and Services

Two-income families with kids and single-parent households give rise to new venture opportunities. Since 1989, the number of newborns has continued to rise, as well as the number of working moms. Home health care for newborns is one of the hottest segments in the baby-boom industry. Helping parents select furnishings and designs for nurseries and children's rooms and catalogs for kids are other expanding areas. In addition, more parents are concerned about every aspect of their children's safety and well-being, from nutrition to physical fitness to improved education.

Many parents rely on special educational consulting, tutoring, and technology to supplement their children's learning. Parents are contacting special consultants to give their kids a head start on learning. For example, toy stores featuring educational learning-based play items have sprung up. The wholesale figures for sales of scientific toys were more than $73 million, and educational toy sales topped $30 million in 1994 and are rapidly expanding. Niche toy stores specialize by creating an entertainment and experiential atmosphere where kids get their hands on computers and brain-teasing toys. New venture opportunities in children's products and services include:

- Juvenile safety products
- Infant and children's organic food products
- Kids' fitness centers
- Kiddie golf
- Nursery design and furniture necessities
- Home health care for newborns
- Kids' educational software for math, reading, science, etc.
- Multimedia computers
- CD-Rom encyclopedias
- Educational toys, games, and puzzles
- Children's learning centers and camps
- Centers for children with learning disabilities
- Children's bookstores

Ethnic Products

Many opportunities abound in designing and marketing ethnically diverse products and services to people from different nations. We are a multicultural nation with people from many different countries living and working together. For example, Asian-Americans are one of the fastest growing, most educated, and affluent ethnic groups in the United States. They are creating new markets for ethnic goods, including cafes, restaurants, specialty grocery outlets, and food courts with such popular cuisine items as chicken satay, noodle bowls, and dim sum, to name a few. Other popular ethnic flavors are Italian, Mexican, and Cantonese-style foods along with hybrid cuisines like French-Vietnamese.

Selling new ethnic medicine is another growing market segment focusing on the medical needs of people from different ethnic groups who have special dietary and nutrition requirements related to ethnic illnesses. Opportunities for ethnic products and services include:

- Specialty lines of cosmetics
- Hair-care products and salons
- Vitamins and dietary products
- Ethnic grocery stores and cookbooks
- Ethnic food mail-order catalogs
- Ethnic cafes, restaurants, and food courts

Home Office Products and Services

A work-at-home trend is sweeping our country. Telecommuters from the corporate world and home-based entrepreneurs are building comforts around them, and they are interested in securing both private security and safety. There are many opportunities for entrepreneurs to spin off new ventures in the following areas:

- Home decorating and furnishings
- Home safety devices
- Home office furniture and technical equipment
- On-site repair services for home offices
- Auto safety alarms and sound systems; personal safety items while traveling
- Home delivery services for computers, printers, etc.

Smart Appliances

Computers have invaded homes and sparked new automations in home gadgets that do everything from running 3-D video games to controlling lights, heat, ovens, and air conditioning automatically by merely calling your home. New markets for on-line banking and home devices that monitor total health and recommend

exercise programs, meals, and lifestyle changes will spring up.
Home techies and entertainment-seeking residents will have
game rooms stocked with digital high-definition TV sets that
hang on the wall like large paintings, improved sound systems,
video cameras, etc. Home videoconferencing will become com-
monplace. The new cyberhome will provide new venture opportunities for:

- Digital cellular phone, radios, and interactive TVs
- Digital imaging products
- Electronic notepads
- Multisensory robotics
- Smart homes and appliances
- Voice recognitions products
- Electronic film cameras

Pet Pampering

Specialized care products and services for pets for people who
treat their pets like children have created new markets for entrepreneurs. Dog treat sales surpassed $1 billion in 1994 and contin-
ue to expand. The *Three Dog Bakery* in Kansas City, Missouri, is an
example of a multimillion-dollar business that started in the
kitchen of one of the founders and has seen its revenues grow over
500 percent. The company is currently opening up new bakeries
all over the United States and selling its packaged treats to some
280 national PETsMARTS locations while opening franchises
worldwide. Opportunities for pet pampering include:

- Pet hotels
- Pet grooming and traveling vans
- Pet home-care visits
- Pet emergency clinics (veterinary care from dusk to dawn)
- Old-age homes for pets
- Pet television and radio shows
- Doggie day care
- Doggie bakeries

- Cat furniture and clothing stores
- Seat belts for pets

Three Dog Bakery

With three stores currently serving the Kansas City area, and a fourth to open in September, Kansas City's canines have given up chasing cars and have started "pawing" for rides to the world's first bakery for man's best friend. The *Three Dog Bakery* concept is the brainchild of 1993 FastTrac graduate Dan Dye and his partner Mark Beckloff.

"The whole thing was really a mistake," said Dye, 35. "Mark's Mom had given him a bone cutter as a gag gift for Christmas. He used the little recipe that came with it to make a dog biscuit. That's literally how the business got started."

By 1993, Dan and Mark had moved their business to the tourist suburb of Westport. It was then that they got their big break. During those first three years of business the store had attracted some local media attention, but when *The Wall Street Journal* "picked up their scent," business would never be the same. "We had no idea what being on the front page of *The Wall Street Journal* meant. From that point on we have received tons of publicity."

With radio interviews, newspaper stories, and television programs all beating down their door, the owners of the *Three Dog Bakery* could barely keep up with mail orders. Business was booming, but they needed help managing the new demand for their products.

"I read about FastTrac from a little blurb in the newspaper. I saw that it was sponsored by the Kauffman Foundation and I knew it was going to be something of substance and not some dog and pony show. The FastTrac program was the best money we have ever spent as a company. I would come back to work and tell Mark what I was learning and we immediately started putting that information to work."

For Dan, the most valuable aspect of FastTrac was the interaction with other entrepreneurs. "Hearing the actual real-life stories of other entrepreneurs enrolled in the FastTrac program was so beneficial. To hear it from other entrepreneurs who are experiencing the same things you are really helped."

Since completing the FastTrac program, the *Three Dog Bakery* has seen its revenues grow by over 500 percent. Today, Dan and Mark are celebrating a new deal with PETsMARTS, Inc., the nationwide pet supply chain. *Three Dog* is opening new bakeries in its stores and is selling packaged treats to some 280 national PETsMARTS locations.

Company: Three Dog Bakery

Location: Kansas City, MO

Founded: 1989

Founders: Dan Dye & Mark Beckloff

Owners: Dan Dye & Mark Beckloff

Service: Baked dog biscuits & treats

Employees:120

Revenue: $2.74 million in 1996

Retail Boutiques

Large national chains have expanded throughout our country with the concept of "bigger is better and cheaper" in home ware, hardware supplies, books, music, videotape rental, office supplies, toys, groceries, kitchenware, lawn and gardening, beds and bedding, interior decorating, and personal computers. Such expansions have opened up many sales niches for individual boutiques, including the Internet with cybermalls. Opportunities for mega one-of-a-kind stores include:

- Clothing
- Jewelry
- Record stores
- Delicatessens
- Bakery cafes
- Specialty shoe stores
- Travel-related outlets
- Paint-your-own pottery stores
- Customized breweries

Personal Shopping and
Errand Services

People are trying to squeeze more into 24 hours as work hours increase and leisure hours decrease, which results in their willingness to pay others to run their errands and handle many family and home time-consuming tasks. In addition, the increasing numbers of elderly make even greater use of errand services.

Personal errand and shopping services perform a variety of tasks, including grocery shopping; picking up laundry, dry cleaning, theater tickets, and shoe repairs; taking cars for servicing and repair; taking care of pets; mailing packages; choosing gifts; wardrobe consulting. Many of these new venture opportunities fall into the home-based businesses category and include:

- Wardrobe consultants
- On-site customer apparel shoppers
- Gift services
- Corporate pickup and delivery service
- Messenger services
- Rent-a-butler
- Rent-a-chef
- Rent-a-driver
- Publicity escort services

How to Recognize
Opportunities

As Thomas Edison once said: "Make it a practice to keep on the lookout for novel and interesting ideas that others have used successfully. Your idea must be original only in its adaptation to the problem you are working on." Discovering creative ideas and venture opportunities is a learned process. The Center for Creative Leadership, for example, holds regular workshops that teach people how to unleash and enhance their creative skills. The key to creativity is the ability to discover new relationships and to look at subjects from new perspectives.

As entrepreneurs learn more about their industry, trends, competition, etc., innovative ideas will be necessary to sustain and grow ventures. It is nearly impossible to create innovations in a vacuum. Therefore, astute entrepreneurs are always gathering information. With more information, they can look beyond the obvious mode and watch for new trends. Therefore, thinking "outside the box" or bottle as suggested by the following example is one skill essential to becoming a successful entrepreneur.

If you place an empty Coke bottle in front of several people and ask them to name alternative uses for the bottle, they would list many uses. Some suggestions might include using the bottle as a flower base, as a container for liquid, or as a candlestick. However, if you break the bottle, look at how many new ways you could use it. The base could be used as an ashtray, the mouth could be used as a ring or pendant. The smaller pieces could be used for a covering in a fish tank. There are a multitude of other uses for it.

It is important to go beyond the obvious and think outside the box to discover a myriad of possibilities. Successful entrepreneurs cut through conventional perceptions to find new ways to succeed and compete in the marketplace. Domino's Pizza applied this thinking to the pizza industry. The conventional pizza business created new crust styles, flavors, and toppings. But Domino's Pizza thought outside the box and found a way to develop a new distribution channel by starting home delivery of pizza to satisfy the customer. Rather than revolutionize the pizza, they revolutionized how it was offered, using a unique grid system that reduced delivery time to 30 minutes or less. As a result of thinking outside the box, the Pizza business will never be the same.

Becoming an entrepreneur requires becoming a trend spotter by analyzing sources of opportunities, observing, asking lots of questions, and listening. Use the following creative idea sources to help you identify new business opportunities.

Creative Idea Sources

Idea Source 1: **Keep Abreast of Demographic Changes.** Demographic changes are continual, but often their consequences are not noticed until too late. Population statistics change more rapidly today than in the past. There are many business opportunities in demographic changes regarding the numbers of births and deaths, age distribution, education, occupations, and geographic locations. For example, Peter Francese of American Demographics, Inc., points out that the fastest-growing age group in America are those 85 years or older. Their needs for assisted-living centers, recreational activities, and delivery service are fertile ground for new ventures.

Idea Source 2: **Look for the Unexpected.**   Unexpected successes or failures are often disregarded by businesspeople. Yet they can provide a harvest of opportunities for those who observe these experiences in the marketplace and improve on the mistakes of others. Scan business journals and newspapers for unexpected business experiences.

Idea Source 3: **Study Problems.**   Problems are fertile grounds for opportunities. Can something be done better or quicker? People are perpetually looking for cost-effective solutions to their problems. Entrepreneurs are problem-oriented and good listeners. They are trouble-shooters uncovering ideas that will make people's lives easier, more economical, or more pleasurable. Audit the media to determine what people are complaining about and try to discover solutions to their concerns. Or make a list of daily nuisances you and others experience. See if you can discover solutions to irritations and inefficiencies that people face.

Idea Source 4: **Identify People's Needs.**   What is important to people today? What are their priorities? Entrepreneurs know their current and potential customers and find out what they need. They ask open-ended questions to discover dissatisfactions with today's products and services. A simple but most effective way to get such consumer information is utilizing a focus group. This is discussed in more detail in Chapter 9. Another simple technique: Just ask questions and listen whenever there is a chance to talk with prospective customers.

Idea Source 5: **Engage in People-Watching.**   Observing people can bring meaningful insights to stimulating new venture ideas. Watching people's behavior and listening to conversations provides ideas on new needs and desires. Example: Go into a hotel lobby, pick up a magazine, observe people and discreetly listen to their concerns.

Here's a brief quiz to demonstrate if you are a good or a poor observer.

1. At social functions do you make more than "small talk"? Do you use the occasion as a quasi-focus group where you can ask questions about concerns, such as: What is your greatest concern as you think about aging?

2. In public places, like malls and airports, do you watch to see if you can observe patterns? For example, perhaps the increased use of "golf carts" for transporting older and disabled people in airports might inspire a thought about the multiple use of mobility carts.

3. At work are you noticing new trends with the increasing number of women and minorities joining the workforce, such as more people eating out because of busy schedules?

Idea Source 6: **Monitor Society, Industry, and Market.**   Changes in tastes, lifestyles, and habits are constant and volatile. Example: Miniskirts were the rage in the 1970s, but when designers tried to bring them back during the 1990s, they bombed. Another example: Cajun cooking is out, but low-fat ice cream is in. A third example: jogging is no longer considered the best way to exercise; walking is better. Astute entrepreneurs observe various industries, such as banking, airlines, communications, in terms of how they respond to deregulation and increased competition. Borrow information from one industry and creatively apply it to yours.

Idea Source 7: **Read, Read, Read.**   Successful entrepreneurs spend a significant number of their nonworking hours reading and scanning publications for new knowledge. One study revealed that innovators often spend as much as a third of their business day just reading. They read intuitively, look for what is different, new and exciting, make connections between seemingly unrelated events, and identify patterns. They read publications outside of their own industry as well as major metropolitan newspapers and local business journals which cover community developments and trends in local markets.

Idea Source 8: **Watch for New Trends.**   The secret of this trend-spotting technique is watching the media, Internet, and your professional associations for recurring themes. Entrepreneurs scan junk mail for clues about new products and services introduced in the marketplace. Track the best-selling nonfiction books which may contain trends you could exploit.

***Idea Source 9:* Utilize Groups to Exchange Information.** Trading information among colleagues, competitors, and professionals in the community is a valuable exercise for spotting trends. Establishing a network of professionals who provide state-of-the-art information is an excellent way to spot trends and trade clues on opportunities. Join associations that serve your industry. For new ideas and forecasts, attend industry conventions and inventor trade shows.

***Idea Source 10:* Seek out Recognized Leaders.** Change is triggered by those who have contact with leaders outside their field. Periodically talk to these people or read their comments in the media. Reading should be supplemented by exchanging thoughts with informed experts. Their feedback is often rich with insights.

***Idea Source 11:* Study the Competition.** It is vital to know what your competition is doing. This is known as market intelligence . . . being a detective by gathering and analyzing data carefully. Ask industry people, customers, and suppliers about your present, and possible, rivals. What are they doing right? What are their weaknesses? What kind of promotion and advertising are they using? Before launching a new venture, scour the marketplace to see who is there already.

***Idea Source 12:* Talk to Members in Your Infrastructure, in Academia, and in Government.** The entrepreneur's infrastructure—the accountants, the lawyers, the bankers—are tremendous sources of information about your industry and new trends. Contact manufacturers, wholesalers, and distributors that service your industry and ask about market research they have recently done. Make sure you include them in your network, as well as leading research universities, polytechnic institutes, and professors. The academic world has to keep tabs on changes in the world so they can teach the next generation. Contact various government agencies, such as the Department of Commerce and Labor and the Census Bureau for data indicating new trends. Review their various publications.

Idea Source 13: **Watch the Information Superhighway.** Surf the Internet to spot new trends, exchange information on electronic bulletin boards, and shop various cybermalls. A great source for the latest information in your industry is on-line information.

Idea Source 14: **Use Commercial Research Sources.** There is usually a fee for commercial research sources. Leading commercial sources include research and trade associations, such as Dun & Bradstreet and Robert Morris & Associates, banks and other financial institutions, and publicly traded corporations.

Business Planning—The Key to Entrepreneurial Strategy

There is no mystery in entrepreneurship as to the key to launching and growing successful ventures. It is sound business planning—developing feasibility plans when launching a new venture, writing business plans when operating an existing venture, and producing operational plans when growing a venture.

Trap

Failure to write a business plan is the worst mistake business owners can make in operating their ventures.

Too many entrepreneurs carry their critical planning records in their heads and never transfer any of these ideas to paper. The common myth is that writing business plans is good only for raising capital and for distribution to bankers. Entrepreneurs frequently do not understand why they should plan or how they should prepare the various planning documents essential to operating a successful business. In reality, these types of plans save precious time, prevent mistakes, and in many instances will save your business.

Eager entrepreneurs run off and start ventures with very few, if any, of these planning documents. They operate their ventures by trial and error. In addition, they often lack the planning skills needed from the start-up stage through the growth stages of a business. As their ventures progress, various members of the infrastructure, such as bankers, other types of lenders, accountants, and so on, require that these plans be developed and followed.

The typical entrepreneurs' response—ugh! They feel the process will be a torturous exercise from which they will emerge wounded.

Typically, the first planning document required of entrepreneurs starting a new venture is a feasibility plan to determine what it will take to move forward, in other words, make a go/no go decision. Instead, they get all wrapped up and excited about a new venture idea without thoughtful consideration, research, and evaluation of its potential and pitfalls. Later, the entrepreneur realizes that although the idea was sound, the market was saturated, the profit margin was too narrow, the proper management team was not in place, there was insufficient capital, or there were a myriad of other reasons why the venture failed.

If entrepreneurs thoroughly researched new venture ideas and wrote feasibility plans before starting, many failed businesses would have never been launched in the first place. That is one of the fundamental reasons that so many new businesses fail during the first years of operation. This failure rate could be significantly reduced if properly structured research and planning were conducted in the beginning.

A feasibility plan should contain (1) an executive summary, (2) a product or service section, (3) a market section, (4) price and profitability measures, and (5) a plan for further action.

The *executive summary* is a brief, concise overview of the venture idea and key dimensions contained in each section of the plan. The *product or service section* covers the stage of development, limitation, liabilities, proprietary rights, production, and related services and spin-offs. The *market section* looks at the size of the market, growth potential, industry trends, customer profile, customer benefits, target markets, competition and market penetration methods. The *price and profitability section* measures what customers will pay for the product or service. It is critical that the venture be able to maintain a sufficiently high gross margin to cover expenses and still yield a healthy profit. This section examines the cost of the product or service, sales estimates, gross margin operating expenses, and start-up costs.

The last section, *plan for further action,* focuses on the future, identifies likely pitfalls, strong points, needed capital, license potential, potential corporate partners, infrastructure members, the entrepreneur's role, and whether to proceed with the new venture idea and write a business plan.

Many entrepreneurs use their feasibility plan to attract potential investors, bankers, friends, personal business advisers, and strategic partners. Feedback from these groups will produce useful information and help better focus the venture idea.

Tip

The main reason for writing a feasibility plan is to test the venture idea to determine if it should be further developed. If the answer is yes, you should proceed to write a detailed business plan.

Entrepreneurial education and training are critical components in the success of new ventures. Call the local Small Business Development Center (SBDC) office, the chamber of commerce, or college or university business departments to help develop your plans.

Entrepreneurs constantly fight the battle of writing good and sound business plans that will provide guidance for operating their ventures and attracting financing for growth. They frequently delay in writing them because they are uncertain how to write and prepare the planning documents essential to running a successful venture. Entrepreneurs continually struggle with producing a usable outline for the plan and developing necessary financial documents such as balance sheets, profit-and-loss statements, and cash-flow projections. Entrepreneurs need to develop strong analytical and conceptual skills. These skills can be enhanced when preparing a business plan. They should think of this process as an invaluable training tool that will help them identify potential risks and pitfalls as well as opportunities. Recently, *Nation's Business* magazine reported that only 1 out of every 100 entrepreneurs has developed a good, solid business plan, which is one of the precipitators of business failure.

Tip

Entrepreneurs should develop a sound business plan and use it as an essential tool to developing vision and focus.

The business plan should be used as a management guide to operate a venture rather than as a blueprint that must be carefully followed. It is the best opportunity for entrepreneurs to flesh out their ideas and clarify their goals. Founders take their goals more seriously when they are written. Written goals help entrepreneurs work smarter rather than just harder. The process of goal setting as applied to developing a business plan enables you to understand and clarify risks, thereby devising ways to both manage and reduce risks. Goal setting helps keep you in a future-oriented mode, always anticipating new trends and directions. Last, goal setting develops your strategy for testing the validity of various projections in the business plan.

Business Plan Myths

The biggest myth concerning business plans is that they are only written to raise money. The opposite is true. They are written to help entrepreneurs plan their ventures and better manage businesses, and they may or may not be used to obtain capital.

The next biggest myth is that successful ventures have no fatal flaws. Entrepreneurs often ignore the need to test the soundness of their business concept with knowledgeable outside resources. The key is to identify potential flaws and then determine how to overcome or compensate for them.

Why Write Business Plans?

The process you go through writing a business plan is an indispensable learning experience. It focuses your thinking. It forces you to take an objective, critical, and unemotional view of your venture. In addition, the process:

1. Highlights strengths of the business
2. Helps identify current and potential problems by pointing out weak spots and vulnerabilities
3. Eliminates blind spots
4. Identifies major flaws
5. Is an easy method to communicate your venture idea to others
6. Provides the necessary information needed by others, especially potential investors and lenders, to evaluate your plan
7. Allows you to spot hidden opportunities
8. Provides an operating tool to help manage the business and achieve projections
9. Helps identify additional ways for the business to develop and grow

10. Can be used to attract financing

11. Clarifies the venture's financial requirements

12. Allows entrepreneurs to measure and monitor performance of the business and its managers

✻ Tip

The discipline of writing a business plan is a learning experience that is much more valuable than the money it raises.

Guidelines for Preparing Winning Business Plans

Twenty years ago entrepreneurs could not turn to a book or software program for guidance as to how to develop a business plan. Today, just the opposite is true. With the advent of the microcomputer, desktop publishing, and spreadsheet software, the agony and long hours of preparation have declined while the quality of these plans is continually increasing.

Business plans usually contain 15 sections: (1) summary and executive overview, (2) concept, (3) management and organization, (4) product and/or service plan, (5) production plan, (6) competition, (7) pricing, (8) marketing plan, (9) financial plan, (10) operating and control system, (11) schedule, (12) growth plan, (13) contingency plan, (14) the deal, and (15) appendix. It is not necessary to include all the 15 sections listed, but this outline will give you an idea of what information to include, depending upon the exact nature of your proposed venture. For example, if your venture is a service business, you would not include a production plan. Also, there is nothing sacred about the order of these sections, although this order is commonly used and preferred in the entrepreneurial world. It is more important for the plan to flow logically.

This outline was taken from *The Entrepreneur's Planning Handbook,* by Buskirk, Price, and Davis (EEF), featuring a question-and-answer format. After answering the questions in each section of this book, you have essentially written your business plan. The book also provides you with formatting tips and lists subtitles for each section. Another recommended book for writing a comprehensive business plan is *Launching New Ventures* by Kathleen Allen (1995, Upstart, Chicago).

Developing financial statements for the business plan is a difficult task. Working with an accountant can assist you in developing these documents after you have done enough research to make realistic and meaningful projections. Or consult the *Business Planning Guide* by Daniel H. Bangs, Jr., from Upstart Publishing Co., which has a lengthy segment on developing the financial section for the business plan. Refer to *Robert Morris Studies,* Robert Morris Associates, published annually, available in most libraries, when preparing your financial documents. This reference book lists industry statistics and financial ratios for every industry.

Yes, there are companies or consultants that will prepare your business plan. However, do not pay someone to write your business plan. Most of the benefit of writing a business plan is lost if somebody else writes it. Sitting down and developing the plan, section by section, forces the entrepreneur to do considerable thinking, evaluating, and planning. Without exception, entrepreneurs who have written their own business plans report that they were compelled to rethink many aspects of their venture when it became apparent that there were some serious flaws in their thinking. Also, most entrepreneurs could not afford to pay someone for all the hours it takes to write a professionally prepared plan. No one knows your business better than you do, so it's important that you write the story.

The best news about developing and writing your own business plan is that once you have been through the process, writing additional plans takes half the time. You'll discover that you have learned valuable planning skills that will be critical to your success as an entrepreneur.

Common Pitfalls in Developing a Business Plan

Entrepreneurs writing a business plan for the first time make some common mistakes that can be avoided. The following are the 10 most common pitfalls to be aware of when developing your business plan:

1. The business plan is too long. Reviewers of the plan look for concisely written plans in bullet form that do not read like term papers.

2. Competition is inadequately assessed. Too little competition may indicate that there is no market for your venture idea.

3. Expectations and projections are unreasonable. Grandiose estimates regarding sales projections or money requested can be disastrous.

4. Financial assumptions do not match data in the financial statements.

5. Business does not provide a realistic exit for the investors.

6. Founders fail to demonstrate that they have the necessary management skills to operate the business.

7. Unrealistic projections that the product or service can be produced or delivered in a reasonable time period.

8. Business plan demonstrates little business operational knowledge.

9. Inadequate price to cost ratios.

10. Plan describes technical product or manufacturing processes with technical jargon only experts can understand.

Value and Uses of a Business Plan

The value of writing a business plan cannot be overemphasized. Every time you prepare a business plan, you become a better entrepreneur and increase your venture's chances of success. Writing a business plan helps entrepreneurs better describe their ventures and shows others how well thought out the venture is. It can illustrate why a business is a good investment and credit risk. It explains the financial plan and strategy that are essential when working with investors or lenders. Last, it proves that there is a market for the product or service.

Tip

Business plans should be used as a road map to follow when operating the business.

The business plan forces entrepreneurs to consider many of the essential aspects that are otherwise overlooked. It forces you to take your goals more seriously. It helps expose flaws and develop plans for contingencies. It outlines your plan of action in the present and during the next several years of growth and expansion. Therefore, it lays out your operational and strategic plans for the upcoming years.

Goals in the business plan can also be used to help your managers set their operational goals for their respective responsibilities. You can obtain greater commitment and a higher level of motivation when performance is tied to achieving the goals outlined in the business plan. In turn, you can use these goals to evaluate performance. Most entrepreneurs find the business plan to be even more beneficial after start-up phases of the business. It can be especially helpful in product pricing, competitive strategy, and financial planning. Potential lenders and investors will almost always require a business plan. Giving them a professional-looking and well-developed plan builds credibility and helps cement your relationship with them.

Most thriving entrepreneurs recognize the importance of business planning to develop and grow successful ventures. Business ventures fail because critical factors are overlooked and pivotal steps in the planning process are omitted. The planning process begins by first developing a feasibility study and then a business plan from which other entrepreneurial planning documents, such as the operational plan and the strategic plan, can then be produced. Planning should be used to reduce the uncertainty of the future and to better manage continuous changes in the marketplace. When you write your business plan, you do a lot of research and expose many flaws. Each one you identify and address enhances your chance of prosperity. Planning is key to success in all entrepreneurial ventures.

Entrepreneurial Trends
Resource Guide

Books

Rosalind Resnick, *The Internet Business Guide: Riding the Information Superhighway to Profit,* Sams Publishing, a division of MacM Computer Publishing, 201 W. 103rd St., Indianapolis, IN, 46290-1097, Tel. no. 1-800-858-7674.

Marvin Cetron, *Crystal Globe,* St. Martin's Press, NY

Kim Long, *American Forecaster Almanac,* published annually by American Forecaster, 2546 S. Broadway, Denver, CO 80210.

Newsletters

The American Forecaster Newsletter, American Forecaster, 2546 S. Broadway, Denver, CO 80210.

Magazines

American Demographic Magazine, Ithaca, NY

Associations

The World Future Society, Suite 450, 7910 Woodmont Ave., Bethesda, MD 20814, Tel no. (301) 656-8274, Fax no. (301) 951-0394.

2
Personal Issues First

Planning permeates every aspect of an entrepreneurial venture. Entrepreneurs cannot successfully operate new ventures without making numerous strategic and planning decisions. The very decision an entrepreneur makes about starting a business as a means for exploiting a business opportunity is a strategic decision. It is important to recognize the strategic alternatives available.

This chapter focuses on the fundamental personal and business strategy issues that drive an entrepreneurial venture and are so critical to its success. The authors maintain that it is important to consider the personal issues that will ultimately affect the entrepreneur's life and that of the business. Use this chapter to evaluate potential start-up opportunities. Or, if you are in business, review your responses to the questions raised here to determine if you are in the right business.

Tip

Assess your personal strategies since a business reflects the personal values of its founder, which then become the foundation of the corporate culture.

For instance, if you hate debt, your business will not likely use borrowed funds to expand, even though it might be the best approach from an economic viewpoint. A venture is but an extension of the founder's values.

Personal Strategy Issue: Why Do You Want to Start a New Business and What Do You Want from It?

Job Security

Is the purpose of this enterprise to provide you and your family with a good living? To what extent is the venture your personal money machine? Is the goal of the business to provide a job for you and/or your family? If your goal for being in business is to make a comfortable and stable living while being in total control of the business, then these values should permeate every business decision. What role will the business play in your life? What do you want from it?

* Tip

Make your business decisions in accordance with your personal desires for operating and harvesting your venture.

Money

How much money do you expect from the business venture? Mike Markulla, cofounder of Apple Computer, wanted wealth from the beginning. That's why he left Hughes Aircraft, a job he loved, for the start-up venture called Intel. That move made him wealthy as did later going to Apple Computer. Apple Computer appealed to him because he forecasted that a great deal of money could be made from it. Mike wanted money and undertook ventures that could give it to him.

Some entrepreneurs put making money lower on their list of priorities. For example, one entrepreneur listed making money fifth on her list of priorities. Unsurpassed customer service and employee satisfaction were among the primary goals. It's more meaningful for some entrepreneurs to create ventures to improve the environment and support their communities than it is for them to make money.

Trap

Never start a business just to make money.

Lifestyle

Is there only one lifestyle that you are comfortable with? How important is it to maintain your present lifestyle or seek a better one? Hugh Hefner started *Playboy* because he wanted to live in the environment that the business created. He keeps the business because it is comfortable for him. If he sold the business, he would be selling his present lifestyle.

Power

Is attaining power important to you? Are you more comfortable running an operation than taking directions from others? Some people crave power while others find it distasteful. Howard Hughes wanted an abundance of power. He would buy businesses just to obtain a power position in some industry. A power player usually has a strategic game plan outlined. Who can predict what game Ted Turner is now playing? He wants power in the cable TV industry.

Many people become bankers for the power it gives them in the community. The owners of media often are power-driven. William Randolph Hearst is such an example. Why do radio and television stations sell for such high multiples? Or look at the sports industry. Why are the prices for professional sports franchises so high? Could power be the answer? Decide if power is important to you and then pursue a business venture that will fulfill your needs.

Personal Strategy Issue: How Will Your Business Idea Affect Your Personal Life?

Age

How many years have you to look forward to? If you are young, you can undertake demanding ventures in ways that an older person cannot. If you are starting a business at an older age or because you plan to retire soon, then you may need to look for a venture opportunity that will produce a quicker payoff and be less physically demanding. Or, you may need to plan for an injection of outside capital to speed up your growth rate.

Health

Are you in good physical condition to withstand the stresses that starting a new venture will cause? Will spending long hours each day be a detriment to your health? Your medical condition will dictate how many hours you can work and the amount of stress you can manage. Weigh the physical requirements of the business with your current physical condition. How much exercise do you get every week? What are your dietary habits? Are you over- or underweight? How does weight affect your energy level?

Family Considerations

What role does your family play in the business? Will they work in it? Will they eventually take it over? Some entrepreneurs refuse to allow their families to play any part in the venture. They even refuse to hire them to work in the business.

On the other hand, are you building the business to pass it on to your children? If so, this makes a hugh difference in what you will do and how you will plan. If you want the business to be a family affair, then you will probably not seek outside managers. Your partners may not be overly excited about working with your kids or other family members.

For example, L.L. Bean, a catalog mail-order company located in Freeport, Maine, is a perfect example of a business whose strategy is almost totally directed by family concerns. The company was founded by Leon Leonwood Bean in 1911 and prospered for approximately 54 years under his direction. When he died at the ripe old age of 94, his grandson, Leon Gorman, became president and still runs this successful company.

Location

Where do you want to live and work? Many people work hard all of their lives in a cold climate so that they can retire to Hawaii or Arizona or Florida. You can live in any of these vacation wonderlands by locating there and starting or buying a venture.

For example, one entrepreneur wanted to move to Vail, Colorado, and looked for a venture to start which would give him that lifestyle. He started an audiovisual equipment rental business for hotel lodgers and coventioneers. Today, this entrepreneur operates a profitable business in the Colorado mountains, and he has many opportunities to ski every day during the season.

Investment

Are you bringing money to the party by investing your own money in the venture? Decide in the beginning how much you are willing to risk. Some entrepreneurs strategically refuse to invest in their own ventures. Instead, they insist on using their talent and others' money. Remember certain types of businesses require a definite amount of cash investment.

For instance, a McDonald's franchise requires approximately $350,000 to $500,000 while a Dunk'n Donuts costs approximately $100,000 to $150,000 to start. The venture's cash requirements will limit the type of business you can pursue.

Attitudes

Personal attitudes and values directly affect your business strategy. Often the only reason why a company does something is that its leader(s) want it that way. Some of the areas in which personal attitudes affect business decisions include:

Use of Debt.   Many people do not function well in highly leveraged situations. Debt places stress upon them that adversely affects their decisions. If you are uncomfortable using debt, then try to avoid it.

Unions.   Many entrepreneurs prefer not working with unions, so they operate their businesses in ways to avoid them. The founders of Texas Instruments adamantly rejected any thoughts of unionization to the extent that they passed up many business deals that might have resulted in a collective bargaining agreement. For example, Texas Instruments had an opportunity to purchase the Benrus Watch Company at a most attractive price from the bankers who were holding the Benrus debt. It needed the watch-case production of Benrus for its watches. But it passed up the deal because Benrus was unionized and located in New England, a union stronghold.

Employees.   Some entrepreneurs do not want to hire anyone. They are uncomfortable supervising other people and don't want the hassle that goes along with being an employer. Since managing employees is a most challenging task, they prefer to subcontract everything.

Religion.   Some firms strongly reflect the religious values of their founders. The firm seems to follow the dictates and values of the church of its founder. For example, Von Frellick, founder of Cinderella City shopping center in Denver, Colorado, followed the beliefs of his church in its attitudes toward the use of alcohol. He prohibited the sale of any alcoholic beverages in the center, thus preventing many restaurants from leasing there. It hurt business, but his value system dictated that he stick to his principles.

Government.   Some entrepreneurs detest government regulations and interference in business so much that they do everything to avoid government interface. They refuse to bid on government contracts and avoid as much regulation as they can by staying out of highly regulated businesses.

Provincialism.   Many people have strong prejudices toward countries, regions, and other cultures. There are Southerners who will refuse to do business with Yankees. Many Texans are uncomfortable working in New England, while others avoid doing business with Texans.

Checklist for Personal Issues

Answers to the following questions and those on page 49 [from *The Entrepreneur's Planning Handbook* (EEF)] will guide your decisions about what type of business to start or whether you are in the right business.

1. Does your proposed business concept meet your personal criteria? List the positives and negatives of the business opportunity.
2. Explain how the business will provide sufficient money to meet your minimum needs.
3. Will the business provide the money you truly expect it to make? List the time frame by years.
4. Explain how the business will satisfy your needs for sheltering your income for tax purposes.
5. Explain how the proposed business will provide sufficient security to meet your needs. Or must you secure a job to have a reasonably satisfactory life?

6. How long do you intend to work in the business? How much of your time will the business demand? First year? Fifth year? Tenth year?

7. What type of environment will you be happy working in? (Example: Indoors? Outdoors? Noisy? Dirty? Odoriferous?)

8. What types of people do you work best with? What kinds of people will you be working with in the proposed business?

9. Are status and prestige important to you? How will your business provide it?

10. How much travel will be required? Can or will you do it?

11. How much political or community involvement will the business require? Can or will you do it?

12. How does the business satisfy your power needs?

13. How much energy is required to get the venture launched and developed? Explain. (Example: Physical demands? Hours of operation? Mental stress?)

14. Explain if your age is an asset or liability in the business?

15. How many years are needed to build the business?

16. Can you afford a failure? Explain why or why not. What level of risk can you tolerate?

17. What does your spouse and/or family think about the venture? How much support will be forthcoming from them?

18. Have you the education or credentials needed for the business? If not, can you get them?

19. Where do you want to live? (Example: Size of city? Weather? Lifestyle?) Will the business allow you to do so?

20. What are you bringing to the venture? Do you have enough money to do the deal without help? Do you need outside talent for your management team?

21. In the end, what do you need from the business as an exit? Will you be able to sell it for a significant gain? Are you building wealth?

22. Can you live with debt? How much debt will the business need?

23. Will your business likely be unionized? Can you work with unions?

24. Explain why you will be an effective manager of employees.

Do you want employees? Will the venture require them or can the work be subcontracted?

25. How will the business fit into your moral and religious beliefs?

26. How well can you work with governmental authorities? How much government regulation will be encountered in your venture?

Business Strategy Issue: How Will Your Business Strategies Affect Your Venture?

There are many business issues involved in operating a venture that affect what kind of a venture you should start. These include intended size and growth, financial requirements, ownership and control, compensation, and legal and tax strategies. Consider how these business issues will affect the type of venture you choose to operate.

Size and Growth

How big do you want the business to be and how fast do you want it to grow? Many entrepreneurs do not want to operate a large organization. Instead they build a smaller-size business in which they are more comfortable. Others want to be big and grow quickly.

* Trap

A sound and successful enterprise can be ruined by unplanned and unwise growth strategies.

For example, a Denver restaurateur owned a successful chain of restaurants that he ultimately lost because he insisted on growing faster than his financial strength allowed. Other firms try to grow faster than their management base warrants. Others try to grow when neither the market nor the economics of the situation support an aggressive growth strategy.

Growth strategy is a complex dilemma worthy of much thought and deliberation. It is important to chart your growth strategy, evaluate it, and frequently adjust it to be in tune with the marketplace and the economy.

Sources of Money

Financing a venture through debt or equity is a critical question to consider. The entrepreneur's life will be immediately impacted when other people's money is used. If the entrepreneur uses only his or her money, there is wide latitude in how the business is operated. Once money is taken from others, they will dictate and control many aspects of the business.

Tip

Growth using only retained earnings takes considerably longer than obtaining an immediate injection of equity operating capital.

A more aggressive financing approach to growth would require a combination of retained earnings, debt, and equity.

Position in System

What role will the company play in the system within which it operates? Ralph Lauren, owner of the Polo brand clothing firm, does not want to manufacture any goods. Instead, the Polo name is licensed to others to make and market the products. Other firms want to manufacture, not market.

Ownership

Who will own the enterprise? The founder? The employees? The public? The customers? Many plywood manufacturers were organized as worker-owned cooperatives. A $20,000 share of stock entitled the investor to a job with the company. On the other hand, some entrepreneurs strongly feel that they want to own the whole show. They want no "partners" in their business ventures. If the entrepreneur wants to sell shares of its company's stock to the public, this must be part of the venture's strategy. For example, a company planning an initial public offering should have several years of audited financial statements, and keep excellent records.

Control

Many entrepreneurs feel strongly that they must control everything in their system from the ground floor to the consumer's hands. Weyerhaeuser in Tacoma, Washington, from its inception

controlled all aspects of its wood-products system. The founding patriarch's strategy was to control the wood supply—in other words, own the forests. "If you control the wood supply, you'll control the industry." Those words were frequently voiced in the corporate hallways and boardroom and the strategy became part of the corporate culture. From the woods, the company wants to control as much of its distribution systems as possible down to selling finished end products to industrial buyers. Other wood-product companies own as little as possible. As a matter of strategy, they buy their logs on the open market and then sell their output on the commodity markets.

Legal Strategy

Some firms as a matter of strategy try to monopolize their markets by frightening away potential competitors with law suits. They harass the little firm with legal actions. One entrepreneur refused to do business in some states simply because he did not like their legal climate. Many firms refuse to do business in foreign countries for reasons of legal strategy.

If your strategy is to eventually sell your company, then you should design legal strategies that will allow you to do so with ease. Avoid erecting unnecessary road blocks to your strategic plans.

Anytime the entrepreneur wants to play in the public market either as a merger partner or an IPO (initial public offering), legal strategies are critical. Much thought and planning should be given to legal structures, bylaws, stock ownership, rights, and contracts, and a good attorney specializing in that area should be used.

Compensation

How do you intend to pay your people? Will it be money or a piece of the rock? How about employee stock ownership plans (ESOP)? Will you use these methods in the future as an exit strategy? Will the company use bonuses, profit sharing, options, stock grants, and so forth? If so, these compensation methods should become a part of the strategic plan. For example, a bootstrap entrepreneurial strategy is for the initial management team to work for lower-than-market wages in return for generous stock options. They can then make their fortunes from the public sale of the stock, not from company revenue flows.

Tax Strategy

New and changing tax laws require continual tax planning. If a firm's strategy is built around capital gains, different strategies are needed depending on how the venture will be taxed and its legal structure. For example, certain legal entities are better from a tax standpoint if the strategic plan is to sell or dispose of the venture in the next 5 to 10 years.

Checklist for Business Issues

1. How big do you want the enterprise to be in years one through five?

2. What sources of money will be used? How will the business be able to attract the needed funds?

3. What position will the firm be in the total business system in which it will operate? (Example: Manufacturer? Distributor? Retailer?)

4. Who will own the enterprise? (Example: Employees? Public? Money sources?) How will this be accomplished?

5. Explain how you will plan to control the venture.

6. How many legal rights will the business retain? How much will be given up? (Example: Licenses? Distribution rights? Patents?)

7. What legal structure will facilitate the conduct of the firm's business? (Example: Partnership? C Corporation? S Corporation?) Under whose laws will the firm do business? (State? Federal?) (See Chapter 3 for more discussion on legal entities.)

8. What legal procedures should be taken to protect the interests of the enterprise? (Example: Patents, Copyrights? Trademarks? Employee contracts? Nondisclosure agreements? Buy-back arrangements?) (See Chapter 4 for more details on intellectual property.)

9. What risks should be transferred to insurance underwriters and which should be borne by self? (Example: Property insurance? Product liability? Major medical?)

10. How will the key employees be motivated? (Example: High pay? Performance bonuses? Stock ownership? Benefit packages?)

11. What tax strategies are needed to support the business needs in the future?

Entrepreneurs should appreciate how everything surrounding their business concept affects strategies and realize that any strategic plan is not a static parameter. Instead, constant planning is needed to respond to our dynamically changing business environment. The strategic plan should be reviewed and revised often.

Family Issues?

Regardless of the type of business you start, there are critical family issues to consider. Recognize these issues, evaluate their impact on your proposed or current venture, and discuss them with family members. Family issues fall into two categories—balancing family and venture commitments, and hiring family members.

Balancing Family and Venture Commitments

Unless both the goals of the family and the business are met, the venture is likely to be a disaster. Family approval of starting and operating a venture is critical. First, consider how starting and operating a business will affect the amount of time available to spend with family members. Changes in family life are inevitable and the demands of a new venture are enormous.

Entrepreneurs are usually preoccupied with their businesses day and night. The commitment of almost all your leisure time and energies is usually inescapable when starting a new venture. Founders are often obsessed with making their ventures a success, sometimes at the expense of the family. This ultimately can lead to the downfall of the business.

It's difficult to balance family responsibilities with owner responsibilities. Vacations may have to be postponed, weekend outings vanish, school visits are missed, social invitations must be declined, and meals get cold. Consider how you will balance the demands of the business with the demands of your family.

Implement the following action plan for family balancing strategies.

1. Set priorities for nonbusiness activities and try to stick to them.
2. Schedule time when you do nothing related to the business.
   On the positive side, your increased absence from the family

as a business owner will decline over time as you delegate more responsibility to others.

3. Explain to your family how the entrepreneurial opportunity you are considering will benefit them.

4. Elaborate on your business goals.

5. Ask your family to read your feasibility or business plan and ask questions about the proposed venture.

6. Discuss the downside and the risks involved. Make sure that your family fully understands and accepts the inherent risks in starting a new venture.

7. Obtain their commitment to support you and your efforts to launch and manage a new venture.

8. Discuss the amount of money required to start the venture. Explain how much money you will invest and how you will raise additional capital. The amount of money spent on family needs and entertainment may need to be cut. Reduced family cash flow is usually a reality.

All these factors put an added strain on your family. Determine if your family is comfortable with the financial resources required, the amount of collateral you may be required to pledge, and the potential financial sacrifices necessary from family members. Remember, smooth family relationships up front are an essential ingredient to successful ventures. Stress and conflicts within the family will affect your ability to launch a new venture and manage it successfully. An unsupportive family will ultimately undermine the business and subconsciously work against it.

Hiring Family Members

Many midcareer entrepreneurs start family-owned businesses for a good reason—they have a spouse and three kids who can go to work for the business immediately, and eventually become partners or owners. This is an example of the mentality of the farmer with many children who will provide cheap labor and work diligently on the farm.

Trap

Don't assume that hiring family members will solve your staffing problems or that they will make good employees.

First, assess whether family members have the talents and skills you need to operate the business. Consider differences in personalities, experience, working habits, talents, and spousal relationships. Many entrepreneurs make the fatal mistake of assuming family members will work for them without seriously considering whether this is a good match of their desires, experiences, and skills.

Founders often treat their ventures like a family picnic. They manage family members like parents instead of like an employer, which causes numerous problems. It is also hard to hire highly qualified and motivated employees when a number of family members work in the venture.

Second, there are inherent conflicts and personality clashes when family members are involved in the business. Emotions and hidden agendas often interfere with business decisions. Family members have different views of business and styles of management. Likewise, in-laws often become silent partners or consultants and interfere with making rational and sound business decisions.

Third, sometimes family members just don't make good employees. They lack the essential skills, experience, and motivation needed to make the business successful. They may be thrust into a position of power, but are incompetent and undermine the morale of nonrelated workers. Other times they just don't have the desire to work as hard as other staff members. Family fights and power struggles are demoralizing and the results can be disastrous. Unrelated workers can take sides with family members, which will increase tensions and lead to employee turnover. They may try to manipulate the business based on their knowledge of the family's internal problems or struggles.

Last, it is difficult or sometimes impossible to fire a family member who is a menace to the business. Hiring family members can turn out to be a satisfying team effort or a disaster. Careful consideration of these issues is critical before deciding to launch a new venture.

How Much Risk Can You Tolerate?

A certain amount of risk is involved in any entrepreneurial venture, but entrepreneurship is not as risky as previously thought. Sometimes the real risk is associated with changing a comfortable situation for the unknown. That is why some potential entrepreneurs retire on the job. The willingness to take a risk means that you are willing to go beyond the familiar and safe. However, the risk of pursuing a venture opportunity may be less risky than trying to keep a job. Today, it is risky to be an employee because more and more employees are having to justify their very existence in a company. What do they bring of value?

Entrepreneurs take both personal and financial risk to get what they want. A good question to ask yourself is what would be the worst thing that could happen if you were unsuccessful in launching a new venture? What is the downside? Keep in mind that you can always get another job if the business folds. Studies demonstrate that founders who have operated unsuccessful businesses are more inclined than others to find new and different uses for their talents with other organizations. Consider all the risks associated with starting a new business. There are always financial risks in starting a new business, such as loss of savings or house equity, and possibly a reduction in income. There are also risks to your reputation, your credibility, and your personal relationships.

Astute entrepreneurs reduce the risk factor by thoroughly researching their business concepts, industry, and market. As Ralph Waldo Emerson said, "knowledge is the antidote to fear." The more entrepreneurs learn about the marketplace, customers, suppliers, money sources, etc., the more courage they have and the better decisions they make. In addition, if a person has worked 10 or 20 years for another organization, they have accumulated much valuable experience which can be applied to the new venture.

Tip

One way to reduce risk is to start small—at home—and test your business concept and market potential.

Experiment with the marketplace on a small scale and obtain customer feedback. Ask potential customers to buy your product or service. Don't ask your friends if they think your venture idea will work. Instead, ask customers to give you a "letter of intent" to purchase. This forces potential customers to seriously think about whether or not they would really buy your product or service. If you are unable to obtain a letter of intent, then maybe it is not such a good idea.

Another way to minimize risk is with business planning. Entrepreneurial business planning can reduce, if not altogether eliminate, risks. That is why writing a feasibility plan first is so important to determine if your business idea is sound, if it can become profitable, and if it will give you what you need. Then develop a comprehensive business plan to use as a management tool to operate the business successfully.

Failure is another key consideration. Entrepreneurs are not afraid of failure, but learn from it. They become stronger, wiser, and more determined as they seek criticism and continual feedback. They discover that failures build character, stamina, and business skills. Entrepreneurs don't consider themselves weak because they have failed. Failure means finding out what does not work, deciding how to eliminate it, and discovering what will work.

Trap

Don't let the potential risks, money, or time keep you from achieving what is important.

If you have the drive, then properly research the industry, test your market, and write a feasibility and/or business plan. You will significantly increase your chances of starting and operating a successful venture if you follow these steps.

Many entrepreneurs have turned their ventures into exciting adventures and rewarding experiences for their families. The rewards of entrepreneurship are great including a sense of social contribution, professional satisfaction, esteem of peers, and being in control of one's life.

Remember, starting a business is more fun than anything else. It is a lot more fun and rewarding to solve problems in your own business and operate it as you think best instead of solving problems in someone else's business. There's no denying that it takes hard work and long hours in the beginning along with sound business planning and defined strategies. Your business plan helps reduce the personal and financial risks inherent in starting new ventures by identifying pitfalls up front and developing contingency plans to overcome them. The risk aversive also pay a price. If you never risk anything—in the end you'll risk even more!

3
Starting a Business

Choosing a Legal Structure

The form of organization you choose to operate your venture is crucial to your strategic planning and potential success. Many entrepreneurs make the mistake of ignoring a legal structure for their business assuming it is not that important. The law then assumes that your business is a sole proprietorship, which means that you and your business are legally one and the same. Key considerations in choosing a legal form of business include personal income level, tax implications, ability to raise capital, and limiting liability.

There are four major legal structures for business: sole proprietorship, partnership, corporation, and limited liability companies. Each is discussed below.

Sole Proprietorship

A sole proprietorship is the easiest of the various legal structures to start since there are fewer formalities and legal restrictions, which means it's easier to set up and terminate. The founder also has complete control of the business and is the sole recipient of any earned profits. For tax purposes, the IRS treats you and your business as one, and your reporting goes on Schedule C of your 1040 tax form. If the business ends up losing money, you deduct these losses on your tax return against any other income that you may have earned during that year. For these reasons, it is the legal form most used by small businesses.

However, there are several drawbacks to this form of ownership. First, the owner is fully liable for all business debts and actions. If the business is unable to meet its financial obligations, creditors will pursue your personal assets including your home and car.

Another major obstacle in sole proprietorships is the owner's ability to raise capital since he or she is generally relying only on his or her personal financial statement. The life of the business terminates with the life of the proprietor. It is difficult to attract good management, which can hamper growth and performance. Finally, the sole proprietor cannot deduct many of the expenses that are deductible to corporations, such as defined benefit pension plans, insurance expenses, and health benefits.

Trap

In a sole proprietorship personal assets are not protected from business lawsuits.

Partnerships

Partnerships are a tricky proposition. It is easier to raise capital and build your management team with this form of ownership, but it can be loads of trouble. Finding someone with the cash, similar goals, needed expertise, and compatible work habits can be difficult. Consequently, many partnerships end up in disaster.

Some of the advantages of partnerships include the ability to raise money, recruit and motivate key people, and provide companionship. The disadvantages include losing control, losing wealth, being stuck with other owner(s), and answering to others.

Issues to consider include deciding who will contribute the most money; how much equity will be distributed; the kinds of exit strategies or buyout provisions to choose; who will make the spending decisions; who will sign checks; and who will hire, supervise, and fire staff.

Tip

Select the right partner who complements your skills and then structure a partnership agreement that reflects the division of ownership and buyout provisions.

Find a partner who complements your strengths and weaknesses. Look for someone who specializes in your weakest area and someone you can trust, are compatible with, and can communicate with easily. Evaluate whether he or she has the ability to compromise. Entrepreneurs commonly involve friends or family members in their ventures; often they gain a partner, but lose a friend because of the stress of starting a business.

Trap

Be wary of considering friends as partners. Consider a trial period before settling on a partner and giving ownership.

There are two different legal forms of partnerships—the general partnership and the limited partnership. In a general partnership, the owners are liable for all business debts, even if the partnership agreement specifies a certain split in profits. Each partner is 100 percent responsible for all liabilities, so personal assets of the partners may be attached to cover the partnership's liability.

In a limited partnership, one partner or several general partners operate the business and are personally responsible for all the partnership's debts. The limited partners are liable only up to the amount of their investment in the business and do not participate in the management of the venture. Limited partnerships are created by filing a certificate of limited partnership with the Secretary of State in the state where the company is located.

If one partner dies or withdraws, the partnership terminates. For tax purposes, the income of the business is considered the income of the partners, so they are individually responsible for the taxes on their personal income tax return. Profits and losses may be divided in any way agreed to by the partners.

When considering any type of partnership, there should always be a formal written contract with a provision for the "parting of the ways" if an unresolved dispute arises. Either the partnership agreement or the corporate bylaws should require any owner to sell back shares at a predetermined price upon separation. Always have the terms of the partnership spelled out in detail, and have a good attorney review it.

Corporations

Most entrepreneurs are strongly advised to incorporate their ventures to protect against potential liabilities. A corporation is a legal entity that exists separate from its founders. It is created by filing articles of incorporation with the Secretary of State of the state in which the company incorporates. The company is owned by its shareholders and run by a board of directors elected by the shareholders. The owner can become a one-person corporation, the sole shareholder, and the only director. However, the founder cannot be both the president of the corporation and the secretary. Another person must be appointed to act as the secretary, but no ownership needs to be given to anyone else.

Three primary characteristics distinguish a corporation from other legal structures. First, a corporation limits a shareholder's liability to the amount of the investment in the business. Second, if shareholders are active in operating the business, they are considered employees and must be paid a reasonable wage subject to both state and federal payroll taxes. Finally, a corporation must pay tax on income as a separate legal entity. If profits are distributed to shareholders as dividends, these profits are subject to taxation as part of the shareholders' income.

Corporations shield shareholders from the claims of creditors and contractual relationships—unless the shareholders sign personally instead of as officers of the corporation. The corporate shield does not relieve any shareholder from personal negligence, civil wrongs, or torts, when acting as employees of the corporation.

Great care must be given to preserve the corporate shield and keep the affairs of the corporation at arm's length. This means the shareholders must file separate corporate tax returns, hold regular shareholder meetings, record minutes of the proceedings, and file a report with the state every two years. Following these procedures takes time and a few dollars.

Compliance with all such requirements is mandatory to maintain the corporate shield and receive limited liability protection. For example, shareholders should always identify themselves as officers of the corporation and keep the affairs of the corporation separate from their personal lives.

Tip

Whenever possible, avoid signing personally for any corporate debts.

Shareholders should never pay corporate debts personally and should never pay personal debts from corporate funds. However, this is not always possible when the founder is starting out and the corporation doesn't have assets. The lender will require that the debt be collateralized and many times the only way to accomplish this is to sign personally for the loan. If shareholders follow legal procedures to keep the corporate shield intact, their personal lives should be protected.

∗ Tip

The realities of the business world dictate that incorporation is usually the best legal structure for most entrepreneurs.

The main disadvantage of operating as a C corporation, is that there is double taxation. That is, the corporation pays a tax on earned profits, and those receiving salaries and/or corporate dividends are taxed again. A way to overcome this problem is to take some of the yearly corporate profits in salary, bonuses, and/or commissions. Entrepreneurs seldom distribute corporate dividends anyway. However, if a founder eventually wants to sell the corporation, not having profits will lower the price he or she can get for the business. The founder's exit strategy will determine if this is a good legal structure. Under our current tax law, the tax advantages are still in favor of the corporate structure.

There are several good resources available for making the job of incorporating easier, such as the *Do It Yourself Incorporation Kit* by S. J. T. Enterprises. Also, check with your state about a business start-up kit for owners. Many states provide these kits free of charge. However, if your corporation is complex or you have multiple shareholders, it's wise to seek the council of an attorney.

S Corporations.   The S corporation was designed for the owner-income enterprise, since profits or losses are reported on a shareholder's 1040, as in a partnership. Income or losses pass through the corporation to the stockholders.

S corporations are not actually separate legal structures, as are corporations, but constitute a special tax status granted by the IRS. S corporations do not pay corporate income tax, but divide the expenses and income among their shareholders. Shareholders report profits and losses on their personal income tax returns.

Consult qualified tax counsel to answer specific questions and take advantage of the tax laws' provisions.

Most entrepreneurs form S corporations to avoid the C corporation's double taxation, but this should not be the primary reason for forming an S corporation.

There are several restrictions on the organization and activities of an S corporation. First, it must be a domestic corporation. It may only have one class of stock issued and outstanding, which is common stock. However, common stock can be issued with or without voting rights. An S corporation may not earn more than 25 percent of its gross receipts from passive investment income (royalties, rents, dividends, interest, etc.) during any three-year period. It must have a tax year that ends December 31. It cannot have more than 75 shareholders, and all shareholders must be citizens or residents of the United States. Last, all shareholders must agree to elect S corporation status.

While the S corporation can be ideal when the venture is losing money, problems may occur when profits are realized and passed on to the stockholders if the company is not in a healthy cash position. They must pay income taxes on these profits while no cash is passed on to pay the taxes. This is one compelling reason for obtaining qualified tax counsel to assist you with this decision.

Deciding to become an S corporation requires careful consideration of the amount and type of income the company might generate in the future, other income or losses you might earn independent of the company, and whether you plan to sell either the assets or the entire company in the foreseeable future. An S election can still be a viable tax-savings device depending on your personal circumstances. It does provide a way to operate the business as a proprietorship or partnership for tax purposes and still benefit from the protection of the corporate shield. For more information about S corporations, obtain a copy of the *Internal Revenue Service Publication 589—Tax Information on S Corporations* by calling 1-800-829-3676.

Limited Liability Company

The limited liability company (LLC) is neither a corporation nor a partnership and is a relatively new type of business entity which when properly structured, combines the benefits of liability protection afforded to shareholders of a corporation with the favorable tax treatment provided to partnerships and their partners. Essentially, it is treated as a corporation, but it is taxed like a partnership. Income is distributed as ordinary income to the members, thus avoiding the double taxation of a C corporation.

Owners of interest in this form of business are called *members,* and their liability is limited to the extent of their investment in the business. Members must designate an operating manager, but unlike limited partnerships, there is no restriction upon the shareholders. The LLC permits an unlimited number of owners, who can be individuals, general or limited partnerships, or corporations. Members can also be nonresident aliens, which are restricted by the S corporation.

Other advantages of the LLC are that it provides tremendous flexibility in planning distributions and special allocations as compared with only one class of stock allowed an S corporation. The LLC can choose how to divide up profits and losses among its members. The LLC is not subject to the cumbersome and often confusing rules related to electing S corporation status. Creating an LLC is much like forming a corporation. Articles of organization must be filed with the Secretary of State of the state where the company is formed. The filing fee is the same as for a corporation. In addition, there must be an operating agreement, which resembles a partnership agreement and is a contract among owners. It is recommended that you consult a small business attorney to draw up the operating agreement. It takes the place of corporate bylaws.

The disadvantage of forming an LLC is that the IRS has not yet ruled on the tax treatment of limited liability companies. It has publicly ruled in Wyoming that the LLC would be treated as a partnership for tax proposes. That is why many business consultants have recommended that founders form their business as an LLC in Wyoming, where this form of ownership has been in operation for many years.

In addition, it is not clear whether the LLC retains its limited liability protection for members if the company conducts business outside of the state. For example, if your business is sued in another state, there is uncertainty as to whether the members would be afforded liability protection. The LLC has not yet been tested in several states, and there is risk involved.

As of 1997, 46 states permitted LLCs. However, businesses and professionals have reacted most favorably to this type of entity.

The trend is for other states to adopt the LLC status and many have legislation pending.

Last, the LLC requires unanimous written consent of all members to admit new members or to permit the transfer of a member's interest. Members can transfer their rights to share in the profits of the LLC.

The LLC is not the ideal legal structure for every business, but its simplicity and flexibility make it an attractive legal structure for many joint ventures, real estate ventures, oil and gas and mining businesses. Keep in mind that as your business grows, it might require a different legal structure to accommodate changing tax laws and the individual situations of its members. Consult a tax accountant or small business attorney for advice.

Protecting Your Business Interests

Operating with Buy-Sell Agreements

There should always be a "buyout" agreement, whether you have formed a partnership or a corporation. Inevitably clashes between partners occur, and there should be provisions for parting company if the dispute cannot be resolved. Either the partnership agreement or corporate bylaws should provide that any owner must sell back interest or shares at a predetermined or agreed-upon price on separation. If a dispute arises and you either want to buy back your partner's share or sell your share, then the other partner must agree either to sell at the offered terms or to buy at those same terms.

Tip

Include in your buy-sell agreement a "shoot-out clause" which stipulates that a partner wishing to buy out another partner must be willing and must offer to sell at the same price he or she wants to buy.

The trick with these types of agreements is how to price the shares. There are two approaches you can take. One way is to establish a predetermined price that is agreeable to the partners. The disadvantage is that as the venture grows, the value of the shares will change. The other approach is to agree to make a yearly evaluation determining the price of the shares for that year. This evaluation can be done by the partners or an outsider or it can be arbitrated. Regardless of how the evaluation is made, you should have a provision for pricing the shares of the venture.

Buy-sell agreements also make provisions for a death of a partner. They typically provide for redemption by the company of that person's share, possibly paid for by a life insurance policy carried by the company on the person. Or it provides for cross-purchase of the person's shares by the surviving partner(s), possibly paid for by insurance carried by the surviving partner(s). The preferable provision depends largely on tax considerations. Consult your lawyer and accountant about the best type of buy-sell agreements for your particular situation.

Operating with Key-Partner Life Insurance

Tip

Purchase "key-partner life insurance" which provides money for the corporation to buy out the shares of any partner who dies.

An advantage of purchasing this type of insurance is that the premiums are tax-deductible expenses for the company.

Consideration should also be given to insuring key employees of the business whose loss could have substantial financial consequences. The loss of a key person could mean the loss of key customers, loss of services or special skills provided by that person, or loss of capital. Many entrepreneurial ventures purchase key-employee insurance. Key-employee life insurance pays compensation to a business on the death of a partner, while key-employee disability income insurance pays compensation caused by permanent and total disability.

Normally, the company is the owner of the policy, the premium payer, and the beneficiary, although a business and key employee may agree to split the premium payments. A key employee must agree to the company's purchase of the insurance on his or her life. If the key employee is terminated, the company may continue the policy in force, surrender the policy for its cash value, or sell it to the employee.

Contact your small-business insurance agent for more details on purchasing key-person insurance. Or if you don't have one, contact Western Insurance Information Service at (303) 790-0216. It is a consumer education and information organization that provides helpful facts for business owners.

Securing a Patent

The first step in securing a patent and getting a product to the marketplace is to write a letter to the U.S. Department of Commerce, Patent and Trademark Office, Washington, DC, 20231 and ask for information and brochures about the patenting process. Or you can call them with questions about the filing process at the Public Service Center, (703) 557-INFO. Also, write for a copy of the book *General Information Concerning Patents*, which is available for $2 from the Government Printing Office, Washington, DC 20402.

You can obtain a patent by yourself or use a professional patent attorney. If you choose to try it on your own, refer to *Patent It Yourself* by David Pressman Polo Press, which clearly outlines the patenting process. Consider contacting an experienced patent attorney who can expedite the process. Obtain referrals for competent patent attorneys or agents.

The next step is to undertake a novelty search to determine whether your concept or a closely related concept has already been patented. You can conduct the search on your own, contact an independent informational broker (listed in the *Yellow Pages*), or have a patent attorney perform the search. The Patent and Trademark Office is located in Alexandria, Virginia; however, patent depositories are located at major public libraries, and on the Internet at www.USPTO.GOV.

Inventors should file a disclosure statement that documents the date of conception of the invention. In the event that two people are working on the same idea at the same time, the one who files the disclosure document first has the right to file for a patent. The disclosure document is a detailed description of the invention and its uses, which may include photos. The inventor has a two-year grace period in which to file a patent application, but must demonstrate diligence in completing the invention and filing the application.

Trap

Do not mail a dated description of the invention to yourself by certified mail; It has no value to the Patent Office.

Consider applying for a Provisional Patent Application which allows the inventor to obtain an early filing date with few formalities and at a lower cost than filing a regular application. To file a Provisional Patent Application you must:

1. Prepare a clearly written description of the invention which is adequate to allow a person skilled in the art to practice the invention; however it need not include traditional patent claims.

2. Present any drawings needed to understand the invention; they need not meet the traditional patent application requirements.

3. Pay the filing fee of $75 for individuals who qualify for small-entity status ($150 for nonsmall entities).

4. Complete a cover sheet identifying the application as being a Provisional Patent Application, the invention title, the inventor's and any coinventor's name, residence, a docket number if applicable, and a correspondence address.

5. If you are claiming small-entity status, present a declaration in support of that claim.

A small entity is an individual or group of individuals, a company having less than 500 employees, a charitable organization, or a university, all of whom have no duty to license or to assign the application to a nonsmall entity.

The provisional patent differs from a regular patent application in that the provisional application is not examined for patentability by the U.S. Patent and Trademark Office and cannot mature into a patent unless a regular patent application based on the Provisional Patent Application is filed by you within 12 months of the filing date of the provisional application.

When a regular application is filed it is then entitled to claim the benefit of the provisional application's filing date. If a regular patent application is not filed, then the provisional application is automatically abandoned by the Patent Office 12 months after it has been filed.

Historically, the life of a U.S. patent had been 17 years from the date of issue. Now, according to the provisions of the GATT Treaty, a patent application filed on or after June 8, 1995, regardless of the date on which it issues and so long as maintenance fees are paid, will have a life of 20 years from the filing date of the formal patent application, or 20 years from any prior U.S. or foreign application from which it claims as a priority filing date.

Acquiring a patent can be an expensive project. Using a patent attorney to file a simple mechanical patent by completing the application process, preparing the necessary written documents, and submitting one sheet of drawings will cost $3000 at the low end, depending on the invention and the attorney's hourly rate. Costs can increase significantly depending on whether you receive a patent applied for status after your initial application, which does not occur often. Usually modifications to the claims are required. The whole process could take from six months to two years.

Tip

Because of the intricacies and detailed regulations, research the patenting process first, perform as much of the ground work yourself, and then consult a professional patent attorney or agent.

Once the patent application is received, the Patent Office will conduct a search of the patent records and during that period the invention is said to be "patent applied for." This status establishes the inventor's claim and dates it. If the Patent Office accepts the patent, the invention is in the "patent pending" stage and awaiting the issuance of the patent.

Worldwide Patents

If you need to file a valid U.S. patent application on any invention, you must do so within one year of any public use, sale, or offer for sale in the United States, or publication of the invention in the United States or anywhere else in the world. Under most foreign patent laws, any nonconfidential disclosure of the invention prior to the filing of your patent application may make it instantly impossible to file an application that will result in a *valid* foreign patent.

Tip

For a valid patent in most other countries, you must file your foreign patent application before making any nonconfidential disclosure of your invention.

Fortunately, most countries are adherents of an international treaty which allows the *effective date* of filing of your foreign patent application to relate back to its U.S. filing date, so long as the foreign application is filed within one year of the U.S. filing date. It is a typical strategy to file an application in the United States (and in foreign countries that are not adherents to the treaties, such as Taiwan) before any nonconfidential disclosure of the invention is made. Subsequently, applications are then filed in foreign countries that are adherents of the international treaty within one year of the U.S. filing date, thereby making the U.S. filing date the effective date of the foreign filing.

Securing a Trademark

It's a good idea to obtain and federally register company trademarks. These are words used as adjectives, symbols, or any combination which a business uses to identify and distinguish its products or services from others. Your business reputation allows you to introduce a product or service more successfully *simply by using your trademark on it.*

Tip

Trademarks add value to your venture as intellectual property and assist in raising capital.

For example, the symbol for Coca-Cola and the golden arches identifying McDonald's are extremely valuable assets. You can license the use of your trademark to others. Once you have protected it, you have the exclusive right to use it and seek protection from the courts if someone else infringes on it. It not only indicates origin, but also can serve as a guarantee of quality. Words or symbols used to identify and distinguish service are called service marks. They are used in the sale or marketing of services rather than products. Service marks and trademarks are registered the same way.

A trademark on goods automatically acquires "common law" legal rights within the geographic area, and nationally, if advertised. Establish a trademark or service mark by affixing the letters *TM* or *SM*. These letters are usually smaller than the actual trademark and most often follow the mark. These marks can be registered with state or federal trademark offices.

According to U.S. law, a "common law" trademark is obtained by first use, and it is kept by continuous, proper use. Registering a mark with the U.S. Patent and Trademark Office enhances the odds of avoiding infringement, and it provides a stronger weapon for contesting infringement. Before a trademark user may file an application for federal registration, the user must use the mark on goods that are shipped or services that are sold in interstate commerce.

Registering a federal trademark involves completing a written application form, including a drawing of the work, and providing three specimens showing the actual use of the mark in connection with the goods or services, and sending the required filing fee. Trademarks have a 10-year life that is renewable for additional 10-year periods unless abandoned. Proof of continued use and a fee must be filed between the fifth and sixth years or the registration will be canceled. Issuance of registration takes about 9 to 16 months. It is also now possible to apply for a registration for a mark which you have a bona fide intent to use in the future.

It is advisable when applying for a federal trademark, to perform a search to determine if another person or organization is using the mark in the same channels of trade. If so, then you probably cannot qualify for the same trademark. Using such a mark can hurt your marketing efforts if you must change it after using it for some time. Names in use can be found in the *Trade Names Dictionary,* the *Thomas Register of American Manufacturers,* and in the *Yellow Pages.* There are also database searches available through most libraries with federal depositories.

Once a trademark is federally registered, the ® symbol or the words *Registered in the U.S. Patent and Trademark Office,* may be used.

Trap

Failure to register a trademark may prevent you from recovering damages for trademark infringement.

To register a state trademark, contact the Secretary of State of that state. For further information get a copy of *General Information Concerning Trademarks* from the Superintendent of Documents, Government Printing Office. Or call the Trademark Office's automated telephone service (703) 557-4656 to obtain an application or ask questions. It is also advisable to involve an experienced intellectual property attorney to review your search and oversee the registration process.

Securing a Copyright

Obtaining a copyright is the first step to properly protect your intellectual property for specific uses of art, sculpture, books, music, motion pictures, videotapes, photographs, software programs, or other types of creative materials. It is a low-cost procedure administered by the U.S. Copyright Office. According to the current copyright law, a copyrightable work is automatically protected *from its creation whether it is marked or not.*

Tip

It is best to include a copyright notice on your material in the form of the full word *copyright*, the abbreviation *copyr*, or the small *circled* *c*(©), along with the year of completion and the owner's name.

Officially register your copyright by filing the proper form, which can be obtained from the Register of Copyrights, Library of Congress, Washington, DC 20559. The cost is $20, and you can do it yourself quite easily.

Once you copyright your property, you have accomplished only 5 percent of the work necessary to take it to the marketplace. A copyright does not protect ideas, it simply gives you the right to prevent others from copying the particular way in which you express your ideas.

It takes about three to four months to have your application processed before you receive a certification or registration. A copyright is good for the lifetime of the author plus 50 years after the death of the author. If you need additional information, call the Copyright Office Hotline at (202) 287-9100. Another excellent resource is *The Complete Copyright Protection Kit,* Intellaw,

Denver, Colorado. This kit, which costs $25, contains up-to-date information on how to register, transfer, and legally enforce a copyright, as well as various copyright forms.

To be protected by copyright, your work must satisfy three requirements. First, it must be original; second, it must be incorporated in something tangible; and third, it must fall within one or more of the categories of works provided for in the copyright act. Although you are not required to use a copyright notice, it is desirable to do so for proper protection. You should also add warning statements like, "All Rights Reserved," (which also provides protection in South America) or "No part of this material may be reproduced without permission" or similar wording. Place the notice on your material where it can be seen by an ordinary user under normal conditions: for example, on the title page.

Protecting Trade Secrets

Trade secrets are any proprietary information used in the course of business to gain an advantage in the manufacture or commercialization of products or services. They can be formulas, devices, patterns, techniques, customer lists, sales forecasts, databases, manufacturing processes, or compiled information that has a specific business application. *They must have economic value, they must be secret, and you must attempt to protect them.*

Tip
___

The most significant factor in determining whether your confidential information receives legal protection is the degree to which you take steps to protect the information and the ease of obtaining the information from other sources.

Trade secrets are not covered by any federal law but are recognized under a governing body of common laws in each state. To be classified as a trade secret, the information must not be generally known in the trade. The most famous trade secret is the formula for Coca-Cola, which is maintained as a trade secret.

In order to keep customer and price lists a trade secret, you must keep the information secret and take precautions to keep it secret. Such precautions should first include establishing policies on identifying and maintaining trade secret information. Second, require employees to sign a confidential disclosure agreement that protects against their giving out trade secrets either while an employee or after leaving the company. Last, mark these documents *confidential* or *secret,* then employees or others coming into contact with this information will immediately be put on notice of its confidential nature and the need to take precautions to avoid disclosure.

Confidential documents should be locked in a vault or other secure location. Trade secrets stored on or accessible by computer must be protected from disclosure to unauthorized parties. Build passwords into your computer system to prevent unauthorized access. Use the exit interview to remind departing employees of their confidentiality obligation. One overlooked way trade secrets are lost is through conventions, trade shows, seminars, or other similar activities.

Tip

Trade secrets can be sold or licensed and used as a financial strategy for increasing revenues.

In today's competitive environment your continued success may well depend on your ability to protect your valuable trade secrets. This involves continuous, systematic, and diligent monitoring.

Invention Marketing Companies

The invention business is rapidly expanding, with the number of patents alone increasing 40 percent between 1985 and 1990. The problem is that most inventors do not know how to market their products, and thus turn to invention marketing companies to do this work for them.

* Trap

The invention industry is saturated with fraudulent invention marketing companies charging high up-front fees for initial research reports and subsequent marketing and sales plans that forecast great market potential stressing the hundreds of thousands of dollars an inventor could earn.

Many of these companies are currently being investigated by the Federal Trade Commission. Recently, *The Wall Street Journal* reported that less than 1 percent of customers ever get a penny from their inventions despite the fees of up to $10,000 that inventors pay to these invention marketing firms. Most of these companies make overly optimistic claims that the inventor will get rich quick. These companies should be avoided, but if you decide to contract with an invention marketing company, follow these steps:

1. Obtain a list of satisfied clients. Contact them personally to determine whether their idea has been successfully marketed. Inquire as to the exact location of where the product is being sold and if possible visit the outlet. Try to estimate the sales volume.

2. Ask for a list of products that the invention marketing company has taken from the idea stage to the marketing stage. Obtain the names of the product owners and ascertain if the marketing efforts of the invention marketing firm were successful. Inquire how much money they have earned from their invention.

3. Request the names and locations of the manufacturers producing the inventions for the company both in the past and currently.

4. Ask for the names and locations of distributors involved in marketing the inventions the firm handles. Try to discover how successfully these inventions have been marketed and sold.

5. Verify all claims the invention marketing company makes and perform as much "do diligence" as possible. It will cost you time and a few dollars, but it's well worth it in the long run. Remember, there are very few, and some experts say no, invention marketing firms that ever carry out their claims. They make great promises but are short on delivery.

6. If the invention marketing company asks you to sign a contract, inquire as to whether they provide a refund if you are dissatisfied with their services. Inquire under what circumstances clients are eligible for refunds. Then request a list of clients who have obtained refunds in the past and check to see if they are employees of the company.

7. Check with the Better Business Bureau in your area, the Consumer Fraud Division of your local district attorney's office,

the attorney general's office, and the consumer advocate in the local media for any complaints on these types of companies.

Licensing Your Invention

A licensing agreement describes the terms for the use of the product or image and usually includes territory and the length of time that the license is effective. It also provides that the licensee pay royalties to the licensor for the right to use the product or characters, logos, or brand names on otherwise unrelated products.

The first step in licensing is finding a company or person interested in your product idea. Begin by going to your local library and looking through the *Thomas Register of American Manufacturers* for names of companies in your industry. This resource book lists manufacturer names and addresses for thousands of different businesses. Also look at *Dun & Bradstreet's Reference Book of Corporate Management,* which gives a detailed biographical description of many leading companies and their principal officers. All communications with a potential licensee should be directed at top management.

Next, go to the store isles where your competitors' products are displayed. Most packages give the name and location of its producer. Make a list of these competing companies. They may be interested in expanding their product lines and are a good source for a potential license.

Tip

Find out as much about different licensing arrangements as possible and use exclusivity rights as a bargaining wedge.

Some organizations that deal with licensing issues include the Licensing Industry Merchandisers' Association, The National Association of Small Business Investment Companies, and The National Venture Capital Association. Your local chamber of commerce, small business development centers, venture capitalists, or banks can also assist with licensing leads.

After you have located businesses in your industry that might be interested in a license agreement, determine what you want from such an agreement. Will you ask for any up-front money to pay for out-of-pocket expenses for developing, prototyping, patenting, or other associated costs? Success in negotiating for up-front money will depend largely upon how badly the company wants your invention.

How large of a royalty percentage should you ask for? What type of exclusivity will you be willing to negotiate for? Be cautious about bargaining away your exclusivity rights. Usually, if you can find one licensee, you will probably be able to find more.

How much personal involvement do you want in marketing the product or overseeing its production? Should you consider hiring a lawyer to represent you during negotiations? If the potential licensing agreement is complicated, it is wise to have legal counsel represent you.

After you have answered these questions and researched licensing arrangements, begin writing query letters to potential licensees. Incorporate information on the demand for your product including any marketing research and/or testing results. Identify potential purchasers. Describe the applications and alternatives for the product. List any proprietary rights such as potential or existing patents, trademarks, or copyrights. Explain your qualifications and business background.

Last, and most important, demonstrate how the licensee will benefit from your product. Writing query letters takes time, and you will probably receive your share of "we're not interested" letters. Don't get too excited about receiving a letter of interest. Often, the first interested party will not be your last. A sound licensing agreement should benefit both you and the licensee. The size of the royalty is a reflection of your negotiating clout, standards in the industry, and how much risk the licensee is taking. Royalties generally range from 2–12 percent.

Trap

Avoid making a hasty decision in signing a licensing contract.

Once you've come to terms with a potential licensee, use an attorney to structure a licensee agreement that benefits both you and the licensee.

Protecting the Name of Your Business

Many founders operate their business under their own name, which can make the business look small and unprofessional. We recommend using a fictitious business name and registering it.

The choice of your company name is important because like selecting a location, it is recognizable and can serve as a form of advertising. It is a part of the total package you are selling and will promote familiarity and confidence in your product. Your company name should be appropriate to your product, easy to read, and easy to remember.

Tip

Before you order business cards or stationery or design a brochure, check with your county or city clerk to ensure that no one else is using the name you select for your company.

If you use a fictitious name, and if no other business is using that name, you can register it. If someone else is using the name you select, you will have to choose another name. Have several alternative names in case the name you want is already being used. Go to the *Yellow Pages* of your telephone book to see if anyone is using the name you are considering locally.

In most states, you file a fictitious business name statement with the county or city clerk and publish a specially worded notice in the legal section of your local newspaper. Many of these newspapers provide the form for filing, publish the notice, and file the required affidavit.

If you do decide to use your first and last name as your company name, you will not need to register an assumed name. However, if you add words like *Co.* or *Associates* or change your own name in any way, it is considered a fictitious name and should be registered.

In some states, sole proprietorships and partnerships are registered at the state rather than the local level. Corporations are always registered at the state level with the Secretary of State. Register your name with your state's Department of Commerce to prevent its use by any corporate entity.

To protect your company name and to obtain national rights, register it with the U.S. Patent Office. To register the name as a national trademark, the company must first use it on the product in interstate commerce and then file it with the Patent Office.

Some consultants specialize in developing company names, and there are attorneys who research registrability of company names. There are also services that maintain databases on business names that can be used to search names. Names in use can be found in the *Trade Names Dictionary,* and the *Thomas Register,* available in the reference section of your local library.

A good reference is *Brand Names: Who Owns What,* which lists 15,000 brand names of about 750 firms by Diane Frankenstein, published by Books in Demand.

Your company name is an integral part of your intellectual property and should be properly protected.

Finding the Right Location for Your Business

There is no ideal location. In most cases there are just compromises. You must compromise some ideas for the sake of finances or your personal preferences. But that's the fun of being an entrepreneur. You can put your business where you want it, as long as you can afford the space.

Several different types of location decisions need to be considered before selecting the specific area for your new enterprise. Your decision will vary depending on whether the business is a service or a manufacturing venture.

First, the location of retail stores is an art unto itself. The value of a piece of property depends almost entirely upon its location. To the retailer, the key to success rests in the selection of a good location that has a significant amount of consumer traffic. By contrast, a manufacturer needs to be located closer to suppliers and modes of transportation.

Consider the following general factors before deciding on a specific area in which to locate your business.

State of Incorporation. In which state will you incorporate? While the corporate statutes of most states are quite similar, there are some key differences. For example, some states give stockholders more rights than others. The laws of the state in which you incorporate establish the ground rules under which you must operate your business.

Delaware is a popular state to incorporate in because its laws allow management maximum control over the business with a minimum of interference from minority stockholders. However, if you incorporate in a state other than the one in which you are doing business, you must file as a "foreign corporation" in the state in which you are doing business. The matter of determining the state in which you should register as a foreign corporation is complex, may have tax consequences, and requires legal counsel. If you are doing business in several states, legal counsel might advise setting up separate corporations in each state.

Tip
___

Generally, incorporate in the state in which the business will be operating.

Consider the following when choosing a business location:

Taxes.   The success of the southern states in attracting new business-es demonstrates the effect that low taxes have on location decisions. Taxes are an important factor to consider in locating your business, but you may be better off paying higher taxes and selling more goods for a higher price. There are many places to locate and enjoy tax relief, but you may have difficulty generating a profit there.

Costs.   The best location for a business might be in the newest local mall. But the cost of the space may prohibit many from locat-ing there. Entrepreneurs may be forced to go where they can afford the rent or where they can operate more efficiently.

Security.   Many businesses avoid certain areas of a city because they fear for their safety and property. Customers might also be leery to drive to these types of locations. Choose a site where you and your customers will feel both comfortable and secure.

Availability.   Many entrepreneurs locate where there is available space at the time they wish to open. Expediency does have its virtues, but consider the long-term effects of your immediate decision. Don't be shortsighted. Is this the best location for your business?

Infrastructure.   Sometimes location decisions are based on select-ing an area where there are many business professionals to support entrepreneurs and serve their continuing needs. For example, computer businesses often locate in the same area where materials and parts are readily available.

Personal considerations.   The location of a business may depend on how far you want to drive to and from the business each day.

Family commitments may prohibit you from locating in a more desirable area that requires considerable driving time. Your personal happiness is an important factor in selecting a location.

Once you have considered these elements, it is time to focus on the selection of a specific area. For retail and some wholesale businesses:

Determine the Trading Area.   Every location has a trading area from which the venture derives its business. The trading area may be only a few blocks surrounding the store or it may be a 5-mile radius. Each type of store draws customers from varying distances. To determine your particular trading area, start by locating on a map your potential site and your competitor's stores. Everything being equal, customers trade at the most convenient place. Next, you could survey the license plates of cars parked in or around your proposed location to determine which counties or states they come from.

Look Up the Demographics of Your Trading Area.   Determine the sizes of the families living in the surrounding area and the average family income. This information will be helpful in forecasting the sales potential for the proposed location. Can the people living in your area afford your product? Evaluate the buying habits and profile of potential customers in your trading area.

Observe Traffic Patterns.   Where does traffic come from and where is it going? Are cars just zooming by on the way to or from work? Is public transportation accessible? High traffic volume can be advantageous to most businesses if cars stop and trade in the area. Ask nearby residents about their buying habits. Approach a local merchant to find out where his or her customers come from. Don't be fooled about the numbers of cars passing by your site hourly. Vehicular traffic may not stop at this location. The key is to assess the quality of the people exposed to your proposed site, not just the quantity. Both are important, but the quality outweighs the quantity.

Evaluate the Ease of Entry and Exit.   Are there any major freeways, one-way streets, traffic patterns, or other physical characteristics of the area that directly influence where people go to shop? Some locations at first glance appear to be excellent, but on closer inspection, you discover that they are difficult to get to. Keep in mind the principle of convenience.

Evaluate Available Parking.   Does the location you are considering have enough accessible and convenient parking? Is the location so busy that customers cannot find a parking place? Adequate parking is essential to selection of a good location site.

Study Community Growth Patterns.   Would it be more beneficial locating in an area targeted for significant growth and expansion versus situating in a well-established center? To obtain a prime space, it may be necessary to anticipate the direction of growth in an area and locate a store in this path before adequate sales volume is realized. Smaller merchants usually need immediate sales volume and cannot risk betting on growth. You must have sufficient money to wait until the market develops.

Pinpoint the Competition.   Is there any competition located close to your proposed site? You may want to locate your store near a competitor with an established clientele which you hope to attract. Perhaps you want to locate where there is no close competition to capture the market in the immediate area.

Find an "Anchor Store."   Entrepreneurs often locate in shopping centers where there are popular anchor stores, such as established chains, so they can live off of the existing traffic flow and offer a selection of goods the shopper cannot find in the anchor stores. They use the promotional efforts of the larger store to help build their traffic and customer base.

Consider Contacting a Competent Commercial Real Estate Company.   Some of these companies have trained salespeople who are familiar with the availability, traffic patterns, demographic information, and busy centers in the city.

For manufacturing businesses:
   If your business deals in the production of goods, then you will be looking at locations for the following characteristics:

1. *Quality of labor.*   Can the community supply the types of skills you require?

2. *Accessibility to transportation.* Will it be easy and cost-effective to ship goods from this location?

3. *Incentives from the city or county.* Are there governmental programs that will provide tax breaks for your business if it locates in the community?

For service businesses, follow these two rules of thumb:

1. If clients come to your site, choose a location that meets the requirements of a retail site.

2. If you go to the client's site, choose a location that allows you to keep overhead costs down.

Selecting a location is one of the most critical elements of your potential success. Base your decision on facts, rather than on subjective perceptions. Research the area well. The rewards your business will reap are the direct result of the time you spend today investigating various available locations.

Selecting a business location is a complex process that often takes considerable research and much time. However, one of the common traits shared by entrepreneurs is their eagerness to get the door open. They want the business to be open right now. Thus, they fall victim to the following common pitfalls.

You Get What You Pay For. The bottom line is that good locations cost more money than less desirable locations. Many retailers simply do not have the money to invest in a good location. There are three main factors that contribute to operating a successful store: location, location, location.

Rents are not a function of costs; they represent how much money can be earned from the space. A small location in a large shopping mall can cost more than a larger space in a smaller mall. However, large shopping malls attract more people per square foot than do smaller malls. Entrepreneurs pay for the people the mall delivers to their door.

The Law of the Landlord. Landlords are in business to make money. Often they do not want to risk the successful image of their shopping center, mall, or industrial site by renting to an unknown operation when they can obtain prospective tenants from a host of well-known, established organizations.

They may not want to risk renting a space to an unknown fearing that if the business fails, the lease may be virtually unenforceable.

Illusion versus Reality.   It is not uncommon for the entrepreneur to be lured into a vacant business location by a landlord offering the "deal of the century." They might offer you a few rent-free months until you get settled or a lower than average price per square foot. Beware of "deals." Be careful of space that is consistently vacant. Maybe the location is tucked away in the corner of the shopping center. The store's sign could not be seen unless it fell on a passing customer. Ask what other tenants have occupied the space and for how long a time. Don't fall prey to such great deals. Instead, thoroughly research the site.

Trap

Beware of overly attractive leasing deals.

Be Careful of Claims by the Landlords.   Landlords are eager to rent available space in their centers and tend to be overly optimistic about the virtues of their location. Verify every piece of information provided. Locate other business owners who closed their businesses to determine what problems they encountered.

Tip

Talk to other tenants in the location you are considering. Ask lots of questions about the location, customers, traffic, and the policies enforced by the landlord.

Researching any site location is essential. In-depth research can mean the difference between selecting a really superior site or one that merely appears to be good. Learn about the feasibility of a location by both subjective and qualitative observation. Ask yourself these questions:

1. Is the area prospering? A close look will tell you if many homes are for sale.

2. What is the condition of the homes in the immediate area?

3. Are there many children around?

4. Are the residents prospering? Look over the places of employment, notice the clothes people wear, the cars they drive.

5. Are local shopping centers and entertainment attractions thriving?

6. What is the traffic flow around these areas?

7. What time of day is the traffic count the highest?

8. Do people seem to be spending their disposable income at these shops?

9. Are they just walking around or are they making purchases?

Visit the government document librarians in your local library and ask for the Census of Business and the Census of Population, published by the U. S. Department of Census which are excellent sources of demographics data. Some of this data is also available on line. Also check the "Survey of Buying Power" that tends to contain more current data than the first two sources. Remember, location is the key to any successful retail endeavor.

Getting Advice and Help from Experts

Hiring Lawyers

In this highly complex legal society, entrepreneurs need competent legal advice which ironically, is oftentimes the most difficult assistance to find. Where should an entrepreneur begin to look?

Trap

Avoid contacting your local legal society to ask for attorney recommendations.

In most cases, local legal societies do not recommend attorneys. To find a lawyer, ask successful entrepreneurs who they use. Who represents them? Who seems to win the court cases? Ask your fellow entrepreneurs to describe their experiences in working with local lawyers.

Then go to your public library and consult directories that give information about lawyers and their credentials. The most comprehensive is the *Martindale-Hubbell Law Directory*, which lists lawyers nationwide and provides detailed information on the background of the firm, areas of specialization, and sometimes includes major clients. It gives "ratings" for lawyers based on their legal ability, ethical standards, professional reliability, and diligence. However, these ratings are based on confidential recommendations solicited from other lawyers. Other directories include *The Lawyer's Register by Specialties and Fields of Law,* the *Attorney's Register,* the *U.S. Lawyer's Referral Directory,* the *Directory of the Legal Profession,* and state-by-state Blue Books of lawyers. Most local bar associations also publish lists of local lawyers with some basic information about credentials and expertise.

The demand for legal services is unpredictable. Rarely do you know when you are going to need legal advice or assistance. For example, when a memorandum of agreement to purchase a business needs to be drawn up immediately, where do you go? You cannot wait to interview different attorneys or be put off to meet with a lawyer at his or her convenience. How quickly a lawyer responds to your request is critical.

Should you look for a large or small legal firm? The legal profession is dominated by several very large firms that have dozens of partners with substantial power and many contacts. They can call upon expertise in many different fields like the Securities & Exchange Commission if you have a tax problem. If you are taking a company public, a larger firm will add significant credibility to your venture. Many have connections and political power that can be most useful. Thus, with one legal connection, you can rent expertise in different areas of business.

However, big firms present several disadvantages. If you operate a small business, you may not be important to them and your concerns could be assigned to a rookie who has little experience in small business concerns. Second, they can be quite expensive. For example, a large firm might easily charge you $3000 to $5000 for incorporating your business, while a smaller firm will charge $300 to $500. They may not be interested in your account or their availability may be less than desirable. For these reasons, many entrepreneurs use smaller firms that are more eager for their business.

The process of selecting a business lawyer is a personal one. Start by asking your friends and business contacts for their recommendations. Perhaps your banker or CPA could recommend a competent business attorney.

Tip

The lawyer you hire should have considerable and practical experience in small business affairs.

After you establish a list of several potential business lawyers, make appointments and interview them. Many lawyers offer an exploratory session free. Develop a list of questions to use during the interview. There is an excellent list of checklist interview questions in the book *100 Ways to Cut Legal Fees & Manage Your Lawyer* by Krasnow & Conrad. It is an excellent publication on managing your legal affairs and controlling legal costs that runs the gamut from how to choose a lawyer to how to act as your own. The book costs $10.95 plus $1 postage and can be ordered by calling (800) 638-6582 or by writing to the National Chamber Litigation Center, 1615 H St. N.W., Washington, DC 20062.

Ask for referrals from other entrepreneurs they currently work with. Ask how many years of experience they have had working with entrepreneurial companies. Determine their particular small business expertise. Describe a routine legal matter and evaluate how they would handle it.

Last, how well do you relate to the lawyer? Is there good chemistry? You and your business attorney should have a similar business philosophy. You will most likely select an all-around general business attorney and then use specialists when the need arises.

There is an art to using a lawyer advantageously, and it must be managed effectively. Here are some guidelines to follow when contacting a small business attorney:

1. *Assist your attorney by conducting any preliminary investigation and obtaining necessary information in advance.*   The more legwork, information, and investigation you can conduct yourself, the more money you will save. Bring your attorney all the important documentation required to aid in the decision-making process. Use your lawyer's expertise to review the issues surrounding the legal matter and bring up potential risk factors.

2. *Use standardized forms for conducting routine business.* Entrepreneurs use many different types of forms to operate their business. Use standardized forms to save expensive legal fees and ask your attorney to review such forms so they are structured to fit your particular needs. Reliable form books include *The Complete Book of Corporate Forms* published by NOVA. Lawyers do not regu-

larly write original business forms for their clients but in most cases also use computerized standard business forms and tailor them to the particular situation.

3. *Decide when to involve your business attorney in negotiations.* We recommend you involve a business attorney once you have established some common ground of agreement with people you are negotiating with. Use your business attorney to review the situation, point out risk factors, and then draw up the legal documents to finalize the deal. The ultimate business decision is yours.

4. *Listen to your attorney's recommendations.* There may be some instances when tax or technical problems in the deal require resolution. You may not be able to adequately judge the true impact of the deal you are considering entering into. Lawyers are experts at pointing out the risk factors associated with a business deal.

5. *Beware of lawyers who are in court all the time.* Although litigation is a cost of doing business, it does cost a lot of money. Entrepreneurs have discovered that the winners in a court case are always the lawyers. A competent lawyer should do everything possible to keep you out of court. Litigation is time-consuming, frustrating, maddening, costly, and hazardous to your health, both mentally and physically.

6. *Beware of lawyers who refuse to go to court.* The other side of the coin are the attorneys who lack the necessary skills to properly represent you in court and will do everything possible to avoid it. They will suggest settlements and compromises, sometimes giving away your position to the adversaries to avoid litigation. Posture yourself that you are perfectly willing to go to court to secure justice.

7. *Never talk to another person's attorney by yourself.* Always have your lawyer present when the other side brings theirs. Lawyers have superior knowledge about the law and may try to bluff you. An ethical attorney would never speak with you directly without your attorney present. Never let the adversary's lawyer talk with you alone. All correspondence should be handled through your attorney.

8. *Discuss fee arrangements with your attorney up front.* Determine the costs associated with representing you in all legal matters at the beginning of the relationship.

Tip

Negotiate a written fee arrangement with your attorney before any services are rendered.

In summary, select a lawyer with the experience and expertise that fits your needs, and collect any necessary information in advance of meeting with your attorney.

Hiring Accountants

Entrepreneurs need an experienced accounting person who specializes in working with small business owners. As your business grows, the duties of the accountant become more numerous and demanding. Use an accountant as a good business adviser who understands the importance of building and managing sound cash-flow documents and assists with tax planning. An accountant should provide assistance in securing loans and become a good source of business contacts. You need someone who can design customized accounting systems for your business.

Shop around for a competent accountant and consultant. This member of your management team will become one of your most trusted and most frequently used advisers. Ask other business owners about accountants they would recommend. Ask your banker or lawyer or your trade association for suggestions.

Tip

If you are planning to significantly expand your business, consider hiring an experienced certified public accountant (CPA).

Hiring a nationally recognized firm will lend credibility to your financial statements and enhance your chances of attracting growth capital. Major accounting firms offer numerous professional manuals, books, and other programs to assist owners. If you plan to raise venture capital or go public, contact an accounting firm with an established track record that works with IPOs or private placement ventures. If they are interested in your business, the cost for their services will most likely be below their usual fee until you become more profitable. Then their charges will rise accordingly.

If you feel that you don't need a national accounting firm, look for an experienced independent person who could work part-time or for a retired accountant. Local colleges and universities with accounting departments are another source for referrals. Contact the Society of Certified Public Accountants in your state, most of which have referral banks.

After collecting a list of potential accountants, interview each of them. Check the chemistry and make sure you are compatible with each other. Ask about their services and fee structure. Accounting fees vary significantly depending on the experience level of the person working for you and the size of your venture.

Tip

To reduce costs, perform the routine work yourself and use professionals to review your work.

Setting up and maintaining your books at the beginning is critical to successfully managing your venture as it grows. Become familiar with the numbers associated with managing your business before seeing the prepared financial statements at the end of the month or quarter. You must have a feeling for the money going out and the money coming in—your cash flow. Carefully track your sales, expenses, how much money you are owed and owe. Do not delegate this function to your accountant.

Hiring Business Consultants

Hiring consultants is usually less expensive than hiring staff especially when you need a specific problem solved or have a project and need outside assistance. Carefully select consultants after thoroughly researching and interviewing them. Many skilled consultants provide invaluable services. Nowhere are your options so abundant with the quality so variable. Prices vary tremendously. Typically, consultants charge anywhere between $100 an hour to $1000 + a day. Well-known consulting firms usually charge higher fees. It's difficult to judge consultants solely on the fees they charge.

First, consider whether you need a generalist or a specialist. Be wary of "can do all" types. Second, consider their prior track record. Who have they worked for and what services did they render? Obtain referral names so you can verify the results of their performance. Ask for a written proposal based on your needs. Evaluate proposals by looking for the outcomes and objectives they say they will accomplish.

The best way to find consultants is through referrals from your banker, lawyer, accountant, fellow entrepreneur, etc. The government is another source. The Small Business Administration (SBA) provides consultants, sometimes at no charge. College and universities are a source for consultants on a private basis or sometimes through federally funded programs. Also, look for consultants in the *Yellow Pages* under "Management Consultants."

Interview consultants, asking about their expertise and approaches. Evaluate their enthusiasm and openness. Try to determine their interest level in your project. Ask about their fee structure. Is it hourly, daily, or a fixed-fee? You want to hire a consultant who works fast, but effectively.

A good book for choosing consultants is *Choosing and Using A Consultant* by Herman Holtz (John Wiley and Sons). Ask your librarian for other similar reference books or articles. Don't underestimate the amount of time it will take to find a consultant who has the expertise you need and the right chemistry.

Tip

Once you select a consultant, work out a written agreement specifying the consultant's responsibilities and objectives and including the compensation.

Using a Board of Directors

Every corporation is required by law to have a board of directors, and the people you choose to serve on this board is up to you. Many give little thought as to whom to select. Instead, they take the easy way out and appoint family members, spouses, sons or daughters, etc. Such boards usually contribute little business experience or provide reliable advice.

Board members should be selected on the basis of who will make a significant contribution and act as a sounding board for new ideas. The people you choose can also be used as references for banks, investors, and lawyers. Expect them to bring in business, make introductions to potential customers, assist in securing financing, etc. Some founders recruit influential business leaders to serve on their board as a way to strengthen their management team. Retired executives are a good source for recruiting board members. Selecting a strong board will impress potential lenders or investors who prefer to see outside members participating. A well-qualified board is an asset to any company as founders try to obtain credit from vendors, get goods shipped on time, and so on. One phone call from a board member can accomplish more than chasing up blind alleys.

Tip

Board members with extensive operating experience in your industry are most effective.

The down side of appointing an outside board is that influential business leaders may be extremely busy and not have sufficient time to devote. They may also be reluctant to serve because of the personal liability assumed. Secure board liability insurance to protect board members. In the past few years this insurance has become less expensive. It is a common practice to pay board members a nominal fee for attending monthly meetings or to compensate them with stock options.

Recruiting a board of outside directors is a smart entrepreneurial strategy, although studies show that less than 10 percent of midsized private companies have outside boards. An outside board brings new and creative ideas by brainstorming different ideas, opportunities, and approaches. They are not concerned about what employees might think; they provide objective analysis and give honest feedback.

Many owners think that no one would want to serve on their board. Usually this is not the case. Serving on a board is flattering to one's ego; members find the experience rewarding, and learn from you and your business as well as other board members.

The most frequently expressed objection to an outside board is that the founder wants total control. However, control lies with the shareholders. Limit board terms to two years so members can be easily replaced.

Fast-growing companies desperately need good boards who can anticipate potential problems and develop solutions. The advantages of establishing an outside board of directors far outweigh the disadvantages. Running a business can be lonely if there are few people available with whom to exchange ideas and plan new directions. Having an outside board strengthens decision making and makes risk-taking easier. An outside board is the best investment you can make in the future of your business and its continued success. An excellent resource is John Ward's *Creating Effective Boards for Private Enterprise,* published by Jossey-Bass.

Using an Advisory Board

Using an advisory board instead of establishing a formal board of directors is a strategy entrepreneurs should consider. Advisory boards are easier to establish and can be converted to a board of directors at a later date. Members should be selected because of their business acumen, ability to generate new business, make introductions to potential customers, influence business leaders in the industry, etc. Look for potential members who have specific knowledge and skills that you lack. Also check to ensure that potential board members have no ethical or legal conflicts with you or your business.

  The primary mission of an advisory board is to provide guidance and feedback about the goals, objectives, and the directions your venture is taking. Unlike a board of directors, they have no voting rights nor any legal liability for their suggestions. They are there to provide counsel and make recommendations.

Tip

Look for retired executives, entrepreneurs who run noncompeting companies, business school professors, members of the infrastructure, and key users of your products or services as potential advisory board members.

  Advantages to establishing an advisory board rather than a board of directors are that members can be replaced easily and the costs to assemble and maintain these boards is relatively low. Sometimes advisory board members are paid for meeting expenses, and you can show your appreciation by taking them out for a group dinner or some type of entertainment.

Trap

Avoid making your advisory board a rubber-stamp entity by limiting membership to insiders and not giving them input into the decision making.

An advisory board of outside directors assists growing ventures in grappling more effectively with the many challenges of competing in our global marketplace. They enhance your management team and can bring sound business knowledge and expertise.

Include a half-page biographical sketch of each member in the appendix of your business plan. Investors and lenders like to see entrepreneurs establish either an advisory board or a board of directors. These types of outside advisers strengthen your management team and can bring in new business.

Starting a new business is an exciting adventure if you plan for it. While no plan—no matter how well thought out—will guarantee success, you will enhance your chances of creating a successful business if you take the time to plan for it.

4

Buying an Existing Business

Buying versus Starting
a Business Dilemma

Entrepreneurs are finding that big returns come from the growth and the revitalization of existing businesses. The often-quoted statistic that six out of every 10 new businesses fail during the first five years represents the risk involved in starting a new venture. Most new ventures need a track record of five to eight years to prove that their concept, market, prices, location, and management are successful.

In a start up venture all operation aspects are unknown. There is a high degree of uncertainty starting a new venture from scratch. Some entrepreneurs estimate that they will break even in six months. However, it might take 18 to 24 months, during which time they need operating capital. Typically, penetrating a market with a new business takes two to fives times as long as originally projected. Buying an existing business is different and can be profitable from the first day.

Tip

Buying the right business reduces the time involved in planning, organizing, and launching a new start-up.

One can equate buying an existing business to buying an older house. Those who build a new house have to worry about everything—similar to the worries of starting a new business. However, there is less risk in acquisitions. When you purchase a business, there is an existing reputation, customer base, suppliers, equipment, leases, and cash flow. The infrastructure and management team are also in place.

Some entrepreneurs are more successful as turnaround artists—building ventures rather than starting them. They are not creators, with ideas that could revolutionize the marketplace. Instead, they recognize good business opportunities and make an existing venture more profitable. One successful entrepreneur claimed that he had only two failures out of 10 ventures—the two businesses he started from scratch. The other business successes were all ventures that he had purchased, grown, and harvested.

Trap

When you purchase an existing business, you inherit all the problems and headaches that someone else has caused.

Advantages in Buying an Established Business

Many entrepreneurs feel that purchasing an existing business is like buying a used car. It's a known entity although there is some risk involved. The risk can be greatly reduced by carefully analyzing the potential purchase and structuring a good deal.

There are six good reasons for buying a business instead of starting one from scratch: (1) time, (2) financing, (3) existing operating systems, (4) lower risk, (5) management training, and (6) lower asset costs.

Time

Starting a business from scratch takes considerable time and effort, perhaps taking several years to get it to a level of being profitable. You can own a profitable business from the beginning by purchasing it. Buying an existing business is a quick way to obtain ownership of a mature business that is generating profit.

What if the business you are interested in purchasing is losing money? Should you still consider purchasing it? Buying this type of a venture may still be a quicker way to get to profitable operations than starting a new business. Turning around a business can be both a profitable and rewarding experience; however, it takes special expertise. Many failing businesses are just poorly managed. By bringing in a good management team, an astute entrepreneur can put a struggling business on its feet again.

Financing

Perhaps the most compelling reason for buying a business is to make use of the seller's invested capital. Most sellers ultimately finance a large part of the sale to help sell the business and to obtain a higher selling price. Sellers are the purchaser's biggest financing source and, typically, the lowest cost of funds available. Sometimes, the seller will finance the entire transaction if he or she has faith in the buyer. Many times, the seller does not need cash immediately. Instead, he or she wants an assured income. Most sellers will ask for all cash up front; however, they often have to give more lenient terms to make the sale. It all depends on the buyer's persuasive powers and the seller's alternatives and needs. Bankers and other lenders are more willing to lend to an established business with several years of performance to evaluate. It is a known quantity.

The selling price of the business is not the most important aspect of the deal structure. Instead, terms for purchasing the business are the key to making the deal work.

* Tip

Terms are everything when buying a business; the selling price is not. Negotiate for terms.

Existing Operating Systems

The entrepreneur who starts a business spends considerable time, money, and effort building an organization and developing an effective operating system. The buyer of a business already has one in place and can avoid the pitfalls of start up.

Most often, some changes are needed. It is usually easier to make changes in existing operating systems than to begin from nothing. Some of the value of an existing business comes from the fact that it is a "going concern." All of its parts are functioning.

One of the most valuable parts of the operating system is the venture's current customers. Customers are gold. It takes a substantial amount of time and effort to build and maintain a good customer base. Another important part of a venture's operating system is its sales force and distribution system. A well-trained sales force combined with an effective distribution system are most valuable assets and well-worth acquiring. The operating system, which is another of the most significant values of an existing business, does not appear on any balance sheet.

Lower Risks

The risks associated with entrepreneurship are usually less in buying a business than in starting a new business. It is easier to assess the risks involved in buying a going business than those inherent in developing a new venture. You can evaluate a known quantity with an existing location, current customers, staff, suppliers, and a reputation.

The first two years of any business are often the riskiest. Survival is the focus during this period and the failure rate is high. Depending on the type of business, it can take two or three years to reach the break-even point with a start-up and another five years to become stable and successful.

Two major factors help limit risks. First, the buyer has better information on both the operating characteristics of the venture and its established market than the entrepreneur would have with a start-up enterprise. Much of the market speculation is eliminated, since the business already has a track record. Therefore, better and more accurate sales forecasts can be made.

Second, and perhaps more important, the buyer can usually invest fewer dollars when purchasing an existing business. This relates back to the seller financing the majority of the venture. The more the seller is willing to carry back as debt, the more he or she can expect to sell the business for. These are usually the least expensive funds available. Negotiated terms can be better than those available from any other type of lender. The buyer should be more concerned with how the purchase can be structured than with the actual price involved.

Management Training

Management training provided by the seller is another advantage of buying an existing business. Often, the seller will teach the buyer how to run the business. Much inside knowledge and expertise can be exchanged. Consequently, the buyer of an existing business may not have to learn those important start-up lessons the hard way.

Additionally, a financially involved seller is motivated to hold the buyer's hand for a longer period of time.

Tip

Ask the seller to work with the new owner for the first six months after the sale.

Lower Asset Costs

Finally, it is usually cheaper to acquire assets by buying a business than it is to purchase them new. You can often purchase the building and equipment for 10 to 20 percent of what it would cost new. Some businesses are purchased just for their location or for the lease they have with the building owner.

Frequently, the assets of an existing business are not worth much, except as to how they are used in that particular business. Thus, an entrepreneur may be able to get into this type of business with less capital than by starting a new venture. In essence, you are purchasing used equipment at an attractive price. This happens more often when acquiring a firm that is in trouble.

Tip

The business success a seller has achieved costs the buyer more money. Likewise, business failure costs the seller money.

Disadvantages in Buying an Established Business

Many businesses for sale aren't worth buying. There are some disadvantages of buying existing businesses that you should consider before deciding to purchase. These disadvantages can be grouped into the following categories: (1) inadequate market potential,

(2) serious competitive problems, (3) technological problems, (4) disadvantageous cost characteristics, (5) seller backs out, and (6) nothing worth buying.

Inadequate Market Potential

Many businesses are not going anywhere because there is nowhere for them to go. The founder is doing everything possible and the business is still losing money. Essentially, the market potential is just not there.

Serious Competitive Problems

A business may be experiencing serious competitive problems. The market is saturated with similar type ventures, and the cost of the product has become very price competitive. There are just too many businesses chasing after the same consumer dollar. It is a cut-throat industry where it is difficult to enter into the marketplace.

Technological Problems

Some businesses become technologically obsolete. Would you purchase a business that makes silent movies or 78 rpm records? Sometimes the product or production process can no longer compete technologically in the marketplace because of new inventions.

Astute entrepreneurs may realize that they are losing their technological edge. They quickly place their business for sale before this situation becomes apparent to the general public. In acquiring any business with a technology base, great care should be given to assess what is happening to the technology in that industry. Are new products being tested that will replace yours? It is essential that you determine whether or not the business has the ability to compete in the new technological arena and how prepared it is to advance technologically in the future.

Disadvantageous Cost Characteristics

It is also difficult to make money if your competition has a cost advantage over you. You will always be vulnerable to price wars. Moreover, your cost disadvantage comes right out of your profits.

Unless you have an idea on how to rectify the cost problem, be careful.

Seller Backs Out

Sometimes you will be negotiating with a seller for several months and are just getting ready to sign the deal. But the seller notifies you that he or she has decided not to sell the business. Often, sellers become too emotionally attached to let go of the venture. Yet, you have spent considerable time and money performing due diligence, doing research, securing financing, and negotiating the deal. In addition, you have paid legal and accounting fees that are unrecoverable, plus the incalculable opportunity costs.

Nothing Worth Buying

There are some businesses that are just not worth buying. They are going nowhere fast. Their products may be inadequate and/or defective. The inventory is old and outdated. The business is on a downswing and experiencing a negative cash flow. Overall, it is difficult to find one good feature about the business, except the sales price. When this situation occurs, it is easier to start a new venture than to purchase an old dog.

Tip

Be careful when you find a business where the owner is trying to sell the business in a short period of time.

He or she may be trying to bail out quickly before the market turns sour. When speed replaces price as the primary goal, beware. You might be able to get a good deal, but the business is or could become unprofitable.

Finding the Right Business

Buying an existing business involves thoroughly evaluating and analyzing the business opportunity. It may take up to a year or longer to find the right purchase. It is also a wise strategy to match your interests and industry experience with an opportunity to purchase a business. Review your goals for wanting to purchase a business. After you select the type of business you want to purchase, determine if the business you are considering matches your personal goals. Evaluate your expertise. What are your strengths and weaknesses? Do they complement the potential venture? Will your knowledge and skills be of help in operating the business? No one is strong in all areas of operating a business.

What kind of lifestyle do you want? There is prestige in owning your own business. But, does this business fit your status and image needs?

Once you have answered these questions, use the following resource checklist as a starting point in your search:

1. Newspapers. The easiest place to start looking for a business to buy is in the classified section of newspapers under "Business Opportunities." The Sunday edition usually has the most listings.

Look in the "Mart" section of *The Wall Street Journal* on Wednesdays and Thursdays. *The New York Times* Sunday edition contains several pages of diverse businesses for sale. There are also specialized business opportunity newspapers such as *The Business Opportunity Journal.* Check with your librarian for other similar publications to review.

2. Industry Trade Magazines. Many of these magazines and trade papers contain a classified section with business opportunities that are industry specific. Check with the trade associations for the industries you are interested in and ask about their various publications. Attend a trade show and look for businesses to purchase.

3. Banks. Some banks publish newsletters of business opportunities. One such bank is the First National Bank of Maryland, (800) 842-BANK. There may be a charge for some of the newsletters and/or catalog listings. Ask banks in your area if they have lists of businesses for sale. Bankers can be helpful in your search, and establishing a relationship with them early on is a must. It might not be long before you'll be asking them for lending assistance to help finance your venture.

4. Business Professionals and Members of the Infrastructure. Talk with attorneys, accountants, venture capitalists, investment bankers, insurance agents, salespeople, and other members in the entrepreneurial infrastructure. These professionals often know of business opportunities that are never advertised.

5. Business Brokers.   These brokers have extensive lists of businesses for sale. They work for business owners and are paid a commission to market and sell businesses. A business broker's fee typically runs between 5 and 10 percent of the purchase price. Your response to an ad may very well be to a business broker.

Try to negotiate a "buy-broker agreement" where the broker agrees to seek out companies for you. Look in the Yellow Pages of your telephone directory for listings of business brokers. You can also obtain a list of brokers who belong to the International Association of Business Brokers by contacting them at (617) 369-5254.

6. Business Owners.   Look for businesses you might be interested in purchasing and contact the owners. Ask them if they are interested in selling. On the average, about 3 out of every 10 calls attracts some interest. If they are not interested in selling, they might be able to refer you to someone else.

7. Chambers of Commerce.   Some chambers of commerce have small-business units that maintain buying and selling services for businesses in their locality. Many have "Business after Hours" meetings where you can meet owners and look for purchase opportunities.

8. Economic Development Agencies.   The Small Business Administration (SBA) and other economic development agencies frequently know of businesses for sale and can give you referrals. Call the Small Business Development Center (SBDC) in your area and check to see if they maintain lists of businesses for sale.

9. Trade Sources.   Suppliers, vendors, distributors, manufacturers, and trade associations are good sources for information about potential businesses for sale. They are excellent resources for industry-specific businesses.

10. Business Bankruptcy Listings.   Most local business journals publish a list of businesses that have filed for bankruptcy. If you feel you have the skills to become a turnaround artist, these listings may produce good leads.

11. Friends. Your friends have a wide network of contacts. Let them know what kind of business you are looking for and ask them to notify you of any opportunities they discover. You might want to consider offering an incentive to get people to give you qualified leads. Paying people for their time and effort is a good business practice.

Tip

Present yourself as a fully qualified person so you will receive a positive response from a seller or broker.

You will probably be asked some qualifying questions to see if the contact wants to continue the process. This list is a starting place and demonstrates that there are many sources for you to tap into during your search. A successful search requires diligence and hard work.

Conducting the Due Diligence

After pinpointing the right purchase opportunity, evaluate the location by answering the following location questions.

1. Is the location convenient for you and does it have enough traffic flow?
2. Is the location convenient to your target customers?
3. What has been the location history?
4. How long has the business been in that location?
5. Have other businesses failed and frequently turned over in that location?
6. What are the surroundings and the physical conditions like?
7. Is any remodeling needed? If so, estimate the costs for such remodeling.

Sometimes a location carries a stigma and should be avoided. On the other hand, an entrepreneur may purchase an existing business just for the location and the lease.

Next consider the financial implications by answering the following financial questions.

1. How much money do you want to make?

2. How much money will you need to purchase the business?

3. Do you have enough capital to negotiate a deal?

4. Will you need to find other sources of financing? If so, identify potential money sources.

5. Can you negotiate terms from the owner?

6. When do you estimate that the business can buy itself back from cash flow?

After answering the location and financial questions, obtain assistance from various business experts including an accountant, attorney, and banker to make an in-depth venture analysis.

Tip

Hire a successful business owner of a similar venture in another community (not a competitor) to consult with you.

Such a person can bring a wealth of experience and be able to detect areas of concern that you might otherwise overlook.

Last, choose the right seller. This person should be both cooperative and willing to disclose all the financial, personnel, customer, and legal information related to the venture. If the owner is resistant to sharing this information, you have reason to be concerned.

These are just some of the key questions to ask and information to analyze when considering purchasing a business. A good reference book is C.D. Peterson's *How to Leave Your Job & Buy a Business of Your Own,* published by McGraw-Hill. Evaluating this information is only one-half of the equation. It is important to use a combination of both research and intuition in deciding whether this business is right for you and if you should make an offer to buy it. Although it may be a good acquisition opportunity, you need good management skills and business experience. Remember, all that glitters is not gold.

Evaluating the Business

Once you have determined that this business is a potential candidate for purchase, use the following checklist to guide you while gathering information.

1. Ask the owner for historical and projected profits, after taxes and sales figures.

2. Ask for the past three to five years of audited balance sheets, income statements, and cash-flow statements. Have your accountant review them.

3. Ask if the owner has operating ratios. If the owner does not have any, you must develop your own. You can work with your banker or accountant to crunch the numbers.

4. How do the venture's operating ratios compare with industry ratios? If there are significant deviations ask the owner to explain identified differences. Industry ratios can be found in *Annual Statement Studies* published by Robert Morris Studies, a source of industry statistics and financial ratios, which you can find in your local library or your CPA may have a copy.

5. Ask for a list of the venture's current assets and liabilities.

6. What is the age and condition of the assets and liabilities?

7. What kinds of debts and other liabilities does the venture have?

8. Are there any pending legal actions?

9. Has the owner been involved in past litigation? If so, what was the outcome?

10. How many and what are the amounts and ages of the receivables?

11. How many receivables were written off as uncollectible each year for the past three years?

12. How much tax has the owner paid to Uncle Sam? Review corporate tax returns for the past three years. Remember that a seller won't exaggerate the business's worth to the IRS since this will cost the owner money.

13. Has the owner taken a salary from the business?

14. What is the exit strategy to harvest from the venture?

If the seller cannot provide this financial information, then this is an indication of something amiss. Also check with the Better Business Bureau to determine if customers have filed a complaint about the business. For a fee, Dun and Bradstreet will give you their estimate of the worth of the business. Look for one of their local offices in the Yellow Pages.

Next, assess the current employees. You are not buying just a company, but also the employees. Ask the following questions.

1. Who are they and how long have they worked for the company?
2. How do they feel about the company and its future?
3. Do you have good chemistry with them?
4. Do they appear to be ethical and honest?
5. Have they been disciplined?

Check their personnel files and look for warning letters, disciplinary actions, performance evaluations, attendance records, records of pay increases, etc., to determine who the good employees are.

Next, evaluate the local conditions, both economic and political and ask yourself the following business environment questions.

1. What are the industry trends for this business?
2. How mature is the market?
3. Is the market increasing or decreasing?
4. What is the growth rate and growth potential?
5. What is the market capacity?
6. What is the competitive environment?
7. Is the market overcrowded with competition?
8. Is there any value-added potential?

Meet with the customers to determine their level of satisfaction with the business. Talk to customers who come into the store. Search out former customers and find out why they are no longer buying from this store.

After analyzing historical sales and profits, prepare your own projections of future profitability and growth potential. Ask for audited financial statements.

* Trap

Even if the business owner provides you with audited financial statements, don't rely on them or future projections. Always develop your own financial statements on the prospective venture and then discuss the differences.

Negotiating the Deal

Try to negotiate with the seller to carry back debt and give you good terms so that the business can generate enough cash to buy itself back in five years. Ask the seller to continue working in the business for three to six months to help your transition and provide training.

Checklist for Buying a Business

After you have answered the above questions, use this final checklist to evaluate this purchase opportunity.

1. Is there a good match between what you want out of the business and your personal goals?
2. What is the upside potential?
3. What is the downside potential?
4. What are the opportunity costs involved in purchasing this venture?
5. Will this venture give you the lifestyle you desire?
6. Does this business opportunity fit your risk tolerance?
7. What is the margin for error? Do you have room to make mistakes and be able to survive?

Pitfalls to Avoid When Buying a Business

1. Don't purchase a business without thoroughly evaluating the venture and its financial statements.
2. Avoid accepting nonaudited financial statements.
3. Don't purchase a business with a shrinking market.
4. Be careful about purchasing a business in an industry with many competitors.
5. Don't think you can manage the business better than the owner if you do not have any prior business experience in the industry. It takes time to make miracles from a turnaround situation.

5
The Virtual Company—How to Look Big When You're Not

Among the many challenges facing entrepreneurs, particularly in the early stages, is how to compete against established and often-times bigger companies when you don't have the resources. This challenge is made more difficult by the perpetually changing nature of the marketplace caused in large part by changing customer needs and technology. The particularly dynamic, even chaotic, environments of some industries with short product lives, like software and many consumer products, demand a company that is flexible, fast, and capable of change. Out of these needs comes the "virtual company," which is the focus of this chapter.

What Is a Virtual Company?

The term *virtual* is borrowed from the video game industry where "virtual reality" is a way for the player to become part of the game environment without leaving the safety of the real world. The player wearing a VR headset feels like he or she has been transported into a new three-dimensional world that seems to actually exist but, in reality, does not.

Virtual companies are very much the same idea. To the customer the company seems to be a large, established supplier of goods and services, but actually, it may have its base of operations in the entrepreneur's home and be linked with a manufacturer, a distributor, and a retailer, as shown in Figure 5-1.

In a virtual company, the entrepreneur can operate out of any location desired—a home, an office, a vacation site, a boat. The possibilities are endless because where the entrepreneur has an office is not important. What's important is that he or she is linked via phone, fax, and e-mail with the other companies with which the company does business. These other companies, the shadow team, are doing the actual work of the business. This is called *outsourcing* and will be discussed in the next section.

TLC—A Virtual Company That Enhances a Lifestyle

Some entrepreneurs create virtual companies to maintain a lifestyle that is not compatible with the traditional business office. Let's look at one example.

Suppose that you are manufacturing three-dimensional foam maps for elementary education purposes and are providing them to Rand-McNally, the famous map maker. Could you design, manufacture, and ship these maps without owning a facility, in fact, by operating from home? Actually, this is a real business called TLC, located in Southern California. Its founder, John Rogers, still runs the company today as a virtual organization. Rand-McNally, the customer, places an order with Rogers who then notifies his manufacturing partner of the volume and shipping date. The manufacturer then assembles the maps, packages them, and ships them to Rand-McNally's distributor, who supplies the retailers. Rogers cannot only handle the production of the product in this manner, but he can also contract with a sales agency, should salespeople or manufacturer's reps be necessary, and with firms that do accounting and clerical work for companies.

And the best part for Rogers is that he can take off and go skiing whenever he wants.

The Virtual Company

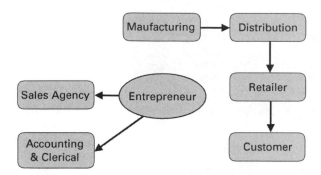

Figure 5-1.

Virtual companies are often the only way a new business can get off the ground in an industry without incurring the burdensome costs of employees, equipment, and overhead. It's a particularly wise move where the resources to manufacture, assemble, and distribute the product effectively already exist in the market. In this case, it doesn't make sense to duplicate this effort.

Tip

For clout in your industry, try networking your company.

If you've decided that a virtual company is the way to go, in some industries there is an advantage to forming a more advanced version of the virtual company called an *agile web* or *networked company.*

Picture a spider web, with your company in the middle. Radiating out from your company are all the other companies with which you do business and the businesses your network partners use as well. Your distributor is represented and your distributor's other suppliers are also represented as pictured in Figure 5-2.

- The difference between an agile web and a virtual company is that all of the companies in the web are linked by agreement with a common goal to provide the resources necessary for your company to produce and deliver its products and services.

- It's like having all the departments of your business located in different geographical areas, but they're all linked electronically to a common purpose.

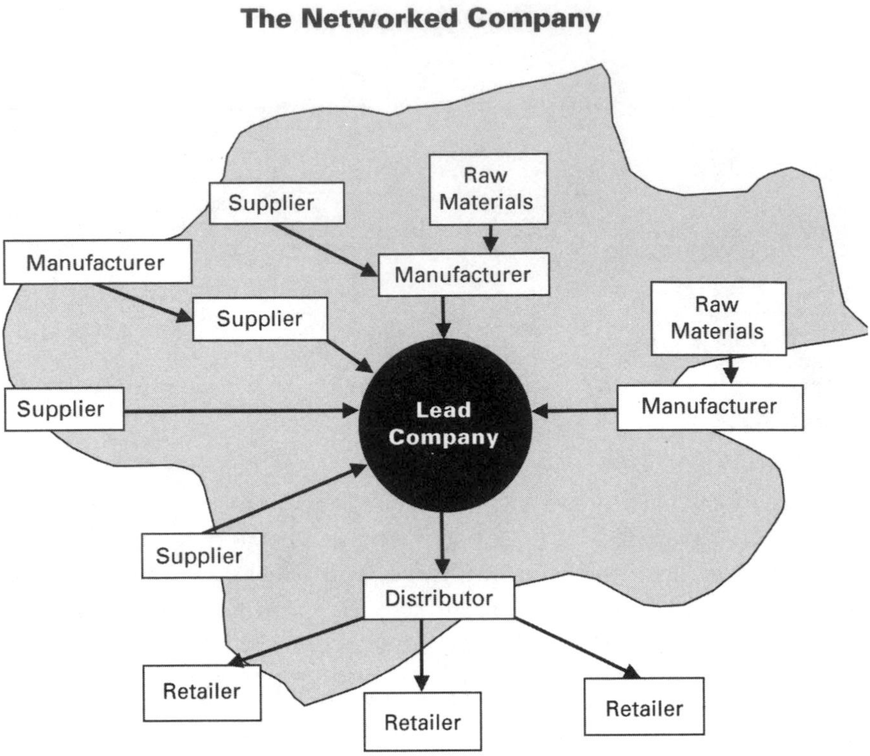

The Networked Company

Figure 5-2.

- If you can over time develop industry partners who share your goals, you will be able to reduce the time it takes to get a product to market, reduce costs and risk, and increase your status in the industry.

Start slowly with one or two members and gradually add more as needed. Remember to choose your partners carefully, because it's very much like a marriage. You will have to live with these people for a long time, and you must be able to trust them.

There are lots of ways to partner with other companies to improve your chances in the marketplace. Briefly, here are just a few:

1. *Partnership.*   This is a legal form that makes two or more companies partners who share the gains and losses of the venture according to their contribution as stated in the partnership agreement.

2. *Joint Venture.*   Not as formal as a partnership but merely a contract between companies to work on a particular project together.

3. *License Agreement or Royalty.*   Your company may give another company the right to produce your products and return a royalty to you based on sales to you.

4. *Outsourcing Contract.*   A formal contract with another company to perform specified tasks for your company.

Trap

Don't be virtual if it doesn't make sense!

Remember that anytime you contract with another company to do work for you, you're implicitly agreeing to trust that company to deliver quality products and services in a timely manner so that you can meet your customers' needs. To avoid problems, be sure to do the following:

- Investigate the company's track record and assure yourself that they're trustworthy or you may be in for a big surprise. You can do this by checking with their customers, vendors, and distributors.

- Remember, the contracting company doesn't know your customers' needs like you do and they're more worried about keeping all their own customers happy than they are about your particular customers. So when they have to choose between their customers and yours, guess who loses? You need to let them know specifically what your customers need.

- Make sure your subcontractors understand the big picture. Outsourcing all of your business' activities can be a coordination nightmare if they don't. Sit down with them and explain how the whole process will work.

- Educate subcontractors as to how your business works and what you must do to satisfy your customers.

- Create a situation where the subcontractors have a vested interest in seeing your business succeed. Usually this will happen if you can demonstrate to them that your company holds the potential to provide them with a new, untapped market.

Don't use a virtual organization if any of the following exist. Going ahead under this scenario is a recipe for disaster.

1. Your company has all the competencies it needs to meet its goals.

2. You can't see a clear benefit to doing so.

3. Your management style and that of your subcontractors are not compatible.

Outsourcing to Compete

With limited resources, a new business must be very creative in how it allocates them. Since labor (employees) is the single largest component of any company's budget, it's the first place entrepreneurs look to save money. Outsourcing tasks to independent contractors and leasing employees are two ways to have as few employees as possible and still grow. As you learned in Chapter 3, there are a variety of places to seek expertise that you don't have.

- Professional advisers like attorneys, accountants, bankers, advisory boards
- Service agencies like temporary help services
- Manufacturing support like job shops, packagers, and design engineers
- Consultants in management, sales, market research, and training
- Governmental agencies like the Small Business Administration, Small Business Development Centers (SBDCs), and the Department of Commerce
- Sales support agencies like manufacturer reps, distributors, and foreign reps

* Tip

Bootstrap your way to building the business.

Bootstrapping is a term of art in business that literally means "beg, borrow, or rent everything." It essentially represents collectively all of the creative techniques employed by entrepreneurs in the start-up phase to gather their resources. The fundamental rules of thumb for bootstrapping are:

- Hire as few employees as possible to handle the aspects of the business that you can't outsource.

- Rent or lease rather than buy equipment and facilities so as not to tie up limited funds. In a lease situation, you can often negotiate no down payment, and the cost is spread over time to coincide with the cash coming into your business.

- Try to get customers to pay in advance, if possible.

- Check local colleges and universities to see if they have an intern program where business students can work in your business for college credit and experience.

You can find outsourcing expertise in the Yellow Pages of your local phone directory under the specific tasks you wish to outsource. Remember, you may only need to outsource one activity of your business, for example, costly manufacturing, where the start-up funding to set up a manufacturing facility is not available or is prohibitive. More and more, particularly for consumer products sold in high volumes, many entrepreneurs are looking to off-shore manufacturing services in Mexico, Hong Kong, Taiwan, Korea, and China. Understanding how your industry works will give you some clues as to what your company should do. In general, plan to outsource anything you can't easily do yourself.

Trap

A handshake may not be enough!

While we would all like to believe that the people we're doing business with are honest, trustworthy, and reliable, unfortunately, it isn't always the case. Even when that person is a friend or family member, problems can arise later that will hurt your business as well as your relationship with this person. How many times have naive business owners

- Made promises to customers they ultimately couldn't keep because their own outside sources did not perform as promised?

- Had no contract with a subcontractor, so they had no recourse under the law when that subcontract failed to perform as agreed?

Today, merely agreeing in principle to do business together is not enough. Any business relationship should have a contract that spells out:

1. The duties and responsibilities of the parties
2. Performance requirements
3. Dates of completion of the contracted items
4. Remedies for failure to abide by the terms of the contract

   A good business attorney can review any contracts to ensure that your company is protected. If your company, for example, contracts with a temporary employment agency to supply salespeople at certain times of the year when your normal staff is not sufficient to handle increased demand, you need to be certain that those salespeople will be sufficiently trained and ready to assume the task when you call. Otherwise, it may cost you time and effort to retrain them yourself, which is an additional cost above the original fee charged by the agency.

Using Independent Contractors

Independent contractors own their own businesses which provide products and services to other businesses under a contract arrangement. Broadly speaking, the only control the entrepreneur has over the independent contractor (IP) relates to the result of the work they do and not the means by which the IP accomplishes the result. That is, you can specify to your IP what you would like in terms of a result—1000 units of toy trucks made to specification—but you can't dictate to the IP the method by which they manufacture the units.

Tip

Protect yourself by understanding the Safe Harbor Law.

The Safe Harbor Law of the Revenue Act of 1978 says that companies cannot be held liable for employment taxes for an employment relationship if:

1. It was reasonable for the company to treat the person as an IP. To prove this, you can supply a previous IRS audit or letter confirming the status, or demonstrate industry precedence, as in the case of real estate salespeople, who although they must work for a broker, are considered IPs.

2. The IP has filed returns as a company with the IRS.

3. The IP has not been classified as an employee in the same duties in which he or she was also an IP.

These are very important distinctions, because if you misclassify an employee as an IP, you may be held liable for back taxes, penalties, and interest for the period of time in which the employee was misclassified.

Independent contractors are invaluable to business owners for a variety of reasons:

- IPs are typically specialists in their field.
- The cost of hiring an IP is often less than hiring an employee because you don't pay withholding taxes and benefits.
- The IP pays his or her own taxes and benefits.

To use IPs correctly, business owners need to be aware of IRS rules regulating the classification of workers as independent contractors. Remember that failure to do so can result in liability for all back taxes plus penalties and interest, which can be a substantial sum. To avoid problems, entrepreneurs should:

- Consult an attorney who will know the most current legislation and laws.
- Draw up a contract with the independent contractor that specifies that he or she will not be treated as an employee for state and federal tax purposes.
- Avoid indicating the time or manner in which the work will be performed.
- Verify that the independent contractor carries workers' compensation insurance.
- Verify that the independent contractor possesses the necessary licenses.

✳ Trap

The IRS can assess business owners with heavy penalties for violating its rules regarding independent contractors.

So, watch out for the IRS who has been cracking down on companies that misclassify employees as independent contractors to save money and paperwork. It is costly to disregard the rules regarding who is eligible to be considered an independent contractor for state and federal tax purposes. The IRS uses a 20-part test to determine employee status. An individual is considered an employee if the individual:

1. Must follow company instructions about where, when, and how to carry out their work.
2. Is trained by the company.
3. Provides services that are integrated into the business.
4. Provides services that must be rendered personally.
5. Cannot hire, supervise, and pay his or her own assistants.
6. Has a continuing relationship with the company.
7. Must follow set hours of work.
8. Works full-time for the company.
9. Does the work on the company's premises.
10. Must do the work in a sequence set by the company.
11. Must submit regular reports to the company.
12. Is paid regularly for time worked, by the hour, week, and month.
13. Receives reimbursements for job-related expenses.
14. Relies on the tools and materials of the company.
15. Has no major investment in facilities and resources to perform the service.
16. Cannot make a profit or suffer a loss through the provision of these services.
17. Works for one company at a time.
18. Does not offer his or her services to the general public on a regular basis.
19. Can be fired at will by the company for reasons other than failure to produce specified results.
20. May quit work at any time without incurring liability.

Employees are often the single most expensive item in a company's budget, which is why there is a growing trend toward leasing employees. This is quite different from a temporary service. Leasing companies or employee management companies hire the employees of the entrepreneur's company and then lease them back to the company. The leasing company then handles payroll, files taxes, deals with insurance and other human resources issues, all for a percentage of the total payroll. This saves the company time and money and usually provides the employee with broader benefits and less expensive health-care premiums.

Before signing an agreement with an employee management company, you should:

- Check with your county clerk to make sure the firm is licensed in the state in which it does business.
- Check to see if the firm is fully indemnified by a large insurance company. If self-funded, the firm should maintain 15 percent of total premiums in reserve. Ask the company for evidence of these.
- Check the banking track record of the firm to ensure that employees will receive their pay on time. Talk to the bank that the employee management company works with.
- Contact current and former clients of the leasing firm to verify reliability and trustworthiness.
- Check to see that the firm has a broad range of insurance options for employees.
- Make sure the company supplies you with regular reports.

Strategic Alliances

Strategic alliances are simply another term for a partnership with one or more other companies. They are a good way for growing companies to structure deals with suppliers, manufacturers, or customers that will help reduce the costs of marketing, raw materials, or research and development (R&D). Since strategic partners invest time and money in your company's products and services and could potentially lose that investment should the company fail, they are considered stakeholders in your company.

Tip

Carefully evaluate a potential partner.

Four criteria should be considered when you're looking for a partner to form a strategic alliance with your company.

1. Find a partner who can bear the financial risk and would not be in risk of losing his or her company should yours fail. This means asking for financial statements and checking with others in the industry who know the company.

2. Complementary to item 1, you should seek a partner who is diversified so that you're not the only company they're dealing with.

3. Choose a partner who has experience in strategic alliances. They will better understand the risks and how to make it work.

4. Find a company that has excess capacity so they don't have to make additional investments in plant and equipment to produce your product.

You can find the company you need by studying your industry: talk to people in the industry, read trade journals, and explore the Internet. Let the appropriate people—industry experts, your banker, attorney, accountant—know of your interest in finding a suitable strategic alliance.

One specific type of alliance is the R&D limited partnership, which is usually employed in technology industries. Here the significant cost of developing a product can be shared with a more established company, private investors, or venture capitalists, who provide the funding to develop a market technology that will ultimately be profitable for both. Limited partners in this type of arrangement can deduct their investment in the R&D contract, thereby enjoying the tax advantages of losses in the early years. They will also share in future profits. Oftentimes, the R&D limited partnership will then license the new technology to your company to commercialize it.

Trap

Avoid the pitfalls of partnerships.

A partnership is very much like a marriage. It starts out with high hopes and usually confidence that the partners will always work well together. Unfortunately, statistics tell a different story. Partnerships have at least as high a failure rate as marriages and for the same reasons—the different personalities and goals of the parties. If no partnership agreement was established, the problems escalate as the partners battle to defend their side of the issue. Failure to take the time to write a partnership agreement is a costly error that may result in litigation by the partners to resolve issues and end the partnership.

A good partnership agreement should spell out:

- Responsibilities of each partner
- Duties
- Profit and loss sharing distribution
- Transfer of partnership interest (in the event of death or termination)
- Length of term of the partnership
- Conflict resolution methods and remedies

Remember that in a partnership, if one partner signs a contract in the name of the partnership, all the partners are bound by that contract. Likewise, each partner has the equal use of all partnership property. We recommend having an attorney advise you on your partnership agreement.

Going Virtual from Home

Approximately 20 percent of the 92 million households in the United States have home offices that produce some income for the owner. In addition, more than 1200 new home businesses begin each day. If you add to that the ever-growing number of telecommuters, those who work part of the week from home using computers, phones, and faxes, you easily arrive at over 38 million people working from home. In fact, some of the most successful companies in the world—Microsoft and Apple, to name just two—were started in garages.

Tip
_____

Establish a professional work space in your home.

When working from home, it's important to establish a work area with as much privacy as possible, particularly if there will be others in the house during normal working hours. The following tips will help get you started.

- A room with a closed door is perfect, but if that's not possible, a decorative screen may create a sense of private space to house all the equipment and furniture you need to run the business.

- Establish working hours that people who call you are aware of. That way you won't be answering business calls during dinner and late into the evening and personal calls during business hours.

- One of the difficult parts about working from home is getting yourself "in the mood" to work and not waste time doing domestic chores because they're there. Some at-home workers have even gone to the length of dressing in a shirt and tie or business suit to make themselves feel more professional when they work.

- If you have children, arrange for childcare so that you won't be interrupted at inappropriate times.

Like John Rogers, whom you met earlier, some entrepreneurs have made it their goal never to leave home and have, consequently, created elaborate virtual companies that they can run from virtually anywhere.

Working from home allows you to work in a comfortable environment, often with no interruptions (if there are no kids at home). All the paperwork of the business can be handled from there, and other activities outsourced to established businesses. If you must meet clients, you can either go to their place of business, to a restaurant, or arrange an agreement with another business to use their conference space on an as-needed basis. One thing you don't want to do is have large delivery trucks and lots of cars going down your street and parking by your house, as it will probably result in the neighbors calling the city to complain.

Trap

Make sure it's legal to operate a business in your home.

How would you feel if one day as you're sitting in your beautiful home office, conducting business over the phone, you are visited by the postal service with a registered letter notifying you that you are in violation of city ordinances for conducting business in a residential neighborhood and for failure to have a business license. Your first thought is, "How did they know?" Actually, they could have found out from a variety of sources.

- You may have a business phone line which you answer with the name of your business.
- You may have regular deliveries of packages, nearly daily.
- There may be an unusual number of cars parked in front of your home during business hours.
- You may be receiving mail under your business name.
- Or you may have been reported by a disgruntled neighbor.

Most communities do not authorize home-based businesses in residential areas. For example, Los Angeles prohibits home-based businesses, even those of typical home-office users like consultants, freelance writers, and artists. Nevertheless, it is estimated that more than 2.2 million households in the Los Angeles area contain a full- or part-time home business.

Bottom line: To avoid penalties for disobeying a city ordinance, it is important to check the laws and restrictions in your local community.

For many types of businesses, the virtual organization is the answer to getting the company off the ground without the need for large amounts of capital. It gives a growing company the flexibility to change as the marketplace changes. We will probably see this type of business structure implemented well into the next millennium.

Resources

Amar Bhide and Howard H. Stevenson. "Attracting Stakeholders." In *The Entrepreneurial Venture,* William A. Sahlman and Howard H. Stevenson. Boston: Harvard Business School Publications, 1992.

Goldman, Steven L., Roger N. Nagel, Kenneth Preiss. *Agile Competitors and Virtual Organizations.* New York: Van Nostrand Reinhold, 1995.

Helgesen, Sally. *The Web of Inclusion.* New York: Currency/Doubleday, 1995.

Robert B. Reich, "Entrepreneurship Reconsidered: The Team as Hero." In *The Entrepreneurial Venture,* William A. Sahlman and Howard H. Stevenson. Boston: Harvard Business School Publications, 1992.

6
Start-up Resources

The Debt versus Equity Financing Dilemma

When deciding how to finance your venture, it is important to consider some business fundamentals that are often overlooked in today's business world. To begin, decide what you are trying to achieve with the firm's capital structure. The ideal capital structure provides sufficient money for financing operations; money is available when needed. Sometimes in obtaining financing from private investors, the unsuspecting entrepreneur has agreed to restrictions upon any future outside financing without approval of the private investor. Thus, the investor is in the position of controlling future growth.

Second, the money must be obtained at a cost that is affordable, if not minimal. (Some firms cannot even afford to pay the minimum costs for loan funds.) Many large U. S. corporations that were caught up in the merger mania of the 1980s paid so much for their capital that their continued existence was jeopardized. RJR Nabisco in its famed leveraged buyout (LBO) ended up paying its stockholders $103 a share with money borrowed by issuing bonds. The resulting debt load was more than the company's operations could sustain. Corporate restructuring and selling off parts of the business had to be undertaken to save the firm.

Tip

You *cannot* make money if you pay too much for the money you buy.

Trap

The high price you pay to use money will usually handicap you until you repay the debt.

Next, the structure should be flexible enough so that changes can be easily made to accommodate rapid expansion or contraction of operations. The capital structure should not block management from undertaking whatever actions are necessary in the future. If the entrepreneur wants to offer members of the management team some stock options, then it should not take more than a vote of the board of directors to do so. It should not require a major restructuring of the capital stock.

Finally, the structure should provide the control the entrepreneur wants while giving the investors and lenders the protection and return they require. Obviously, great compromises must be made, for the achievement of these ideals is difficult.

Trap

Be wary of "professional" money people who profess, "It's better to have 10 percent of something, than 100 percent of nothing."

While it may be true on the face of it, the statement does not always apply. The 10 percent could easily turn out to be 10 percent of nothing if the venture is unsuccessful. On the other hand, 10 percent of a profitable venture may be a small piece of the pie, but that may not be all that bad. There are no hard-and-fast rules to follow; be sure to check out your professional money sources carefully before committing to anything. It really depends on the situation and if the venture achieves success.

Tip

Who has control is a critical factor in any capital structure.

To summarize, the ideal capital structure provides for:

- Sufficient money for operations
- Potential capital loss
- Flexibility
- Control

Debt Financing

The essence of debt is that the borrower *must* repay the funds along with whatever service charges (interest, rent, or whatever) were agreed upon. If the money is not repaid as promised, *and this is most important,* the lender can take several different actions against you to recover the debt, none of which are pleasant. You could lose your business.

Some entrepreneurs seem to be oblivious to the fact that when they borrow money, they are playing a game we'll call "Bet Your Company." You cut a deal with the lender in which you are betting your company that you will be able to perform according to your plans. If your plans are wrong, you may lose your company. We stress this point to emphasize the seriousness of borrowing money. It is not something to be done lightly; it is a serious obligation.

Debt takes many forms which are discussed below.

Direct Loans

Borrowing money from a bank or other financial institution, a private party, another company, the government, or whomever else creates a liability that is recorded as a note payable in the liabilities section of the balance sheet. If you have to pay it back within a year, it is a current liability. If it is due after a year, it is put into the long-term liabilities section of your financial statements.

Depending upon the deal you negotiate, the note is either secured (collateralized) or unsecured (signature loan). On an unsecured signature loan in default, the lender can sue in court for a judgment against you in the amount of the note plus legal costs.

By contrast, if you fail to meet the terms of a secured note, the lender asks the court to take possession of whatever asset or assets were pledged as collateral and sell it. The proceeds of the sale are then applied to the amount due on the note.

Trap

The loss of your collateral may not release you from all liability on the debt.

Suppose you borrow $20,000 from the bank using the company's injection molding machine for security. For some reason you don't pay. The bank goes to court and proves its case to the judge.

It proves that the note is legal, that you are in default on it, and that it wants from the court a legal document that will allow the sheriff to take possession of the molding machine.

The sheriff comes to your plant and hauls off the molding machine. It only brings $5000, some of which goes to the lender and some of which to the attorney. *You still owe the lender* $15,000 plus legal fees and court costs, depending upon your initial agreement. Most lenders insist that you pay all legal costs incurred, which could be substantial. In your case, the $5000 might be just enough to pay the legal costs.

For those reasons, most lenders are wary of collateral that is not almost cash, that is, securities and receivables. Or they want collateral that can be located easily and for which there is a recognized market value. They want collateral that has some liquidity.

This is why most lenders are reluctant to make loans and use great caution when lending money. Typically, they require both a primary and secondary source of repayment for the loan to ensure that they can collect it. The primary source could be from the firm's revenue flow and the secondary source could be from the sale of the collateral. They know how difficult it is to collect on a note, so they are not about to lend money unless they feel certain that it will be repaid. Seldom will they lend money in the hope of getting your collateral when you default. They want their money and interest, not your property or business.

Much negotiation takes place over exactly who is liable for the debt. Who signed the note? Did you sign it personally or only as a corporate officer? Did you in some way indicate that you were accepting personal responsibilities for the debt? Great care must be taken in the promises you make both in writing and orally about your responsibility for the debt.

Tip

Try your best to avoid personal responsibility for corporate debts and signing personally for a company obligation.

The personal guaranty provides that if the business defaults on the note signed by the business, the owner is personally responsible. One of the advantages of a corporation is the protection of personal assets from the debts of the business. The personal guaranty destroys this advantage.

Most banks will insist on a personal guaranty if the company is closely held, that is, the founder holds most or all of the stock. The bank wants to make certain that the firm's management has maximum motivation to pay off the loan. If the borrower fails to pay, lenders want to ensure that the borrower can repay the debt with secured collateral. They don't want the borrower to be able to walk away from the scene unscathed, with the lender holding the bag like in the 1990 Silverado Savings & Loan scandal.

Another problem with the personal guaranty is that typically it is made *continuing*, which means that as long as the loan is outstanding, you remain liable. This happens even if the loan is paid off and a new loan is obtained. The continuing guaranty carries over long after you have forgotten about signing it.

✳ Tip

Insist that your personal guaranty expire when the business loan is paid off. Or, when the loan is paid off, send a certified letter revoking the personal guaranty.

A standard guaranty also allows the bank or other creditors to extend the time of payment of the loan or vary other terms without the guarantor's consent. Negotiate the right to approve these actions.

Government Programs

One of the lesser known financing strategies is borrowing money, some at relatively low cost, from various governmental agencies. Some books provide comprehensive lists of the government agencies that help finance new ventures. For example, see Rick Stephan Hayes and John Cotton Howell's, *How to Finance Your Small Business with Government Money: SBA Loans* (New York: John Wiley & Sons, 1990).

Dealing with the government is a controversial topic among entrepreneurs. Some issue strong warnings against becoming involved with governmental financing programs because of the tremendous amount of paperwork and bureaucratic hoop jumping. Others claim that they have encountered unexpected difficulties and the government can be the quickest one to close you down. While a banker might go a long way if convinced that you are trying to work out a difficult situation, the government may not show much tolerance since they play by a different set of rules.

On the other hand, many entrepreneurs have used governmental funding programs successfully. Paperwork and time-consuming procedures, while a bother, are not insurmountable
obstacles. In all fairness, other types of money people can be
equally slow in responding to your urgent call for capital, and
they all make you jump through their hoops. Today, government
agencies are trying to lessen the amount of paperwork and
respond in a more timely manner to requests for funding.

Some of the sources of governmental financing that entrepreneurs have used successfully include: The Small Business
Administration, small business investment companies and minority enterprise small business investment companies, and state
programs.

Small Business Administration (SBA).   Almost inevitably in any discussion of financing small businesses, the SBA loan comes up. This
agency finances many types of businesses. Basically, there are two
different types of SBA loan programs. The first is a loan guarantee
program in which the SBA guarantees up to 90 percent of a loan
made through normal banking channels. If you borrowed $100,000
from your bank on such a program, and defaulted, the government
would pay the bank holding your loan $90,000. It may guarantee
loans up to $750,000, or in special situations up to $1,000,000.

A direct loan from the SBA cannot exceed $150,000.
Unfortunately, such direct loans are frequently unavailable for
lack of funds. Until Congress votes the SBA money with which to
make direct loans, the line forms at the door. Direct loans usually
carry lower interest rates than the guaranteed bank loans.

Such loans may be for as long as 10 years, unless they are for
working capital in which case they are limited to 7 years. Loans
for constructing facilities can be for 25 years. Typically, the loans
must be paid off in equal monthly installments.

The second major type of SBA loan is the 7 A asset loan program which was established so entrepreneurs could obtain
financing by using their hard assets such as equipment, building,
etc. Much of the SBA's financial assistance is aimed at helping
existing businesses that need to expand their operations. SBA
loans can also be used for start-up ventures although these can
be more difficult to obtain.

There are many other governmental sources of money. The
Department of Agriculture has a program to help finance firms

that will locate in rural areas. In addition, many states have programs to help finance new businesses. For example, North Carolina has a $20 million venture fund for new ventures. Indiana and many other states have similar programs. Sometimes local communities have industrial development programs that will finance ventures that appear attractive to them.

Small Business Investment Company (SBIC) and Minority Enterprise Small Business Investment Companies (MESBICs). These venture capital firms, licensed and regulated by the federal government, must be privately capitalized with at least 3 to 5 million dollars to be eligible to leverage up to three times in SBA low-interest loans for each private dollar invested. While many of these firms are owned by private individuals, many are owned by banks and other financial institutions as a means for making equity investments in small businesses. SBICs can spend up to 20 percent of their capital on any one investment; MESBICs, 30 percent. Research SBICs in your area by going to the reference section of your library and looking at the membership directory of the National Association of Small Business Investment Companies (NASBIC).

State Programs. State, regional, and municipal development agencies are also good sources for financing. Governments want jobs for their constituents and therefore are willing to guarantee or supply loans, work out venture capital deals, or act as resources for financing sources. States such as Michigan, Wisconsin, and Pennsylvania, are attractive because they have start-up funds available to entrepreneurs. Consult with the National Association of State Development agencies (202) 898-1302 to obtain information on what your state offers.

State pension funds are also taking a more active role in helping minority business owners get financing. In addition, municipal or community development grants may be available in your region, especially if the business is located in an economically depressed area. For more information review a copy of *Free Money From the Federal Government For Small Businesses and Entrepreneurs* by Laurie Blum published by John Wiley & Sons.

Suppliers. Most businesses use their supplier's money to finance operations. It appears on the balance sheet as Accounts Payable.

Tip

Money from suppliers is usually the cheapest money you can "borrow" so use it liberally.

Sometimes suppliers are so eager to have you as a customer that they will go out of their way to help you finance your new venture. Look for eager suppliers who will offer lengthy terms of payment to attract your business. The basic principle is: Look to the people who will benefit from the business for money. They not only have a good reason to lend the money, but they have the expert knowledge about the business that gives them confidence in what they are doing. They usually feel that they can pick the winners.

Leasing.   Leasing is a form of borrowing. A lease is a liability. Once you sign, you are obligated to pay the lessor some money in exchange for using whatever asset you are renting. The obligation you take on when signing a lease should appear on the balance sheet, but it seldom does. Sometimes it is footnoted. That is why we call it *off-balance-sheet financing*. It is a way of borrowing a lot of money, yet not having the unsophisticated reader of your financial statements know the actual condition of your company.

Tip

Leasing can be a way of selling equity.

A private investor is interested in your new venture but is reluctant to take a minority equity position in it for good reasons. You need the investor's money to buy equipment. So let the investor buy the equipment and lease it to you, thus resolving many of the investor's fears.

Factoring.   Factoring is a means of financing by which entrepreneurial companies sell their accounts receivable at a discount to a commercial finance company known as a *factor*. It is a mechanism to increase cash flow when cash is limited and accounts receivable are high. It is short-term financing to solve short-term cash-flow bottlenecks. Cash can be made available to the entrepreneur as soon as proof of shipment is provided or on the average due date of the invoice. Most factoring arrangements are made for about one year.

Factors make their money by acquiring a company's invoices and collecting on them, charging the business a fee. Unlike a bank, factors buy, pay for, and own the receivables outright. If your creditors don't pay, the factor may incur a loss. Some factors require that the entrepreneur establish a reserve for bad debt of approximately 5 percent of the account. If the account is not collected within 120 days, the factor will draw against the reserve. If the account is collected, the factor's return on investment exceeds that of conventional lenders.

So instead of using accounts receivable as collateral against loans, your receivables are sold at a discounted value to a factoring company. For example, if the factoring company uses a one-time charge and discounts 6 percent, then for every $1000 in receivables, the seller receives $940.

Some factors discount according to a schedule, paying a smaller percentage up front and then paying an additional percentage depending on whether the receivable is collected within 30, 60, or 90 days. The factor takes over the entire collection procedure including mailing the invoices and other associated bookkeeping functions. Each of your customers is notified that the account is owned by and payable to the factor.

Many business owners use factoring when their banker turns down a loan request that they had tried to guarantee with their accounts receivable as collateral. Many banks steer away from asset-based lending because of the unpredictable nature of the underlying collateral and the difficulty in liquidating it.

However, if you are a new business and your accounts receivable are evaluated as marginal credit risks, you might not be able to find a factor that will accept them. Let's face it: Although factors take greater risks and are more liberal lenders than commercial banks, they need to be assured that your customers will pay their bills. They will execute substantial credit checks on each debtor and carefully analyze the quality and value of the invoice before buying it. They look to the strength of the receivables and credit worthiness of the invoices that you are selling them. Factors will also establish credit limits for each customer.

Tip

Factoring is not the cheapest way to obtain money, but it does quickly turn receivables into cash.

The advantages of factoring are being better able to pay your bills, receiving an injection of cash quickly, obtaining more credit, and fostering better growth than traditional borrowing. Also, the fee is an expense and offsets taxable income. Essentially, the entrepreneur is buying insurance against bad debt.

The disadvantages of factoring are the higher cost of money than traditional borrowing and the sometimes seemingly outrageous returns factors receive. A business concerned with cash flow but not with collection might want to pursue accounts-receivable financing through a commercial bank which would be less costly.

Overall, factoring can be compared to using a credit card for your business. Factors work best with businesses that have long delays between the making and selling of goods and cash collection. Start-up ventures and emerging businesses, along with service industries, are prime candidates for factoring, as well as other businesses that experience cash-flow problems.

Talk to other entrepreneurs in your industry as well as with members of the infrastructure to obtain recommendations and references about which factoring companies to use. Trade associations are also an excellent resource for locating factoring companies in your industry. For more information, call National Factoring Services, Inc., at (303) 592-1919 or (800) 253-6700, or other national factoring companies.

Bonds.   A bond is a form of an interest-bearing note issued by a corporation, but a more formal instrument than a note. It contains many formal provisions that must be observed lest the trustee who oversees the administration of the bond declare the company to be in default.

Mistakenly, many people think that bonds are only for big companies. Small ventures can also use bonds to raise money. They provide the financier with some advantages not enjoyed by a note holder:

- Bonds tend to be more negotiable than notes.
- There are some third parties involved to act as watchdogs.
- Courts are more likely to be responsive to the pleas of a group of bondholders than they are to the complaints of noteholders.
- The inclusion of options, warrants, and conversion features in

the bond can give its owner many, if not all, of the advantages of ownership, thus availing the creditor the joys of the enterprise's prosperity. The investor can enjoy both the virtues of debt and equity.

The company, while it has a more flexible instrument to use in raising money, will find that the costs of floating a bond issue will usually exceed the costs of raising money by note. Yes, it can cost money even to sign a simple note at the bank. The bank may want you to keep an offsetting balance in your account of 20 percent of the loan, thus effectively increasing your costs. The bank may insist on some additional accounting audits periodically, again incurring some costs.

Trap

All of the costs of borrowing money are not paid as interest.

It is not uncommon for bonds to be sold to investors in new ventures in combination with some sort of equity instrument. For example, one unit for $2000 might consist of one $1000 bond and 100 shares of common stock. The stock might be of a special class that gives the investors certain preferences in income or claims on assets or restricted voting rights under some circumstances. One of the advantages of the corporate form of business organization is the tremendous flexibility and options for financing available to the founder.

Money Finders.   There are numerous financial consultants who will not only help you package your deal, but put you into contact with potential investors. But they will usually cost you money up front plus finder's fees. Typically, they work with firms whose capital requirements are below the minimums required by investment bankers. As might be suspected, they are flexible in their operations and vary tremendously in their abilities.

* Trap

Beware of frauds who pass themselves off as money finders and financial consultants. They promise to raise money, but demand advance payment of a finder's fee. Avoid paying up-front fees to fund-raisers.

Many of these deals are cloaked in clever scams involving loans from foreign countries at low interest rates. Just keep in mind that there is no *Santa Claus* in the money market. When you deal in the money market, be prepared for an unusual cast of characters. Money attracts all sorts of people with all sorts of motives, some good and many bad.

First, money often attracts people who cannot be trusted. They look upon the money market as the direct way to riches. Be careful whom you deal with. Don't think it's easy to spot these types of people. They often have the best addresses and the best-looking offices, and they can be very persuasive.

Second, the financial world is loaded with incompetents who will promise you money but not be able to deliver. They don't have the contacts they profess to have.

Third, there are dreamers who really think they can do something for you, take you public or whatever, but they are wrong. Many of these people are simply "unreal." They are easy to spot but, unfortunately, you may not want to spot them. You want what they tell you to be true. You like their dreams.

Finally, there are people working around the fringes of the money market who just don't know what is going on.

Tip

Check credentials of money finders, ask for and call all references. Find people who are interested in and understand your business as well as have a good reputation.

Other Lending Institutions.   At one time the traditional commercial bank was about the only money game in town. But today, there are different organizations that "sell" you money with a variety of deals and terms. A few that deserve some attention are: (1) Savings and loan associations, (2) Credit unions, (3) Commercial finance companies, and (4) Hard-asset lenders.

Savings and Loan Associations
Not too many years ago the savings and loan companies only made loans on real estate; that was the purpose for which they were created. Then in the 1980s, they rushed to resemble commercial banks when Congress allowed them to do so. Many aggressively sought to make commercial loans. The S & L scandals

of the early 1990s dried up this source of money, but it is slowly returning.

Credit Unions

Initially created to serve the financial needs of the workers of large organizations, particularly for the financing of appliances, cars, and home improvements, the more aggressive ones have branched out to help their members finance other activities. In some instances, you don't even have to work for any one company to join a credit union. One in Richardson, Texas, accepts members from any company in town.

Tip

Credit unions offer more reasonable financing terms than other institutions.

Trap

However, money borrowed from a credit union is usually short-term and limited.

Credit unions usually don't lend a large amount of money, such as $50,000 or more, but are more comfortable with loans of $10,000 to $20,000. Also, they can be used for small personal loans.

Commercial Finance Companies

Names such as Beneficial, CIF, Household, GMAC, Associates, and The Money Store are some commercial finance companies who prosper by lending money to people with whom bankers would refuse to deal.

While these firms are most famous for their activities in consumer credit, they still do a large business with commercial institutions. Some of their loans are quite large and in the three- to five-year range of payback. They are worth your time to investigate. But such loans do cost more than loans from your commercial bank. The lenders are professionals, and they can examine your situation and perhaps provide you with some ideas.

Hard-Asset Lenders

Certain firms will lend money against so-called hard assets, such as equipment and machinery, tangible assets with a recognizable liquidating value. Most of the firms with which they deal have exhausted other avenues of borrowing, largely due to a poor credit rating. Prime plus 10 percent is a good deal in this segment of the money market. Hard-asset lenders provide quick, decisive action and much good advice.

Equity Financing

Equity means ownership—the owner's equity in the business. And we all know that the owners get everything that is left over after everyone else gets paid—suppliers, employees, the bank, the government . . . everyone. They don't call it the *bottom line* for nothing.

Equity is a complicated concept and a combination of three things: (1) the right to control, (2) the right to income, and (3) the right to assets.

1. *Right to control.*   Control is gained through the ability to elect the majority of the board of directors, thus, the officers who govern the business. Control is also gained through stock ownership. Majority control may not be necessary if the stock is dispersed widely enough among people who are not likely to get together to oust you from power.

Tip

The majority control of a company's voting stock is the key to control.

2. *Right to income.*   Control is one thing, income is another. Sometimes one class of common stock has voting rights but little else while another class has the rights to income on some preferential basis but without voting rights, unless certain provisions are not met. By these means, entrepreneurs can keep control of their ventures as long as they meet the stipulations of the preference stock.

3. *Right to assets.*   Claims on assets in dissolution can vary according to the financial instruments used. Usually entrepreneurs are not particularly interested in what happens to the firm in dissolution because they figure that by that time they will be out of the picture.

Major Forms of Equity

The major forms of equity discussed in this section are (1) you, (2) friends and family, (3) credit cards, and (4) the "angel network."

You. In most ventures, entrepreneurs are the first person financing the venture out of their own pockets. If the founder believes in the potential success of the venture, then he or she should have contributed cash to get the venture off the ground to convince the next level of investors that the venture warrants more capital. In fact, most investors require that the founder have invested in the venture. This type of equity is always the easiest and cheapest form of capital.

Friends and Family. Friends and family are one of the most-used sources of start-up capital for entrepreneurs. The most common involve M&Ds (moms and dads). They are easy to access, know your situation, and lend money based on their relationship with you versus the soundness of the venture.

There are times when it's OK to use family money, but don't think that there aren't problems involved. Families can be even rougher than outside creditors. They can nag you to death. Many entrepreneurs advise not to use family money. Don't take Aunt Mary's life savings for your surefire venture. Aunt Mary may need the money, and if you lose it, Aunt Mary will either starve or you'll have a new lifetime house guest.

Trap

If you lose family money, you'll pay for it the rest of your life— not in money, but in respect and relationships. *Be most careful with family money.*

About the same advice can be given with respect to friends. Taking money from a friend is a good way to lose a friend, even though you ultimately get the money back to him or her. Many business deals are made between friends. I just warn you to be careful. Friends are not that easy to come by. But this depends upon the deal, since some friends will be offended if you do not let them into your deal. As some put it, "Better they be offended outside the firm than inside it. There is no way I can run a business without doing something that would make an investor mad at me. Sooner or later, my expense account would be too large or I would be paying myself too much money, or something. The minute you let anyone into your company, the rules change."

Social relationships differ from business ones. You cannot treat friends the same way you would treat an outside stockholder. Many businesspeople prefer to keep everything on a businesslike, professional basis by dealing only with the professional money people.

Credit Cards.   Although one of the least-preferred financing options, modest credit card borrowing for financing short-term needs has been used by some entrepreneurs. This is an expensive and more risky method of raising capital. It can be used as a short-term alternative when more traditional sources are not available. A number of struggling entrepreneurs use credit cards in the early start-up phases of their ventures for working or expansion capital—especially when they are not considered "creditworthy" by traditional lenders. Credit card financing can act as a bridge to get new ventures over initial financial cash binds.

Tip

Be certain you have sufficient cash flow to make your credit card payments.

However, only consider this source when there is no other way to secure operating capital. Typically, you should be able to acquire an unsecured line of credit between $1000 to $5000 from each source. Some enterprising entrepreneurs have applied for multiple credit cards to finance their operating capital needs.

The major pitfall is that most credit card bills require payment in 30 days and carry high interest rates. You must consider whether paying higher interest rates is worth the extra money. In addition, you are personally liable for the debt.

The best technique for obtaining money from credit cards is to submit credit card applications simultaneously so you can obtain several cards with a cash advance privilege. By applying for credit to a number of different sources at once, you can truthfully disclose that you have no other outstanding loans.

This type of cash advance is very similar to obtaining a line of credit from a bank. You can get cash when you need it by taking your credit card to your bank to receive cash or have it deposited in your account. However, beware that many credit card companies charge an additional fee or a higher rate than their regular interest rate for receiving cash advances.

Shop for the lowest rates possible. Credit card interest rates are extremely competitive and newer companies may offer lower interest rates and more services.

Avoid using credit card financing to start a new venture or to pay for fixed expenses, such as equipment. Entrepreneurs should have enough cash from their own resources to launch their businesses. But, if you are not yet bankable, credit cards can provide needed capital very quickly.

Tip

Use credit cards as a cushion for cash crunches and then replace credit card financing with conventional loans when possible.

From a tax standpoint, the same tax deductions are available with a credit card loan as with any other business loan. The right to deduct interest rates is determined by the purpose for which the money is used. Regardless of how high the interest rate is, interest is deductible at the time it is incurred, not when it is paid.

Preferably repay the credit cards in full within 30 days to avoid accumulating high interest rates. Any late payments on your credit cards may affect your ability to qualify for future loans.

The Angel Network.   Private investors, known as *business angels,* are wealthy individuals or groups of individuals who put money into local ventures. Often they are the only source of risk capital for entrepreneurs. Recent studies show that there are over one million investors, or angels, in the United States investing equity capital into ventures annually.

They are not typically multimillionaires. Some studies show that the annual income of an angel averages around $250,000. Many are business owners, managers, or professionals who are generally about 20 years older than the entrepreneurs they finance.

Angels invest their own money, in small amounts. The majority of their investments are under $100,000 and usually don't exceed $500,000. The average angel invests about $35,000 in any one company and usually invests in ventures within a 50-mile radius of their home. Angels like to be familiar with the business or industry they are investing in.

The good news is that they love start-ups, and this type of money is easier to acquire than venture capital. Plus, they generally offer better interest rates than banks and have fewer strings than venture capitalists. A majority don't want voting rights in the company; however it depends on the industry and the amount they have invested. They may want to take on an advisory role or become a board member. They expect returns of three to five times their investment after two to five years.

The bad news is they are hard to find. Start by looking in your industry and contact your attorney, accountant, banker, trade associations, or professional groups. Local economic development agencies or chambers of commerce should also have lists of potential investors.

Tip

To find angels, use intermediaries who are advisers to angels, such as merchant bankers, boutique bankers, financial consultants, and planners who specialize in raising small amounts of capital.

Intermediaries develop a small network of angels who invest in the deals they find and recommend. Look in the Yellow Pages under "investment management, financing consultants, or financial planners." One such boutique investment banking firm is the Capital Institute, (800) 748-6887, which has offices throughout the United States. Financial consultants and planners usually work through a brokerage firm and are involved in managing the investments of angels.

Contact one of the venture capital clubs in your area. They can be a good place to learn about the local angel community. The Association of Venture Clubs in Salt Lake City, Utah, at (801) 364-1100, can provide a list of clubs.

Another source is the Venture Capital Network in Durham, New Hampshire, (603) 862-3558, which introduces entrepreneurs and angels through a computerized matching system. They have offices in several cities and have a limited number of members, but are worth contacting. There are also angel networks in Massachusetts, Texas, Montana, Colorado, and Missouri, to name a few.

When working with an intermediary, be cautious. Check out their references and their track records. Try to get referrals from lawyers, bankers, accountants, and insurance brokers. For more information about private investors, refer to *Finding Private Venture Capital for Your Firm* by Robert J. Gaston published by Wiley or *Guerrilla Financing* by Bruce Blechman and Jay Conrad Levinson published by Houghton Mifflin. Both are excellent resources on financing tactics for entrepreneurs.

Factors Affecting Use of Debt and Equity

The theory of debt and equity is all fine and good, but the key question remains, What are the factors to consider in financing your enterprise? Let's examine each of these factors in some detail.

1. Investor Preferences

Unquestionably, the preferences of the money market play a large role in determining your capital structure. You usually have to give investors what they want to get their money. If they are playing the capital gains game, then they want some stock or the rights to buy some. If they want assured income, then you'll have to think in terms of giving them some debt instrument or let them own some assets and have you lease them.

The investment bankers can tell you what their customers are buying and what you have to give them. There are few problems in finding out what the market wants. The key question is, Can you go along with it? You may not want to saddle your firm with an inappropriate capital structure, one that will jeopardize your future plans, just because of the market's whimsy. There are times you should say no to the market, if you can afford that luxury. But first, examine the market closely.

It is easy for investment bankers to say that R & D partnerships are hot in the market; after all, like everyone else, they want goods that are easy to sell. However, rest assured that other forms of financing are also selling, but to other investors.

2. Your Preferences

While it may seem inconsistent to include this factor right after stressing the importance of the investor's preferences, still you are the entrepreneur who hopes to control your own destiny. If you cannot live peacefully with some particular type of financing, then avoid it. It's a matter of your personal philosophy. Determine which types of financing you are comfortable with.

In particular, the use of debt is a matter of great concern to many entrepreneurs. Even though many modern financiers are in love with the concept of leverage and urge the utmost use of debt in capital structure, you may not like creditors nor their hold over you. Perhaps you lose sleep over the pressures debt places on you. Then be comfortable, avoid debt!

3. Time

When do you need the money? Tomorrow you say? Good luck! As one banker is fond of saying, "You say you need my answer on your loan application today. Fine, I'll give it to you right now. It's *no!*" It takes time to get money; some kinds of money take longer than others. If you want to float a public stock issue, you are looking at a minimum of 6 months, more likely 9 to 12 months, depending upon how many Band-Aids the investment banker has to put on your operation to get it in shape to go public. Thus, if it is your intention to take your firm public at some future time, by all means you should make contact with an investment banker early. Let them guide you in how to structure your company so that it will take a minimum of effort to go public when the time comes.

More important, let them have time to get to know you and your operation. In a very real sense, when an investment banker takes you public, he or she is giving some testimony about your credibility and what he or she thinks of your future.

Even a bank loan will take some time. It could take a week or several months, to approve a loan unless the banker knows you well and the amount fits within their lending limitations. Again, let them know about your needs ahead of time. Get to know your banker. Make sure that your banker knows you and is familiar with your venture.

A venture capitalist can act quickly, but seldom does. You may be several months negotiating a deal with one, if you choose to do so. Consequently, if you need money quickly, you'll likely have to borrow it. Most equity takes more time to develop.

Do not underestimate the value of liquidity—the ability to raise cash fast. Naturally, the most liquid money is the cash you have hidden at home. For example, many people are in businesses where the possession of quick cash gives them tremendous buying opportunities. They can take advantage of offers made by people who are in need of immediate cash. With an excellent banking relationship and a good line of credit, you can quickly get the money you need to act rapidly on some matter. It can be most frustrating to see a highly profitable opportunity slip away from you because you could not come up with the cash that was required. Entrepreneurs who buy distressed properties at auctions must have certified checks in their hands at the time. They often profit handsomely from their liquidity.

4. Amount Needed

How much do you need? A small amount may be easily borrowed. But if you need a large sum of money, you may be forced to think in terms of a public sale of securities. Banks have definite limits to what they will lend any given company. Small loan amounts for inventory or operating capital are more difficult to obtain from banks since the administrative cost incurred could be more than the interest received on the loan. Most banks consider a loan of $150,000 or less as a small loan. Bankers feel that you should own more of the company than they do. They don't sleep well at all when they have more money in a deal than anyone else.

Banks are also limited by law as to how much they can lend to any one borrower. Thus, if you foresee that you will be borrowing a substantial sum from your banker, establish a relationship with a larger bank, one that can finance your venture as it grows.

One bitter entrepreneurial truth is that it is easier to raise large sums of money than small ones. A $50,000 deal can be tough to finance. There is not enough in it for lenders or investors to bother with. If you have a $50,000,000 deal, then all sorts of people may work hard to get the financing for your venture because they will make a lot of money doing so.

5. Control Aspects

There are all sorts of ways to maintain control of an enterprise. In some high-tech ventures, the talents of the entrepreneur are so critical to the venture's success, that without that individual's knowledge, the firm would likely flounder. Certainly, the average investor knows that he or she is incapable of managing the company so there is no threat of a takeover from greedy investors. Indeed, they are scared the entrepreneur will leave the firm for some greener pastures. In such cases, you might well sell a good deal of equity with little worry about losing control, particularly if you structured it wisely.

On the other hand, there are deals that look so profitable and easy to do that it would be unwise for you to allow absolute control out of your hands. After all, you are the one who is doing all the work to set up the deal. You want to keep it.

6. Costs

Some money costs more than other money. Going public may cost a minimum of $150,000 up front just to cover the legal and accounting fees for developing the prospectus. If the stock does not sell, and it is not a guaranteed deal, you are out $150,000. Not many firms looking for money can stand for that kind of loss. The investment banker may want between 10 and 15 percent of the money raised. You may have to pay out another 5 percent to various people who helped you find the money (finder's fees).

Even a private placement costs money: finder's fee, attorney costs for preparing the private placement memorandum, and accounting costs. Banks are the cheapest source of money. There are few front-end costs, and they will likely be the least expensive to service (lowest interest).

While the venture capital firm is seen by some as the financial savior of needy entrepreneurs, statistics show they finance a very small portion of new ventures and do so at high prices. They are relatively costly and it takes time to find the right one for your venture. But as one financier says, "The most expensive money is the money you don't get." Perhaps!

7. Confidence in Plan

As we previously stated, when you borrow money, you are betting your company. You are betting you can repay the loan as promised. If you are wrong, you lose. How sure are you of your forecasts? When you borrow money, you are forecasting an ability to repay it plus interest by a certain date. Those who are not quite so certain of their future may prefer equity, which does not have to be repaid on any schedule.

8. Ability to Service Debt in Early Years

Once you borrow money, the lender wants to start receiving interest fairly quickly. At times lenders will give you a little breathing room, but not much. You must pay the interest. Will you be able to do so? Many new enterprises do not have sufficient money in their early months, or even years, to pay much of anything—salaries, expenses, rent, interest, etc. If you have a business that will be slow to get off the ground, then beware of borrowing money. You need equity!

9. Glamour

If you are proposing a new venture into some glamour field with excellent publicity and news values, you may be able to go public from the start with little of substance to show—the genetic manipulators are a prime example. Many other so-called high-tech ventures have successfully gone public far before their time because they had a story that captured the investing public's imagination. And imagination sells for a high price!

10. Purpose of Funds

How are you going to use the money? Fixed assets? Inventory? Accounts receivable? Research and development? Each requires different kinds of money. Usually bankers lend money for R & D work, unless there is sufficient collateral to cover the loan amount. Consider an old-time basic financial principle which says: *Finance long-term assets with long-term money and short-term assets with short-term money, but never finance long-term assets with short-term money.*

Short-term borrowing is usually made for financing seasonal inventory and accounts receivable. They are often referred to as asset-conversion loans by bankers because the funds are invested in assets that will be subsequently converted into cash again with which to pay off the loan.

Term loans, an increasingly rare breed, are made for financing equipment. Suppose you buy a machine with a five-year payback: then five-year money would be needed. If you buy that machine with three-year money, then you will have to rob some other part of your business for some money when payoff time rolls round. The money would most likely come from the firm's income flow. Thus, bankers call this type of loan an *income-repayment loan* inasmuch as the bank must look to the firm's income for liquidation of the loan. As a general rule, bankers much prefer asset-conversion loans to income-repayment loans.

11. Business Contacts

Undeniably, your contacts will play a role in your financing plans. If you have excellent banking connections, you will likely rely heavily on bank borrowing. If you are well-wired into an investment banking house, then you will likely sell some securities. If you know some private investors well, you'll likely look to them for financing. You have to finance with those who know and trust you. It is difficult to get money from those who don't know you.

12. Management Skills

It takes more managerial skill to operate an enterprise on borrowed money than on equity. Stockholders cannot put you into bankruptcy. They can make noise and perhaps jeopardize your ability to sleep at night. But once you have their money, their legal rights are limited largely to whatever voting rights they have. But lenders have other powers.

Conclusion

You should now understand that your firm's capital structure can vary from a most simple one consisting solely of your own equity to a most complex blending of debt, equity, and operations. The type of capital structure best for your venture is not static. It will change as your venture grows and has different capital needs. Use capital structure to your advantage; it is a management tool and an important ingredient of success.

7
Growing Your Business

It may seem hard to believe, but some entrepreneurs consciously or unconsciously choose not to grow their businesses. Consciously, they may have read the many stories about entrepreneurs who fail during the growth period because they weren't prepared or didn't have the skills to manage the company during this volatile time. So to prevent a similar scenario in their own business, they put on the brakes and slow the company's growth to a manageable pace. Unconsciously, they may not understand that growth and expansion are natural by-products of a successful start-up venture. Growth is the way that new ventures establish a foothold in the market and create excitement for their products and services.

Yet another way that entrepreneurs may unconsciously stall the potential rapid growth of their companies is by believing that only high-tech companies experience rapid growth. The reality is, businesses in a variety of industries regularly grace *INC. Magazine*'s list of annual 500 fastest growing private companies, businesses that include service companies, restaurants, product manufacturers, and clothing companies. What makes a business a candidate for substantial growth is not so much the industry (although some industries like telecommunications do regularly experience phenomenal growth) but the business strategy.

Entrepreneurs can certainly choose not to grow their companies or grow at a pace that doesn't keep up with market demand

and opportunity, but for a company to survive over the long term, growth is essential.

Tip

Employ strategies to encourage growth.

Businesses that want to grow should do four things:

- Be first in a market niche you created based on an opportunity you saw. This way you can establish brand recognition early. It may be a tiny niche in the market; but define it, and you dominate it.

- Be the best at what you do and make sure customers know it. Don't just find innovative products; innovate in how you deliver your products and services. In fact, you need to innovate in every area of your business.

- Run a "lean and mean" operation that puts your resources into those aspects of the company that produce revenues instead of non-revenue-producing overhead.

- Offer something unique and clearly differentiated from others in the marketplace. It may be a product, a service, a distribution strategy, whatever—but make it unique to you.

Factors that Affect Your Company's Ability to Grow

Deciding you want to grow your company is certainly a start, but mere intentions are not enough. You must be aware of the factors in your business's environment that will increase or decrease your chances for growth. Here are a few of them:

1. *The characteristics of your target market.* If the niche market into which you're entering is small in terms of sales and the buying power of its customers, then the level of growth you can achieve may be limited. However, domestic niche markets can grow enormously with a global strategy that is easily put in place using the Internet and a company website.

2. *What your competition looks like.* Competing against much larger companies does not automatically keep your company from growing. Today being smaller means you can be more flexi-

ble and change more rapidly with changing market demands than a mammoth company with enormous overhead. Another example: If the industry you're in is very mature and stable, you may be able to create a niche by introducing new technology and new ways of doing things that will give new life to the industry.

3. *How innovative your industry is.*   Innovating in an industry that survives on innovation, like the computer industry, is not bringing anything new and exciting to the table. Being able to innovate more quickly and with higher quality, on the other hand, makes you competitive. By contrast, an industry where innovation is rare provides an opportunity to enter and establish the standards in your niche that everyone else will have to meet.

4. *How unpredictable your industry is.*   If your industry seems to change direction overnight and is totally at the whim of either the customer or certain key players in the industry, you have a hotbed of opportunity from which to capitalize. Growth and success in business come from change. Young and dynamic industries like telecommunications still offer opportunities for very high growth.

5. *How difficult it is to enter the industry.*   There are lots of ways an industry can make it difficult for a new business to enter and gain enough market acceptance to make a decent profit. Some industries have very mature players that have dominated the market with their brands. Other industries are costly to enter in terms of plant and equipment or regulations. Also, if key people in the industry own the rights to core technology that you need to produce your product, you may be barred from entering, so growth is effectively terminated. You will have to consider carefully if it's worth the effort to try to grow in this industry. It may be better to look to a compatible industry for growth opportunities.

6. *Whether or not you as the entrepreneur are willing to delegate authority and responsibility to someone better able to take the company through the growth process.*   Many a successful start-up has moved quickly into the growth phase only to find that it doesn't have the skills it needs to manage growth. If the entrepreneur doesn't recognize his or her shortcomings quickly and delegate to professional management, the company may flounder and eventually fail. The entrepreneur's talents are certainly needed to conceive and give life to the new business, but not many entrepreneurs also have the very different skills needed to manage the business.

7. Whether or not you as the entrepreneur can encourage the rest of your team and employees to think entrepreneurially about the business. It is important that everyone in the organization buy into the vision for the company and be ready and willing to accept the added responsibility and stress of growth to achieve it. You must convey your growth vision to everyone, including customers, and be willing to listen to and accept their feedback.

Trap

Watch out for success!

Just as growth is a trap that often snares the most successful of start-ups, success is perhaps an even bigger trap. This is because often with success comes complacency. "We've made it. The customers love us. We can do no wrong." You forget that while you are enjoying your newfound success, one or more of your competitors is constantly looking for ways to overtake you.

Also with success comes a more healthy cash position, and this is where the biggest trap lies. Business owners begin taking on more expensive overhead to celebrate their victory. To pay for it, they take more money out of the business. In effect, they forget that if the market changes—and it will—they will still be responsible for that expensive overhead even if their revenues have declined.

In business, success can be sustained only if you focus on continual improvement and putting your resources into those aspects of the business that produce revenues for the company.

Small Business Growth Strategies

There are many growth strategies available to businesses. They are standard in any good business text, but only a very few work well for small, young companies. In this section we'll take a look at a few of those strategies that allow a small business to grow in a way that is healthy for the business and the entrepreneur.

Networking

A network strategy is also called an *agile web* or *modular* strategy, which you read about in Chapter 5. This strategy involves focusing on what the company does best and outsourcing all other activities

ABC Database Systems

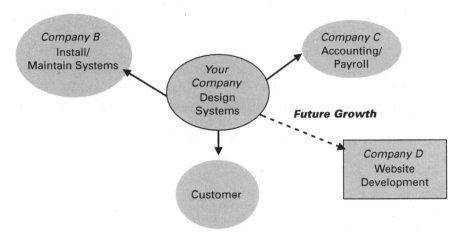

Figure 7-1. Network strategy

to other companies that specialize in them. It allows a small company to grow much more quickly with fewer overhead and production costs than would otherwise be necessary. For example, look at Figure 7-1. If your company specializes in designing integrated database systems for small companies that allow them to keep track of customers, you may choose to focus strictly on the design aspect and outsource installation and maintenance to another company. You can even outsource your accounting and payroll tasks since you probably don't consider them one of your specialties.

You are still the company with whom the customer deals. It's your company's name that the customer knows. As you begin to grow, your customers may, for example, let you know they would like the ability to let their customers reach them via a Website. So one way you can grow is to outsource that expertise, Website development, to an established company but provide the service under your company's name. You can continue to form relationships with new companies as you need them to satisfy your customer's requirements.

Licensing

Licensing is another way for a young company to grow without investing huge amounts of capital in plant, equipment, and employees. Licensing is built on the premise that you own intel-

lectual property that has value to someone else; that is, you have
something of commercial value that is either patented, copyrighted, trademarked, or is a trade secret. You may have invented
a product or process for which you have a patent, or you may
have copyrighted a character, like the children's toy "Tickle Me
Elmo." Or you may have a trade secret for a great new chocolate
chip cookie. In any case, you have the right to license the use of
that intellectual property (IP) to someone else to exploit in the
marketplace either by manufacturing and distributing it or using
it, in the case of a core technology, to produce their own product. You can negotiate a royalty that you will receive on all sales
of whatever product is produced using your property, and you
may also be able to negotiate an up-front fee in addition to the
royalty.

There is another side of this coin as well. Suppose someone
else owns some intellectual property you need for your business.
You can choose to license that IP from them and pay them a royalty to use it. Small companies have often found success and
growth from licensing characters developed by entertainment
companies and then exploiting them through toys, apparel, and
other types of merchandise.

Licensing is a legal transaction, so we highly recommend that
you use the services of a good attorney who specializes in that type
of law, not only to protect yourself against unscrupulous licensees
or licensors, but to make sure you get the best deal you can.

When You're the Licensor

If you'd like to consider licensing as a growth strategy and you
have intellectual property that someone else might pay to use,
here are some steps to take.

1. Decide exactly what you intend to license—a product, the
   design for a product, a process for doing something, etc.
2. Define the benefits to the licensee (buyer). Why should they
   license this intellectual property from you?
3. Do your market research to make sure there is a suitably large
   customer base for the licensed product and so that you can
   convince the potential licensee of the value of the license.
4. Do due diligence on potential licensees to make sure they
   have the resources to properly commercialize your IP and

that their reputation in the industry is sound. You don't want your IP associated with a disreputable company.

5. Decide if you will license the IP as is, allow it to be modified by the licensee, or sell it outright.

6. Determine the value of the license agreement. This is usually based on the economic life of the IP, the chance that someone will get around the patent or other form of IP protection, the potential for legislation that might affect the IP, and changes in market conditions. You will usually want some money up front and then a running royalty over the term of the license agreement. The amount of the royalty will vary by industry and by how much the licensee will have to invest to commercialize the IP.

7. Structure a license agreement with the aid of an attorney who specializes in this area. The agreement will have a grant clause specifying what is being delivered and whether or not it is an exclusive or nonexclusive license. Be sure to include a performance clause so that the licensee can't just sit on the license and keep you from giving it to someone else.

8. If secrecy must be maintained in the agreement, there should be a confidentiality clause defining who may know the secrets and to whom they may disclose them.

9. The manner in which payment will be made will also be specified as well as the currency to be used for the transaction, if other countries are involved. As a U.S. licensor, you would definitely want to take payment in dollars but you may have to take a combination of dollars and the licensee's currency, which could fluctuate up or down during the life of the license. This means that your royalty and the licensee's payments will also fluctuate accordingly.

10. You will probably have some form of improvement or grant-back clause in the agreement that allows the licensee to improve on the product and grant back to you the right to any improvements. You may also have a grant-forward clause that gives the licensee the right to use any improvements you've made on the product.

11. Be sure to set a term for the license agreement, and specify whether or not the licensee can sublicense the IP or assign the rights in any way.

When You're the Licensee

One of the ways you can grow by licensing is to license other companies' intellectual property and develop new products and services from it. Here are some steps to take if you want to license.

1. Identify a product or logo you want to license. Some of the most successful are those of sport teams, universities, TV shows, movies, or cartoon characters. Alternatively, you may be looking to license technology or know-how from a patent-holder.

2. Prepare a business plan to review the product you're proposing to develop and market with the intellectual property. Make sure to include estimated sales, the targeted market, how you plan to penetrate the market, and how you're going to finance the licensing contract.

3. With the help of a good attorney or a licensing consultant, you'll need to negotiate a satisfactory license agreement that will contain all of the elements mentioned previously when we discussed the licensor.

It's important to note that if the product you want to license is famous or very valuable for any reason, you may not have much room to negotiate and you will probably pay a premium for the license.

Franchising

Franchising, like licensing, is one of the more popular ways to grow a company rapidly without the expense of doing it all yourself. It is estimated that franchises account for almost one-third of all retail sales. Franchising lets the business grow in several geographic areas at once and is generally less expensive than setting up a national distribution system. Similar to licensing, franchising is granting to a franchisee the legal right to:

- Do business under a particular name
- Market a particular product, process, or service
- Receive training and assistance in setting up the business
- Receive ongoing training and assistance after start-up
- Receive marketing and quality control support

✳ Trap

Not every business has franchise potential!

Just because you have a great business concept doesn't mean it's a good choice for a franchise growth strategy. Successful franchises must meet the following criteria:

- You must have a successful prototype store (or better yet, multiple stores) that is profitable and has an excellent reputation.
- You must have registered trademarks and provide a consistent, recognizable image for all stores or outlets.
- The business must be easily systematized and replicable.
- Its products or services must have value in a variety of geographic regions.
- You must have sufficient funding. Setting up a franchise system is a costly undertaking.

Tip

Franchising comes in three flavors.

There are generally three types of franchise opportunities.

1. *Dealerships:* This type of a franchise allows manufacturers to distribute products without having to do the retail side of the business. An example is an auto dealership.
2. *Service franchises:* Tax preparation, temporary employees, payroll preparation, and real estate services are examples of this type of franchise opportunity. Examples are H&R Block Tax Preparation Services and Century 21 Real Estate Services.
3. *Product franchises:* These are the most popular types of franchises, offering a proven product, a recognized brand name, and an operating model. Examples are Burger King and Chief Auto Parts.

The franchisee, the one who purchases the franchise opportunity, pays a fee and royalty on sales to the franchiser, the owner of the business concept, in much the same manner as a license agreement. For this the franchisee will normally receive:

- A product or service with a proven market
- The use of trademarked names

- Perhaps the right to a patented design, process, or formula
- An accounting and financial control system
- A proven marketing plan
- The benefit of volume purchasing and advertising

In short, the franchisee receives somewhat of a turnkey operation.

Putting together a franchise opportunity to sell is a fairly complex undertaking that can easily cost up to $150,000 or more. You will need a well-documented prospectus that spells out the rights and responsibilities of the franchisee, a training and support manual, and system for franchisees both before they purchase and after. You will also need to establish some site selection criteria for franchisees so that all future locations of the franchise will be similar in appearance and quality of location. And you will need to maintain some type of quality control procedures so that customers of your franchises can expect uniform quality everywhere they go. This may mean periodic on-site inspections, controlling vendors' quality level, and getting feedback from customers.

Trap

Franchising is risky!

Franchising can be risky both for the franchisor and the franchisee. Watch out for these risks:

For the Franchisee

- Franchisees typically pay 2 to 10 percent of *gross* sales to the franchisor for monthly marketing and royalty fees, which can significantly affect cash flow.
- It may take up to three years to earn a profit.
- The failure rate is high, especially for eating and drinking establishments.
- Bankruptcy of the parent company can leave the franchisee with no support and virtually in limbo.

For the Franchisor

- The work to prepare to present the franchise opportunity is like starting the business all over again.

- It is difficult to accurately screen all franchisees for financial strength and skills necessary to run the business effectively.
- The costs are high and include legal, accounting, consulting, and training.
- Research has found that nearly 35 percent of franchises go out of business in four years.

Growing by Buying Another Business

Another way to grow your business more rapidly is to acquire an existing business—your competitor, perhaps, or a complementary business that allows you to extend your product line. For example, if you manufacture a product, you may acquire the supplier of your raw materials or you may purchase a retail outlet to control that end of the distribution channel.

Today a popular strategy is the "Pac Man strategy," a concept taken from the popular video game of the same name. The goal is to enter a very fragmented industry where there are a lot of "mom and pop" type small businesses and start purchasing them and putting them under one name to achieve economies of scale and synergies among them. Wayne Huizenga did this with the garbage industry to form Waste Management, and Todd Smart did it with independent tow truck owners to form Absolute Towing and Transportation. What you need to know to purchase another business can be found in Chapter 6. However, make sure when you purchase a business to grow your own business, that it has a compatible culture and a good reputation. These are the hardest things to deal with and correct if they're not right to begin with.

If you are interested in growing your business avoid the following:

1. Don't try to get customers by discounting, giving rebates, or coupons. It's a short-term fix, and you won't win the best customers, those who will stay with you. What you will get is the scavengers—those customers who are seeking the best deal, who will move on as soon as the deal is better somewhere else. The loyal customers won't.

2. Don't go global unless it makes sense for your business. Also be sure you have a partner in that country and carefully research the opportunity.

3. Don't buy a business that isn't compatible with your company's culture and goals or you will find you have employees who don't "fit in" and who may not buy into your vision for the company.

4. Don't forget about sharing the success with your employees and relieving the stress of growth through laughter and recognition.

5. Don't fail to plan for growth and how it will affect every aspect of your business.

Expanding Globally

Today expanding the boundaries of your company globally is not something that only large companies need to concern themselves with. The reality of the global marketplace today is that it is touching every business no matter how small and no matter where it's located. Your competition, your suppliers, your manufacturers can as easily come from a country you've never heard of as they can from the business down the street.

Fortunately, technology has made it possible for your business to have a global presence and deal in a global market alongside very large companies for very little money, time, and effort. Technology, which has become a part of everyday business life and which makes small businesses competitive with much larger ones, includes e-mail, videoconferencing, teleconferencing, networked databases, and the Internet, to name just a few.

✳ Tip

Take advantage of computer-related technology to help you grow your business.

Here are some examples of technology that will enhance your company's ability to grow in a global marketplace.

- *E-mail.*   Electronic mail lets your company communicate quickly, easily, and inexpensively with customers, vendors, and others around the globe as well as within the company. All it requires is a computer and a modem.

- *Teleconferencing and videoconferencing.* These let you conduct meetings with several people, all of whom may be in different locations. Teleconferencing requires a phone system that allows conference calls. Videoconferencing requires a computer and video cameras.

- *Networked databases.* These are sources of information available on computer to be accessed by anyone in the company. They may be company databases or on-line databases accessed via the Internet. They require computers, database software, and an Internet service provider.

- *Modems and laptop computers.* These let your employees work and remain in contact with the office and your customers from anywhere in the world.

- *Voice mail.* A voice mail system lets growing businesses receive messages when they're not available to answer the phone. They're available from commercial vendors.

- *Satellite systems.* These can be leased from a vendor and will permit the company to receive broadcasts from major manufacturers or suppliers in its distribution channel without having to incur the costs of producing a broadcast.

- *Laser color printers and publishing software.* Today small businesses can produce professional quality marketing materials every bit as good looking as those produced by much larger companies.

- *The Internet.* Having a Website and an automatic global presence is as easy as securing an Internet service provider and using the latest word processing software, which allows you to create Web pages the way you do any other document and then save them in HTML format to upload to your Website.

Tip

Do careful research to find your global market.

It's not easy to decide which global markets to go after with your product or service—there are so many from which to choose. Fortunately a variety of resources are available to business owners to help them choose.

- *The International Statistics Yearbook of the United States.* In this book, which can be found in any major library, you can use the

United Nation's Standard Industrial Trade Classification (SITC) codes to identify commodities used in international trade and the demand for products and services in specific countries.

- District Office or the Washington, D.C., office of the International Trade Administration. This office has a wealth of information on international trade.

- Department of Commerce. The DOC's database links all International Trade Administration offices and provides an abundance of information.

- U.S. Chamber of Commerce International Business Exchange (IBEX). Here small business owners can actually sell products and services or purchase supplies anywhere in the world electronically. The entrepreneur enters the required information and the system searches its databases for potential matches.

Once the country or region you're going to target has been chosen, several steps should be taken to ensure a successful launch:

1. Develop a well thought out marketing plan and budget based on understanding how business is done in that country.

2. Consider hiring a consultant who is expert in the country you're targeting. This person will make sure that you do not make costly errors.

3. Attend foreign trade shows to learn about businesses in the country you're interested in. You'll also get an idea of how business is conducted and who the competition is.

Franchisers have taken the global market by storm, particularly those in the fast-food industry—McDonald's, Burger King, and Kentucky Fried Chicken. Those that have been successful have usually had a local partner that made their entrée into the culture easier. Franchisers consider many things before going into a foreign market. These same considerations apply equally well to all businesses:

- The compatibility of their business with the country's culture. Will people in other countries understand the business concept? Does it run counter to local customs?

- Given all the costs particular to that country and setting up business there, is there the potential for sufficient profit?

- What does the customer base look like? How and when do people buy? What's important to them—packaging, design, quality?
- The country's current infrastructure: roads, transportation, utilities, etc., How will they affect your ability to do business?
- The availability locally of supplies needed to run the business.
- The stability of the foreign currency. Make sure your profit margins leave room for currency fluctuations.
- The nature of the competition. Many countries are fiercely loyal to local business owners and may not purchase from you.
- The legal system of the country. For example, will your intellectual property rights be protected?
- Real estate issues for facility purchasing, building or leasing.
- The availability of skilled labor to do the type of work you need.
- The tax structure and ramifications to the business.

Trap

When in Rome...

What works in the United States may not be suitable or acceptable in another country. One well-known fast-food chain failed miserably in Malaysia because they didn't understand that two-thirds of the population does not eat meat. Another fast-food chain failed in Japan because they regularly used a type of fish that is considered inferior by the Japanese.

The bottom line: Understand the culture and habits of your customers in other countries before you do business there!

Using the Internet to Grow

The Internet and the World Wide Web, a commercial area of the Internet that connects large and small companies in a global network of information and resources, are the latest frontier for growth, and it's the Wild West all over again. Anyone can set up shop on the Internet. All you basically need is an Internet service provider (ISP), a computer, a modem, and software that lets you create web pages. Web pages are very much like a storefront in the form of an interactive brochure. They let visitors learn about your company, purchase products on line, and link to other sites and sources of information that you've included in your site.

  Most of the money being earned on Websites today is through advertising; however, more and more products and services are being sold as well. Other companies with products or services compatible with yours will pay to link to your site or to place an ad on your site. An alternative is to do a trade with a company so that you help each other find new customers.

Tip

To succeed on the Internet you must plan how to stand out in a crowd.

The Internet is like riding a crowded subway. It's still on the slow side and there are millions of Websites vying for your attention. So how do you stand out in a crowd? Here are some tips.

- Link up with a compatible, but noncompeting, website so that customers who stop at your partner's site become aware of and can easily jump to your site. For example, a bookstore could link with a record store.

- Use colorful, simple graphics but be careful not to use memory-hogging graphics and animation, because most users are still working with 28.8 baud modems and the wait to download those graphics so they can be seen may discourage a potential customer enough to leave the site prematurely.

- Keep your main selling points clear and concise—sound bites. People who surf the Web have short attention spans.

- Offer something free like information or an invitation to join a forum.

- Make sure your graphics clearly identify the product and the company so as to be understood by global readers.

- Make it easy for your customers to sort through lists.

- Give people a reason to come back. Update the site regularly.

Getting Started on the Web

Besides going directly to setting up a Website on your own or with the help of a designer, here are three additional suggestions for how to get a business started on the Web that can be used alone or in tandem with the Website.

1. *Start with a forum where users can come to ask and answer questions and state their opinions.* Some of the larger Internet providers like America Online (AOL) have forums on particular topics or in particular areas of interest. Get involved in a forum in an area related to your business and when you sign your name, use your company name as well. This is a subtle but effective way to start to gain a presence in the Internet marketplace.

2. *Start an on-line newsletter in your area of interest.* The newsletter can be sent via e-mail to a start-up list of potential subscribers you identify. Then ask these people to recommend others by forwarding the newsletter to them. This was the strategy of author/consultant Azriela Jaffe who started *The Entrepreneurial Couples Success Letter* and now has well over 500 subscribers worldwide. From this she has gotten consulting jobs and speaking engagements as well as book deals.

3. *Operate a forum for an on-line service.* This involves soliciting a service provider like AOL with a proposal for the content of the forum. If you create enough interest, the provider may even front the money to set up the forum. It will then receive a percentage of the on-line fees paid by the users of the service, from advertising, and from sales to users. But understand that competition is enormous for this approach.

Trap

Be sure to register your company's domain name.

When the Internet became a popular site for businesses, Internet domain names, your Internet address (i.e., www.fitscapc.com) became valuable. Some service providers went around registering domain names for big companies and then went to the companies to sell them back their name. One company, Kaplan Educational Centers, took the company that pirated its name to court for trademark violation. An arbitration panel required the pirate, Princeton Review, to give up the domain name, kaplan.com.

Immediately register your domain name through your Internet service provider.

Hiring an Internet Service Provider

When seeking an ISP, you'll want to check around, because the cost and quality of their services vary significantly. Here are some questions you should ask:

1. What are their standard rates?.
2. How long have they been in business?
3. Which modem rates do they support?
4. What security measures do they have and how many backups do they do?
5. Are e-mail and electronic ordering blanks available?
6. Which reports do they provide and how often [i.e., the domain names of the visitors to the site and the number of hits (visitors) per day]?
7. Who owns the rights to the Website? If a designer is used, do they have copyrights to any graphics and icons they design?
8. Who owns the programming code for the Website?
9. Who owns the data on the Website? Be sure you protect the rights to the data you generate on the Website.

Once you have your ISP, look into the latest software that makes it easy for you to create your own Website as easily as you create any other document.

As you can see, there are a number of ways for small business owners to grow their businesses effectively while minimizing the chance of failure. Growth is a natural and important part of the life of a business. It should be planned for and enjoyed because it can be one of the most exciting times for an entrepreneur.

Resources

Buying a Franchise and Business Opportunity, Entrepreneur Magazine business guide. 800-421-2300.

Commerce Department, "Flash Facts," a 24-hour free fax line for information on specific international regions. Eastern Europe, 202-482-5745; Mexico, 202-482-4464; Pacific Basin, 202-482-3875; Africa, Near East, and South Asia, 202-482-1064.

IBEX: 800-537-IBEX. Requires IBM-compatible, Windows-capable personal computer with a modem. There is a one-time software and registration fee of $250. Users pay by function, not by minute. Average usage costs are $50 to $100 a month.

Trade Information Center, 800-USA-TRADE (800-872-8723). Ask for an industry desk officer who is a specialist in your industry.

TradeNet, an Internet electronic mailing list for international importers and exporters. *TradeNet@cerfnet.com; TradeNet@ix.netcom.com; TACC5BA (Prodigy); TradeNetWS (America Online); 75144,3544 (CompuServe).*

Uniform Customs and Practices for Documentary Credits (UCP). *ICC Publication 500.*

U.S. and Foreign Commercial Domestic Field Offices: 800-USA-TRADE.

Whiteley, Richard and Diane Hessan. (1996). *Customer-Centered Growth.* Reading, Mass.: Addison-Wesley Publishing Co.

Wolf, J.S. (1992). *Export Profits.* Chicago: Upstart Publishing Co.

8
Finding Resources for Growth

Venture Capitalists

Venture capital firms specialize in investing money in return for an equity position, if they think the business has a strong potential for success in a short period of time. They look for ventures with extremely high growth potential where they can at least quintuple their investment in five years. They are interested in businesses with a potential to go public, since a public offering allows the venture capitalists to liquidate their investment.

Venture capital is defined as a professionally managed pool of participation through stock, warrants, or convertible securities. These firms only fund about 1 percent of the deals that come across their desks. Only a smattering of venture capital firms are interested in raw start-ups. The majority prefer to have several years of an established track record before considering investing in the project. Most statistics show that less than 14 percent of investments made by venture capitalists were in start-up ventures.

Trap

Avoid going to a venture capital firm for seed money to launch a new start-up.

Most money invested by venture capital firms is in older, more developed companies, where there are many opportunities for high growth—like 60 to 70 percent annually. Some of the smaller funds prefer to invest upwards of $250,000 while the mega funds do not invest in deals less than $1 million. This heavily depends on the size of the venture, its growth potential, and its stage of development.

Venture firms all have stringent criteria for their investments, they look for ventures with extremely high growth potential, and some only invest in certain industries like high-tech, software, bio-tech, or health care.

Finding the Right Venture Capital Company

The first step is identifying several venture capital firms that might be interested in your venture. There are over 2300 venture capital firms in the United States and more overseas. Also, there are more foreign investors coming to the United States looking for deals. Many are aggressive in initiating projects in markets and technologies in which they have special interests.

Most firms specialize in one or two technologies or markets, because they are familiar with the industry and/or have experienced past success. Some only invest in specific types of deals, such as computer software, robotics, etc. Others specialize in stages of investment such as "seed only," leveraged buyout only, mezzanine financing only, and so on. Some firms specialize by region. Others like to be the lead investor negotiating all the terms and structuring the deal before bringing in follower investors. A few firms become actively involved financially and managerially often becoming board members.

Tip

Seek advice and referrals from your professional advisers when looking for a venture capital firm.

For more information consult these books available in your library: *Venture's Guide to International Venture Capital* (Venture Magazines, Inc.); *Pratt's Guide to Venture Capital Sources* (Venture Economics, Inc.); *Who's Who in Venture Capital* (John Wiley & Sons); *Handbook of Business Finance & Capital Sources*

(Dileep Rao); and *Venture Capital at the Crossroads* (Harvard School Business Press). These books contain lists that indicate the amount of money each venture capitalist wants to invest (minimum and/or maximum) and the types of ventures preferred.

Contact the National Venture Capital Association who publishes an up-to-date list of its members and will send out free copies when requested. Economic development centers and/or the SBDCs in your area have lists of venture capitalists. Local colleges and universities with outreach business development programs are another source.

Trap

Beware of advertisements that ask you to send $150 to $200 for lists of venture capitalists.

The lists you receive from many of these mail-order companies are the same lists you can obtain *free* from the library.

Tip

Always secure an introduction before contacting a venture capital firm.

The more you can network with the entrepreneurial infrastructure and other business owners to obtain referrals to venture capitalists, the better chance you have of securing financing from these investors. The referral may only be a telephone call alerting the venture capitalists that your business is deserving of their consideration. In a few hours venture capital firms reject about 90 percent of the venture deals they evaluate.

Start by contacting several venture capital firms to which you have obtained an introduction and where there is a reasonable probability of their being interested in your venture.

Trap

Avoid mass mailing your business plan to different venture capitalists.

"Safety in numbers" is not the case when trying to obtain financing from venture capital firms. Do not shop your business plan to several venture capitalists at once. It's a close-knit community and word will get around. During the first contact, describe your venture, its products, the experience of your management team, the amount of capital sought, and the expected performance of the venture two to three years down the road. You must be able to persuade the investor to find out more about your venture.

After an initial call, the venture capitalist will quickly evaluate whether the venture is worth having you submit a business plan or perhaps make a presentation. Usually the business plan comes before a presentation. Experts estimate that between 60 to 80 percent of all ventures presented to venture capitalists are rejected during the first contact. They will only agree to review your business plan if they believe that your idea has a large enough growth potential in an expanding market, your management team is well qualified to operate the venture, and they will potentially earn an appropriate return on their investment in terms of capital appreciation.

Studies of the investment screening process by venture capitalists reveal that they usually evaluate six major areas that include: the caliber of your management team including a successful track record and relevant experience; the industry, market and growth potential; available technology for the venture; the distinctive characteristics and uniqueness of the venture; your financial data, including pro forma cash-flow documents, balance sheets, and profit and loss statements; and finally, the terms of the deal. The management team is of key importance to them. In most instances, a venture capitalist would rather invest in a first-rate management team and a second-rate product than the reverse.

If no major flaws in the above areas are identified, you will be asked to make an oral presentation to the investor. At this stage, no more than 10 to 20 percent of all entrepreneurs who originally contact a venture capitalist are still being considered. Don't be discouraged about being turned down at this point. Your venture must fit the investment objectives and philosophy of the firm. The firm must decide on the number and portfolio mix of businesses, buyout opportunities, the types of industries and the geographic region for the investment, as well as the intuition and gut feeling of the venture capitalist to your deal.

Tip

Rule of thumb: Entrepreneurs usually give up between 35 to 60 percent of their equity to attract venture capital.

The venture capital game concludes with the structure of a deal and the negotiating of terms. Venture capitalists may insist on a "lockup" agreement which provides that the entrepreneur will not negotiate with any other investor for a fixed period of time (usually 30 to 90 days) without any commitment from them to invest. They argue that this time is necessary to perform their due diligence. Resist making a lockup agreement if possible or limit the amount of time.

✶ Trap

Venture capital negotiations begin with a term sheet that is badly leveraged for the entrepreneur. Don't blindly agree with the term sheet.

A *term sheet* is a brief summary of the terms of the investment contract. The venture capital is usually structured with convertible preferred shares for the investors and common shares for the entrepreneur. Common shares are given to the entrepreneur because this has the best tax implications. Venture capitalists contribute money, which establishes the value of their shares. If the entrepreneur were to receive the same shares for no investment, this granted stock would be immediately taxed. Without cash, the entrepreneur would not be able to meet the tax obligation. But, if the stock is of a different class, and the other class has advantages (preferences), the common stock can be valued at a fraction of the preferred class of shares.

Preferred stock has preference over common stock in receiving dividends, rights to assets, and voting. Preferred shares usually contain a wide variety of terms, including assigning all of the proprietary rights to the company, signing a confidential disclosure agreement, the right to a board seat, conversion ratios, dilution rights, dividend provisions, conversion rights, liquidation and exit strategy, etc. Therefore, it is critical for founders to understand the venture capital game, and all the various negotiating techniques and strategies, as well as to have strong legal representation.

Initial Public Offerings

An IPO, which takes a company public, raises capital through federally registered and underwritten sales of the company's shares. It is a more complex form of a private placement in which the founders and equity shareholders agree to sell a portion of their company (via unissued stocks and bonds) to the public by filing with the Securities and Exchange Commission (SEC) and listing the stock on one of the stock exchanges.

The decision whether to go public is difficult because once the process begins, the business, decision making, and the position of the founder(s) significantly change. Trying later to return the business to private ownership is almost an impossible task.

Trap

The legal, accounting, and administrative costs of raising money via a public offering are much higher and more disadvantageous than other ways of raising capital.

For example, legal fees can easily cost as much as $75,000 or more. Filing fees with the SEC and filing fees in the state in which the company does business can add another $50,000 to $100,000. Audited financial statements, pro forma statements, and summary financial statistics could range from $20,000 to $150,000 depending on the size of the company and the complexities of the audit. Financial printing fees for the prospectus, SEC registration statement, and official notices could run anther $40,000 to $100,000. It is not uncommon for a small IPO of $6 million to cost up to $500,000 before any proceeds are realized, if the offering is successful.

Also much time is spent by management complying with SEC regulations and reporting requirements to maintain a public company. This time, which should often be devoted to operating the company, could adversely affect its performance and future growth opportunities. Management time is a real cost to taking a company public, along with other standard expenses.

Another consideration is that the required disclosures about company products, performance, and financial condition made to stockholders and other outsiders may be better kept secret, especially from your competitors. In addition, there is always the risk that the public will not purchase the entire issue or even a major portion of it; yet you will still incur the costs of preparing to go public.

Trap

The stock issues may not be successful but, the company must pay costly up-front expenses out of earnings.

Once the company goes public, you become more focused on maintaining the price of the company's stock and computing capital gains than in operational matters. Short-term goals for maintaining or increasing a current year's earnings could be counterproductive and take precedence over longer-term goals of slowly strengthening the business. Trying to consistently increase earnings when the best strategy is to temporarily retrench can seriously damage the company in the long run.

Last, the value of the company's stock achieved through the public offering may be an illusion. If there is no real market for the stock, there will be no active trading after the opening day, which could cause the value of the shares to decline to practically nothing. This is an inherent risk when taking a company public.

Only a small number of new or young ventures go public on one of the stock exchanges. New ventures suffer from lower evaluations placed on the company and usually the company gives up more equity. Because your stock is listed does not mean that you will realize a liquid gain. SEC restrictions about the timing and the amount of stock that officers, directors, and insiders can sell in the public market are restraining. It may take a number of years after the initial public offering before you could realize a liquid gain.

Going public may be a terrific way to raise substantial sums of capital, but it is also a costly gamble. This strategy could backfire and your company could be worse off financially.

* Tip

The stage of growth, finding the right underwriter, and economic conditions must be right for the initial public offering to be successful.

How to Find an Investment Banker for an IPO

Once you have decided to proceed with an IPO, find a competent underwriter to handle and sell the issue. An underwriter will probably charge an initial fee of 1 to 2 percent of the issue's value, plus commissions of 7 to 10 percent of the value of the actual stock issued.

The best way to locate a qualified underwriter is to get references from either a national accounting firm or through your legal counsel. Usually accountants and lawyers with experience in SEC regulations are the best referrals for finding an underwriter. Most underwriters are located in major cities, particularly in New York.

The underwriter should be interested in your industry and your company and should believe in you. Some focus on taking only those firms public that are looking for over $10 million. Some specialize in new ventures, while others prefer to deal with firms that have several years of "seasoning."

Private Placements

A private placement is a means of bypassing the strict and costly registration requirements of an IPO, which is closely regulated by the Securities and Exchange Commission. A private placement is a capital formation transaction that is quicker, easier, cheaper than taking a company public, and is encumbered with fewer legal requirements. Private placements may be made for either debt or equity financing or a combination of both.

Most private placements are governed by Regulation D of the Securities and Exchange Act of 1933 and fall under alternative rules and requirements depending on the size of funding, and nature and number of investors. Regulation D defines three separate exemptions that are based on the amount of money being raised. Obtain a copy of Regulation D from law offices, the library, or by writing to the SEC to become familiar with its restrictions. Under Regulation D there are no specific disclosure or information requirements and no limits on the kind or type of investor the entrepreneur is seeking when raising under $500,000. Regulation D provides a safe harbor from SEC registration requirements. Private placements may take the form of service debt, subordinated debt, convertible debt, preferred stock, various equity derivative securities, common stock, or combined forms of these instruments.

Most private placements are handled by a business attorney, an investment banker, financial packager, or venture capital firm.

Tip

Do not undertake a private placement without the advice of a competent attorney who is skilled in this matter.

Trap

If any violation of security law occurs, management as well as the company's principal equity holders can be held liable individually, in addition to the liability of the corporation.

Most business and legal consultants will strongly advise that a disclosure document, sometimes called an offering memorandum, be prepared for potential investors. You are subject to state and federal fraud provisions and should take great care to disclose all information as accurately as possible. The offering memorandum varies significantly since the length and detail depends heavily on your business structure and the type of investor you hope to attract, the level of sophistication of the investor, and how much money each investor will contribute. The length of memorandum will vary depending on whether you are providing a service or selling intricate computer hardware.

Finding potential investors is key. Sometimes your lawyer or accountant will know of some private investors or have contacts with underwriters who might be looking for this type of investment opportunity. Whoever the offering will be made to will dictate how the private placement is structured.

Another consideration is whether you will go out of state to raise funds. Although a private placement is exempt from full registration requirements under federal law, a registration statement must be filed with each state in which stock is to be sold. These so-called blue-sky laws must be satisfied regardless of the size of the issue.

Blue-sky laws regulate any type of security sales made in a state. They are designed to eliminate possible fraud. The majority of states have agreed that if the issue is qualified under Regulation D, it fulfills the provisions of state law. Consult your securities attorney to ensure all state registrations are met.

Reasons to Consider the Private Placement Market

1. Traditional money sources may not be available if your company is in its early stages of development, or if it is highly leveraged, lacks collateral, or has a shortage of assets.

2. The founder wants the company to remain privately owned.

3. The founder desires to gain ultimate financing flexibility and

tailor financing needs around the specific needs of the company and its shareholders.

4. Capital is needed to fund recapitalization, expansion, acquisitions, or management buyouts.

5. The founders want to attract outside investors to meet financing and growth needs.

6. The founder wants to "take the company public" but the venture's current financial status prevents it from securing a quality underwriter.

7. Public market conditions are not right to take the company public.

8. The founder needs bridge financing until public market conditions improve.

Small Corporate Offering Registration

The small corporate offering registration (SCOR), also called SCOR U-7, is a stock offering that is administered on the state rather than federal level. It makes the registration process much simpler by providing 50 fill-in-the-blank questions that ask for the basic financial, management, and marketing information for the company.

SCOR provides several advantages for entrepreneurial firms. First, it is far less expensive than a regular IPO and there are no high fees to an underwriter. The size of the offering is relatively small—a company can raise only $1 million in a given year, although it can do multiple offerings. The company must have $25 million or less in annual revenues. Companies must also register with each state in which they want to offer stock.

Mezzanine Financing

Mezzanine financing is a layer of subordinated debt between senior term debt and equity used to raise capital for expansion, leverage buyouts, or taking a company public. Loans to finance this type of debt are typically unsecured and used by companies with revenues of $2 to $5 million who have a demonstrated performance record.

Mezzanine lenders look for a company with a strong market niche, an attractive growth prospect, several years of financial history, a strong management team, a solid business plan, and an identifiable exit for the investor. This type of capital is usually available for companies considered too high risk for conventional debt.

Tip

Mezzanine financing enhances your borrowing ability and allows for flexibility in structuring deals.

The mezzanine investor looks at a company's cash flow, asset value, business valuation, and the ultimate rate of return on the investment. Like the venture capitalist, this investor wants to cash in the investment usually through a buyback provision. Repayment is usually due within 5 to 8 years.

In addition to a fixed interest rate, mezzanine debt is usually structured with an "equity kicker" in the company usually in the form of warrants or options, such as a conversion feature into common stock. Warrants to purchase equity in your company typically range between 5 to 15 percent of common stock. In some situations, options can take the form of "redeemable preferred stock."

Generally, these lenders arrange for loan payment of interest only for the first two or three years, while senior debt is being repaid. Interest rates tend to be relatively low and fixed at prime plus 3 to 6 percent.

The interest combined with the equity provision is designed to give the lender a total return of 20 to 30 percent. How the deal is structured depends on the current interest rate, equity valuations, and the risk-reward ratio. The cost of mezzanine capital is much higher than you would pay for collateralized or other senior debt, but lower than the rate-of-return requirements from a venture capital investor.

Other negotiated variables involve setting maturity dates, call features, covenants, and put and call options. The deal usually contains a performance trade-off or "claw back provision," where you and the lender agree that if certain agreed-upon performance measures are met, the equity component will be adjusted. Historically, mezzanine financing was used in specialty retailing, broadcasting, communications, environmental services, biotechnology, and consumer business services, where large sums of capital were needed for a certain period of time.

Mezzanine players involve various types of financing institutions, including large commercial finance companies, commercial banks, insurance companies, pension funds, public and private investment funds, venture capital firms, and some banks that specialize in this stage of capital. Ask your banker, accountant, and attorney as well as other owners in your industry for recommendations.

There are several disadvantages to using mezzanine capital compared to equity capital. First, you will lose some equity and the lender may demand a seat on your board. In addition, the principal must be repaid if not converted into equity. Last, mezzanine financing presents a large claim against cash and can be burdensome if your expected growth and profitability do not materialize.

Trap
_____
The interest on debt is payable on a regular basis and may hurt your cash flow.

Bridge Financing

Bridge financing is a short-term interim loan and, like mezzanine financing, is a layer of subordinated debt between senior term debt and equity. These are loans made as a bridge until repayment by either the borrower or creditors. It is often used by owners for inventory expansion or for increasing production or to provide funding when preparing for a private placement or a public offering.

Repayment of the bridge loan is built into the process of the underwriting. Loans for bridge financing are usually unsecured and used by companies with revenues at the low end over $1 million who have a demonstrated performance record and solid growth potential.

Obtaining a bridge loan is like securing a line of credit but paying a higher interest rate. It can take the form of debt or equity. Bridge loans are usually structured with stock options or warrants to sweeten the deal.

Potential private placement investors may want to make a bridge loan to "get in on the action" prior to the memorandum. Angels or wealthy investors may also be a source for a bridge loan for a favorable interest rate. Ask your banker, accountant, and attorney as well as other owners in your industry for potential investors. Bridge financing is a good option to pursue while raising money for a private placement.

Retained Earnings

If some entrepreneurs do not want outside investors such as venture capitalists or angels, they can try to finance growth by reinvesting profits into the business. The founder's ability to use retained earnings depends on the capital requirements of the venture.

Tip

It takes significantly longer to grow a business from retained earnings, but the founder controls the business.

Summary

Raising money to grow a business is truly an art. Your success depends on your venture, its age, your industry, financial contacts, referrals, how much money you have already invested, how much capital you need, your exit strategy, balancing debt and equity injections, and matching outside money sources to your business. Forecasting your financial needs and choosing the right source at the right time is key to your future growth and success. You can't know too many financial contacts or funding sources in the money market. Continually network with all money sources.

9
Building Customer Relationships

Let's face it. Traditional market-driven strategies to establish brand recognition and loyalty from customers don't work well anymore. Mass advertising and promotion designed to identify customers, find ways to convince them to buy, create an image to entice them, and sell that image to them are not compatible with the current changes in customer behavior. Customers today are smart. They demand choice, quality, and a high level of service. And since technology and innovation have made this variety and customization more feasible, customers are demanding more individualized products. Keeping your customers satisfied today is like trying to hit a moving target.

That's why to be competitive today, business needs to market the qualities and philosophy of the company as much as the product. Brand loyalty today means being market driven not marketing driven, that is, putting the customer on the team from the very conception of the product or service.

Tip

Get your business name right!

Business owners often forget that the name of the business is one of the first marketing tools they use—it's actually the first point of identity for the customer. A good business name should be:

- Easily remembered
- Related to what you're selling
- Dependent on the type of business, convey some style

For example, a name like *Useful Products* probably won't grab a lot of attention or win any prizes for style, but the name of one Oregon-based coffee company might. It's called *Higher Ground*. Or consider a restaurant that caters to dogs and their owners which is in the planning stages by young entrepreneur Jessica Cutuli in Southern California called *Bone Appetite*.

It's very common to see a plaque on the walls of many small businesses that reads "The Customer is King," suggesting that they already have a deep-seated commitment to the customer. The reality is, if anything, they've made a commitment to after-the-sale customer service but are still trying to entice new customers with mass advertising. This is certainly OK for a start but what they really have to do is put in place policies and processes that will allow them to effectively serve the customers' needs *before* the sale.

Since it's so difficult to get and keep customers today, it's important not to rely on familiar, traditional marketing techniques—strategies that are out of touch with today's reality. Entrepreneurs need to use "guerrilla" marketing strategies to grab attention and relationship marketing to build long-term relationships with their customers.

Guerrilla Marketing

Guerrilla marketing is really a set of tactics used to attract customers to your business. They are based on the premise that small companies don't have the marketing dollars of major corporations, so they have to use creative techniques that conserve limited resources but get directly to the customer they're targeting. A few of the more successful tactics that fall under this category are the following:

Database Marketing

Database marketing is actually a way to gather and use information on customers and prospects. A database is simply an electronic filing system into which you can put and keep track of data on your customers, their purchasing habits, preferences, and any other information that might help you meet their needs better. A database makes it easy for you to analyze all this information so that you can better target your marketing dollars to the exact people you want to reach for any particular product or service.

Right now, do you know:

1. How many of your customers are women?

2. How many purchased from you more than twice in the last six months?

3. The dollar volume of the top 10 percent of your customers?

With a well-constructed, low-cost database system, you can answer those questions and more. You will actually be able to profile your customers so you can target specific messages to them. If you are in the retailing business and use computers to "ring up" sales, you will find that you are also ringing up important information for your database file on that customer—what they bought, when, for what reason, what color, how many, how much it cost, and so forth. As individual pieces of information, they may not seem very useful, but aggregated with all your other customers, or one customer's information over an entire year, they can be a very powerful information source.

To ensure a successful database marketing effort means collecting information every chance you get.

- Call customers after a purchase to check how they liked the product or service.

- Put in a "hotline" where customers can call in and leave messages—suggestions or complaints, both are valuable. Better yet, use a Website and e-mail to give your customers a quick, private, and low-cost way to reach you and give information.

- Offer incentives to provide you with more information. A discount coupon might be given if the customer completes a questionnaire on tastes and preferences.

Database marketing helps entrepreneurs increase their response rates, aids in the development of new products, helps to forecast sales, and generally improves marketing decisions. It also lets the company personalize advertising, cross-sell related products, and increase customer loyalty.

The Yellow Pages

The Yellow Pages of the phone book are a relatively inexpensive way to advertise your business in a local area. If you're a retail business or other nonprofessional service, it's likely people will look for you in the Yellow Pages. If your ad is creative and presents your key benefits well, customers will be more likely to call you before they call someone who has not spent the time and money to attract their attention.

Coupons and Contests

Couponing has been an advertising staple, and today every community has coupon magazines that are distributed free of charge to households. Also many telephone books now offer coupons as well. It has been an excellent source of new customers for businesses because it entices the potential customer to at least try what you have to offer. Some couponers offer "buy one, get one free" or a large discount on your first purchase. Putting an expiration date on the coupon makes it more likely that the customer won't put it in a drawer somewhere and forget about it.

Contests are another way to introduce your business to potential customers. Sometimes you can even partner with another business during its grand opening to provide a drawing that will bring customers to your business as well. Be careful about the use of contests, however. Many disreputable businesses have offered prizes to unsuspecting customers who then found they had to sit through lengthy selling presentations to receive their prize. This will ultimately hurt the business, because the disgruntled contest winner will probably never come back, if they even stay to collect the prize. If you give a prize, give it freely. The customer will remember who gave it, and your business will demonstrate a lot more integrity and goodwill.

Publicity

Publicity is one of the best forms of guerrilla marketing there is because it's free. Publicity is essentially free advertising by the media who are interested in the story your company has to tell. There are several keys to gaining a shot at good publicity for your company:

1. You must have a unique or newsworthy product or business. Do you have a new environmental product that will solve a current problem? Have you opened a center for rehabilitating victims of corporate downsizing? Look at what news shows typically report about and you'll have a good idea of what attracts their attention. Vidal Herrera certainly knows the value of free publicity because he has probably received more of it than he can begin to count. The reason is the uniqueness of his business, which is Autopsy Post Services, essentially "autopsies to go." His company performs private autopsies to fill the gap left by underfunded county coroner's offices, and business is booming because he'll never run out of customers.

2. Write to a reporter and tease them with an idea; then follow up with a phone call or take him or her to lunch.

3. Issue a press release answering the who, what, where, when, and why of the business, but make it exciting.

4. Send reporters a press kit containing your press release, bios and photos of key players, any necessary background information, and copies of any other articles written about the company. Make it easy for the reporter to write the story.

5. Use reprints of articles written about your business in your future advertising and brochures to extend the positive effect of the publicity.

6. Check into monthly publications that distribute information to editors and reporters nationally like the *Contact Sheet* and *PR Newsletter*, a membership electronic service.

These are only a few of the hundreds of guerrilla marketing techniques available to entrepreneurs. For more check out the series of books by Jay Conrad Levinson and others on this topic.

Relationship Marketing

Developing relationships with customers that will create value for both the company and the customer is a process that evolves slowly over a long period of time. The results will not be seen immediately. In the United States we tend to become impatient when our efforts don't provide immediate feedback and results, but the reality is, developing relationships with customers over time is a fact of life in many other countries. Certainly, in the Middle East or the Pacific Rim, people expect to build a level of trust with you before they're willing to do business with you. Americans tend to rush the process, and this is not well received by businesspeople in other countries.

Relationship marketing means changing the way the company does business. As a company, you want to learn from your customers:

- What they want
- When they want it
- How they want it

In other words, your customers will help you differentiate yourself from everyone else in the market. Economically, relationship marketing makes sense because it costs 5 to 10 times as much to secure a new customer as it does to keep an existing one. So establishing a loyal customer base that will last over the life of the business should be a top priority.

Relationship Marketing Techniques

How are customer relationships built? The traditional method of marketing was transaction focused; in other words, it didn't matter who the customer was, but rather how many customers bought the product. Consequently, mass marketing was very dependent on customer demographics: age, income, gender, etc. But savvy marketers today understand that two customers with the same demographics can have different tastes and preferences. Therefore, it's important to gather more information from personal contact with the customer. In this way, you learn not only how to better market your products and services to that customer, but also ways to provide new products and services to those same customers. So marketing today is very much a contact sport. Here are some tips for gathering information over time on your customers:

1. Don't try to sell something every time you talk to the customer. They may not be as willing to talk to you in the future.

2. Give the customer lots of ways to contact you: phone, fax, e-mail, voice-mail, Website.

3. Establish a customer information file that contains three general areas of information: When did the customer last purchase from you? How often do they purchase? How much did they spend on average over the last six months?

4. Include contact information: how to contact the customer, when, and how the company contacted the customer.

5. Include complaints and their resolution as well as perceptions of the company's products and services.

Unless you take the time to study the buying patterns of your individual customers, you may never realize that often as few as 24 percent of your customers account for 95 percent of your revenues. These are the customers that it's important to keep. There are a number of techniques that will help ensure that your best customers stay with you:

- *Frequency programs.* Most of us are familiar with the frequent flyer programs of the airlines. But these types of programs work in other businesses as well. For example, some food service companies issue cards to their customers who, after they purchase 10 pizzas, receive the next pizza free of charge. Rewards as incentives to purchase more are a good way to keep customers.

- *Clubs or memberships.* Clubs make customers feel special because they receive special benefits and privileges for being a member, such as discounts, newsletters, and other offers that the general public does not receive.

- *Just-in-time marketing.* Keeping track of important dates for customers—birthdays, anniversaries, etc.—gives the company an opportunity to make another contact with the customer and potentially another sale.

- *Complaint marketing.* Customers should be encouraged to air their complaints about company products or services and it should be easy to do. A complaint, while certainly not eagerly anticipated, does provide an opportunity for a dialogue with the customer. The successful handling of a customer complaint can lead to a loyal customer in the future.

*Tip

Lifelong customer relationships make the company.

There are many benefits to establishing lifelong relationships with your customers. They include:

- You create more successful products and services because customers let you know exactly what they want.
- When there's a problem, the customer won't automatically shift allegiance to another company because they've invested too much time in yours.
- You can realize the full value of the customer. It costs five times as much to acquire a new customer as it does to keep your current customers happy, and a satisfied customer will tell at least nine other people.

Trap

Don't waste time on bad customers.

If, typically, 24 percent of your customers account for 95 percent of your revenues, that means 76 percent of your customers only account for 5 percent of your revenues. This is a very powerful statement about where business owners need to focus their efforts. Too often we spend 80 percent of our time trying to please the 20 percent of customers who will never buy, will buy very little, or who have a bad debt history with the company. It's important to get rid of the worst customers because they're costing you money you'll never recoup. Many of the other customers accounting for 5 percent of revenues over time can be encouraged to become better customers through dialogues to find out what they need to be satisfied.

Why You Need a Marketing Plan

A marketing plan contains the overall strategy for building customer relationships and establishing the character of the company in the minds of the customers. It will also contain the tactics you'll use to carry out the strategy, such as advertising, promotion, trade shows, and so forth. Ideally, you should be able to write your complete strategy in one paragraph. If you can answer the following questions, you'll have a good start on a successful marketing plan:

- What do you expect your plan to accomplish? Are you trying to introduce a new company or product to the marketplace? Are you trying to position an existing product differently? Do you want to educate your customers about something? You need to know the reason for writing the marketing plan.

- What are the benefits of your product or service? How will they meet customer needs? Why should they buy from you?

- Who is your target customer? Which is the primary group that will purchase the product or service and why?

- What is your market niche? Where does your company fit in the market, and how will you differentiate yourself from everyone else?

- Which marketing tactics will you use to bring the benefits of your product or service to your customer?

- What is your company's identity? How will customers perceive the company?

- What is the percentage of sales that will be represented by the marketing budget? Usually this figure is based on industry norms for businesses of your size in your market, but they could vary if you're using a new marketing strategy as a competitive advantage.

Tip

Do your homework before writing the marketing plan.

All your key management should be involved in writing the marketing plan. The following steps will ensure that the plan will meet the company's and the customers' needs.

1. *List your options.* Learn about the different ways to promote your company and its products or services by reading books and articles and by talking to other business owners, customers, and suppliers.

2. *Think like a customer.* Ask yourself, what would entice the customer to purchase from you?

3. *Study your competitors.* What are they doing that you could do better? What are they doing that you should be doing?

4. *Analyze your options and rank them.* Get rid of the strategies

that either don't meet your needs at this time or aren't possible yet. Then rank your top 10 choices.

5. *Write the marketing plan!*

Promoting the Company and Its Products and Services

A promotional plan's purpose is to establish the identity and vision of the company that will be conveyed in everything the company does, from advertising to billing. This is quite different from image, which is what the company wants the public to perceive it as. The identity of the company, on the other hand, is defined by its vision and company beliefs.

Tip

Don't woo customers with product or service features.

Don't always look at the physical aspects of your product or service because these quickly become commodities in the eyes of the customer. Instead, focus on those things that are difficult to measure—the intangibles:

- Quality
- Innovative technology
- Service
- Reliability

The intangible aspects of your product or service are crucial to differentiating yourself from other companies in a very competitive marketplace. A good promotional plan will contain the following elements:

- The core values of the company—What the company and its owners believe.
- The purpose of the company—Why do we exist? Why are we in business?
- The mission—What is the big, measurable goal the company wants to achieve?

- The strategy—The plan for achieving the mission.
- The tactics—The specific techniques the company will use to implement the strategy (i.e., advertising, trade show, publicity).

✳ Trap

Not researching your market is a recipe for failure.

One of the biggest mistakes entrepreneurs make is not doing market research on their target market, those who are most likely to purchase the product or service. They ask a few "friends," who give them positive responses and assume the marketplace as a whole will agree. Nothing could be further from the truth! Some key questions that should be asked to avoid spending time and money on a product or service for which there is no market are:

1. Who is the customer? Be specific.
2. What do they usually buy?
3. How do they learn about these products or services?
4. How do they like to buy them?
5. How often do they buy?
6. How can we, as a company, best meet their needs?

The following is a checklist of the various types of tactics that can be used to promote the business and its products and services.

Product or Service Promotion Checklist

Advertising	Print media (newspapers, magazines, direct marketing, Yellow Pages, signs). **Tip:** *Check out the target market audience for any print media so you don't waste dollars on an uninterested audience. Create professional looking ads and brochures that attract attention.*
	Broadcast media (radio, television, cable TV, infomercials). **Tip:** *Use shorter spots like 30 seconds with music and sound effects. Catch the*

	listener's attention in the first few seconds. Run ads three out of every four weeks for good coverage.
	Internet (World Wide Web, on-line forums). **Tip:** *Link up with compatible sites so you increase your visibility and hit rate.*
	Miscellaneous advertising (coupons, demonstrations, video tapes, seminars). **Tip:** *Use guerrilla marketing tactics such as those in the series of books by Jay Conrad Levinson.*
Publicity and public relations	Free media attention in articles, TV, radio. **Tip:** *The key to publicity is having a product or business story that is newsworthy. Get to know media people on a first-name basis.*
Personal selling	Working directly with the customer to create sales. **Tip:** *Today personal selling means building relationships over the long term that emphasize benefits to the customer, total quality, and continual customer contact. Use a contact manager to keep information on your customers at your fingertips.*

Tip

Protect that brand name!

Establishing a brand name for your products and services is a long and expensive process, so it's important to protect that brand name from those who would try to use it for their own benefit. Here are a few suggestions:

1. Always use the trademarked name of the company as an adjective in the product's name, as in *Sanka Brand Decaffeinated Coffee.*

2. Check ads and advertisements to make certain that the media are using the brand name correctly.

3. Choose a unique typographical treatment for displaying the brand name.

4. Choose a brand name that is unique and not already in use or covered by copyrights.

Pricing the Product or Service

One of the more difficult aspects of marketing is pricing the product or service. It doesn't matter how good it is or how attractively it's packaged; if it isn't priced right for the market, it won't sell. Determining an effective pricing strategy requires that you understand your industry thoroughly and know what your competitors are doing and why. If you're a new company with new products, remember that you probably won't be able to compete on price with established companies in the industry because your costs of production will no doubt be higher in the beginning.

The following guides will help you arrive at an appropriate price for your product or service.

- Where the demand for the product is strong and a shortage of supply exists, you can realistically command a higher price.

- Where customers need the product no matter what the price, you can charge a higher price. This is usually only true when there are no substitutes for the product. An example is milk.

- Where there is a lot of competition, the price of your product or service will need to be lower.

- Features not offered by others may warrant a higher price.

- New technology often justifies a higher price initially unless it's merely "bells and whistles" that customers won't pay for.

- The position of your product or service relative to related products or services can determine price. For example, if you position your product among luxury items, it will in many cases justify a higher price.

The important point to remember about pricing is that ultimately the customer determines the price—what they're willing to pay. You must be certain that you can provide the product or service at a price that also allows you to cover your cost to produce, a portion of the overhead, and a reasonable profit.

Trap

Failure to heed warning signs can lead to pricing problems.

Many business owners don't heed the warning signs that their products or services are not priced correctly. Consequently, they fail to change a strategy that isn't working until it's too late. Watch for these warning signs of impending pricing problems:

- Your prices are always based on the cost to produce (i.e., cost plus markup).

- Different people in your company set prices for different products and services, so there's no continuity in the pricing strategy.

- Your prices always follow the competition.

- You always set new prices as a percentage increase over the previous year's prices without regard for the market.

- You charge exactly the same to all customers (i.e., no discounts for volume, etc.).

- You standardize your discounts to everyone rather than basing them on something variable like volume.

The way you promote your company and its products and services will have an enormous impact on your profitability and longevity in the market. Building lifelong customer relationships and using guerrilla marketing tactics can help your business survive over the long term.

Resources

Bangs, D.H. (1995). *The Market Planning Guide,* 4th Ed. Chicago: Upstart Publishing Co.

Regis McKenna, (1991). *Relationship Marketing.* New York: Addison-Wesley Publishing Co.

Don Peppers and Martha Rogers (1993). *The One to One Future: Building Relationships One Customer at a Time.* New York: Currency/Doubleday.

B. Joseph Pine II, Don Peppers, and Martha Rogers. (March/April, 1995). "Do you want to keep your customers forever?" *Harvard Business Review.*

Reynolds, D. (1993). *Crackerjack Positioning: Niche Marketing Strategy for the Entrepreneur.* Tulsa: Atwood Publishing.

Treacy, Michael and Fred Wiersema. (1995). *The Discipline of Market Leaders: Choose Your Customers, Narrow Your Focus, Dominate Your Market.* New York: Addison-Wesley Publishing Co.

Zaichowsky. Judith Lynne. (1994). *Defending Your Brand Against Imitation.* Westport, Conn: Quorum Books.

10
Employees: Your Most Valuable Asset

It has probably become a trite phrase or cliché but your employees really are your most important asset. It's not management or equipment or ideas or a great product that make the company a success—it's the employees. Wes Zimmerman, a noted marketing consultant and corporate trainer says,

The tree grows from the bottom up; it dies from the top down.

How perfect this metaphor is for an organization. It grows because of the employees and their belief in the company and what they contribute to the company's success. When problems occur, look to management for the source. All business failures can be traced back to management—that's the bottom line. What management does or fails to do directly impacts the success of the business.

As the founder of your business, it's your job to have a vision for the company and convey that vision to everyone who works with you. It's also your job to see that everyone, down to the lowest employee, understands what he or she contributes to the profit potential of the company and to the satisfaction of its customers. Until and unless this happens, you will have employees who don't feel they have a stake in your company. Therefore, they won't work to their fullest potential, and they won't feel an obligation to be loyal to you or to treat the company with respect. Much of the cause of employee theft can be attributed to the fact that employees are treated like pieces of equipment or machinery to turn on and off when needed. They are not treated as essential and valuable members of a team that has come together to create and sustain a successful business.

Why Your Company's Culture Is Important

Imagine a business where the employees come to work in costume, where they spend time juggling, break dancing, or reciting poems to make their customers laugh. Now picture a line of customers out the door enjoying the entertainment while they wait to buy a scoop of ice cream or a chocolate shake. Is this your basic ice cream shop? Hardly. It's Amy's Ice Creams, a seven-store chain in Austin and Houston, Texas, and its owner, Amy Miller, believes the secret to her success in selling what can only be called a commodity is her corporate culture.

Culture is a set of values, beliefs, attitudes, and ways of doing things that defines a company. You can look at it as the personality of the company. Every business has a personality, whether its people are aware of it or not. Customers will feel that personality or culture from the moment they enter the door of the business or talk to the receptionist on the phone. They'll see it in many more ways:

- In the manner of dress of the employees
- In the way the office is laid out
- In the way everyone talks to each other and to the customers
- In the amount of empowerment the employees have

Essentially the culture you create in your company reflects your values and beliefs and those of your employees. In the case of Amy's Ice Creams, what they value above everything else is entertaining the customers so they'll come back for more. So the culture is one of laughter and fun and creativity. When they hire new employees, they hand them a white paper bag and ask them to do whatever they want with it but return in a week. The people who get hired are those who do the most unusual and creative things.

The most important thing about the company culture you create is that it will be unique to you; therefore, it may make the difference between getting and keeping customers and not. And certainly it will differentiate you from your competitors.

Tip

Define your company's culture.

Here are some questions that will help you better define the culture in your company.

1. Do people work in teams or individually?
2. How do you deal with change?
3. How do you deal with failure?
4. How are decisions made in the company?
5. How is work prioritized?
6. How is information shared?
7. How does the company ensure that it gets the right employees?
8. How are employees treated?

Why Your Company Needs a Vision

There's an old saying, "If you don't know where you're heading, any road will get you there." Unfortunately, that's a truth that many business owners live by. They start a business with the goal of getting sales and making money and then get so wrapped up in the day-to-day operations of the business, they never look up to see where the business is going. This is a mistake. If you know where you're going and why, you will make the kinds of decisions you need to make along the way to get you there. On the other hand, if you don't know where you're going, a decision you make may lead you in a direction that you don't want to take, but you won't know it until you get there.

The vision you have for your company is the driving force for everything you do. It's what helps you build your company and make decisions that will take it in the direction you want it to go. In their groundbreaking research on visionary companies,

Collins and Porras developed a framework for understanding this notion of vision.[1] They said that vision is comprised of the company's

Core values and beliefs

Purpose

Mission

Let's look at each of these to see how they can be applied to your business.

Core Values

Core values are really your fundamental philosophy of life—what you believe is important, what your personal values are. So core values are beliefs that you've held over a long period of time and are not likely to change. They are the mortar that holds the bricks of your organization together. They're a set of guiding principles that help you make decisions as your company grows. Some examples of core values might be:

- We believe in total integrity.
- We believe the customer is the center of the company's team.
- We will treat everyone fairly and honestly.
- We have a deep respect for individual values.

If these are beliefs you hold, then you would never do anything in your company to compromise them. For example, you would never cheat a customer or fail to deliver on a promise. You would respect your employees and encourage their input in every area of the company. You would focus on doing things that show your company has integrity and considers the customer an important member of the team.

You don't get your core values from a book. You can only find them in your deepest beliefs. The key thing to remember is that a core value stands the test of time. No matter what changes around you, your core value stays firmly in place.

---

[1]James C. Collins & Jerry I. Porras. (1994). *Built to Last: Successful Habits of Visionary Companies.* New York: HarperBusiness.

Tip

Test your core values.

Successful companies have three to five core values they've identified to guide them in their growth. How can you arrive at a set of values that everyone agrees on?

1. The owners and people who best represent what you're trying to achieve in your company should first draft a list of potential core values based on each person's inner belief system.

2. Then put each potential value to the test. Ask, "If circumstances changed in the marketplace or within the business, would we still be able to keep this core value?"

3. If the answer is yes, you have found a true and enduring core value. If it would hurt your business to keep the value under the new circumstances, then it's not a core value.

Purpose

Purpose is the fundamental reason you're in business. It's your raison d'être. It comes directly out of your core values, and it's a goal that's always on the horizon. You're always striving to reach it, but you never actually do. The purpose of your business is broad, fundamental, and something you can constantly strive to achieve. For example, your company's purpose could be stated as follows:

We are in the business of providing business solutions.

Notice that this purpose gives your company a very broad area to operate in—business solutions. This is important, because it allows you to change with the times and respond to customer needs without having to change your whole purpose for being. If, by contrast, your purpose were to read, "We are in the business of providing computers and software to businesses," you'd be limiting yourself to solutions that revolved around computers and software. What happens when computers and software as we know them today don't exist any longer? You're out of business, or you have to drastically change your purpose for being in business. With the purpose as written above, you have the option to expand the business with the needs of the customer and the changes in the marketplace.

Tip

Ask "Why?" five times.

To get at the fundamental purpose for your business or it's reason for being, try using a technique Toyota developed to get at the root cause of problems.

1. Start by stating what you believe to be the purpose of your business.

2. Then ask and answer "Why?"

3. Continue to ask and answer "Why?" until you've reach a broad general statement that will stand the test of time.

Mission

Your mission, unlike your purpose, should be a clear and compelling goal that focuses all your efforts and is always achievable. Once it's achieved, you can use your purpose and core values to define another mission. A good mission statement gives the company a bold, big, outrageous goal (Collins and Porras called them big, hairy, audacious goals) that's the business equivalent of climbing Mt. Everest. So, this goal may not be 100 percent achievable, but the probability is high enough to excite everyone in the company to try to achieve it. And that's what's important about a mission: it must excite enthusiasm. It must also be clear and measurable; that is, you have to have a way to determine if you've actually achieved the mission. Here's an example of a good mission statement:

To become the leading producer of XXX by the year 2000.

Here we know how to find out if we've achieved this goal or mission. We want to be number one and we want to do it by the year 2000.

Once you've established your core values, your purpose or reason for being in business, and an exciting mission you want to achieve, you can begin to look at strategies for achieving your mission. Remember, your core values, purpose, and mission are enduring; but strategies, the actual plan for achieving the mission, change as you adapt to the marketplace changes on the way to achieving the mission statement.

Using Total Quality Management as a Strategy to Be the Best

Total quality management (TQM) is a concept that has been around since the 1980s when it was considered a "fad" because companies hurried to implement it thinking it was a quick fix. But in many cases the results were not what they had hoped, and so many people believed that TQM was an impossible goal. Total quality management is about achieving the highest quality levels possible in all four broad areas of the company: product, process, leadership, and organization. It's aiming for defect-free products and processes, the highest quality of visionary leadership, and a total quality organization focused on continual improvement. This is certainly not an easy task, and it definitely will not happen overnight. The reason so many companies have failed in the implementation of TQM is that they usually try to use it in only one area of the company, forgetting that the company is a system. As such, a change in one area will affect other areas of the business as well.

It is not within our purpose for this book to get into an in-depth discussion of TQM. What is important is that you begin to consider improving the level of quality in all areas of your business, from soliciting sales to billing to working with suppliers. To help you do that, you need a process or systematic way of going about it. You also need to train your employees in the skills they'll need to fully participate in the company.

* Tip

To improve your company, use a mini TQM process.

To begin to use total quality in your company, answer these questions for every area of your business:

1. What is the problem?
2. What are the basic causes?
3. What areas of the business are affected by this problem?
4. What do we need to have and do to improve the situation?
5. What was the result of our attempts to improve the situation?
6. How can we maintain the improvements?

7. Which problem do we need to deal with next?

Traditional TQM encompasses the four components: product, process, leadership, and organization. We believe there is also a fifth component to the TQM concept, and that is the customer. Very simply, without the customer, there is no business, so it makes no sense not to consider the wants and needs of your customers in everything you do. With customer input into the design of the product or service, as well as the design of the company, you can move forward assured that you are creating something the customer wants. The commitment of everyone in the organization to achieving customer satisfaction in every function of the business is what will ensure the success of your company.

The Company Is Only as Good as Its Employees

If it's true that you have no business without customers, it's also true that you'll never achieve customer satisfaction unless your employees are 100 percent committed to it. Employees need to see the customer as the person who pays them. Your company is only the vehicle by which that happens. If the customer is happy with the product and service you provide, they will be loyal to the company and buy more. Your company will enjoy higher profits and your employees will benefit through raises, bonuses, and perhaps profit sharing. It's a win-win situation for everyone.

On the other hand, if employees aren't 100 percent committed to satisfying the customer, product quality and service will suffer, your company may lose customers to competitors, profits will decline, and rewards for performance will not be possible.

Success starts with the input of the customer and is sustained by the satisfaction of the customer. The link is your employees. Only with their 100 percent cooperation and commitment to the customer can real success be achieved. How do we get employees to commit to satisfying the customer? Here are some suggestions:

- Give employees a feeling of control over their work by giving them a choice as to how and when they do it.

- Help employees prepare to take responsibility by providing training and team support. If an employee doesn't feel competent to do a task, they'll never achieve a feeling of control.

- Help employees understand the value of what they do. Employees want to control tasks that are important to the company rather than trivial tasks, so give them tasks that directly impact the business in big ways.

- Help employees believe that what they are doing makes a difference; it has a significant impact on the company. They need to understand how what they do results in satisfaction for the customer and profitability for the company.

- Make employees take responsibility for the consequences of their decisions and also share in the rewards of success. Incentives such as bonuses, days off, theatre tickets, and/or vacations should be tied to performance that positively affects the company. Reward employees also for suggestions they make that improve the quality of any area of the company.

✳ Trap

Don't empower employees by simply telling them they're empowered.

You can't just tell employees that they're empowered to make decisions and then take the consequences. To empower employees entrepreneurs must do the following:

- Make a sincere effort to give employees decision-making power over things that matter, even if it means changing the way the company is structured and how jobs and roles are defined.

- Create interdependencies among all the functions of the company so that the business operates like an integrated system. Your employees in production need the input of salespeople to plan for demand. Similarly, your salespeople need to know production's capabilities so they aren't promising customers things they can't deliver.

- Use small teams so that individual empowerment is not lost in a large group environment. Entrepreneurs need to encourage employees to also take control of their personal growth.

- Provide meaningful incentives to offset the increased responsibility.

- Provide support and learning opportunities.

You Need a Human Resource Policy

At start-up and during the early stages of growth in a new company, entrepreneurs focus on keeping overhead costs down, so they generally find ways to avoid hiring employees or hiring as few as possible. But as the company begins to grow more rapidly, the need for employees increases, and the need for a human resource policy becomes real.

Today human resource planning is not just something that occurs in a department of a very large company. Instead, planning for employees is a strategic issue that affects the successful growth of your company from day one. The human aspect of your company affects everything your business does and particularly determines how your company deals with change.

A good human resource policy will include the following fundamental components:

- The customer as part of the team from product design to marketing and service.
- Rewards that celebrate team effort over individual effort, customer satisfaction, and quality.
- The means for everyone in the company to know the customer.
- A way to share company information with employees so they can use it and provide feedback on the direction the company is taking.

The concept of open book management (OBM) is an important one for young, growing companies because they are in the best position to implement it. What OBM essentially means is sharing company information with employees so they understand where they fit into the picture and how they directly impact the satisfaction of the customer and the profitability of the company. It's a way of operating a company that gets every employee focused on helping the business become and stay profitable. Where OBM has been implemented, it has ranged from giving employees the basic understanding of the nature of the business they're in and what role they play to actually opening the financial records of the company to employees and giving them a say in strategic decisions that will affect the profitability of the company. Most open-book management programs focus on profit sharing and teach the fundamentals of business. Jack Stack, CEO of SRC authored a book, *The Great Game of Business,* published by Doubleday/Currency which is all about how SCR instituted open book management. Stark says if you have equity, and understand it, you know why it's the key to building for the future and achieving lasting success. Another good book is John Case's *Open-Book Management: The Coming Business Revolution* published by HarperBusiness. There are a lot of variations on open book management, but what is important to remember is that your employees need to understand the importance of their performance on the company's performance and profits. And they need to be able to share in those profits either through profit-sharing plans, bonuses, or stock-options plans, to name just a few ways of giving employees a vested interest.

Trap

Bonuses cost employees money too!

When entrepreneurs think of ways to reward employees or themselves, one of the first things they think of is bonuses. But if you have an S or C corporation, you need to be aware of the tax implications for employees who receive bonuses. Since bonuses are treated like wages, any bonus you pay yourself or your employees will incur a Medicare tax and a Social Security tax unless you've achieved the maximum wages for those taxes. Then there are federal and state taxes as well.

That's why many entrepreneurs look into other forms of compensation such as retirement plans, stock options, and so forth. The interesting thing is that employees, even knowing the tax ramifications, prefer cash bonuses to other options.

Bottom line: Check with your accountant before you give that bonus and educate your employees about the tax effects!

Recruiting and Hiring Employees

Getting employees who can share your vision, who fit into the company culture, and who understand that it is really the customer who pays them begins at the point of hire. Recruiting and hiring the right employees is a challenging task that is crucial to the successful growth of your business. Unfortunately, many entrepreneurs don't have a plan for recruiting and hiring. They often do it in a haphazard fashion, making lots of mistakes along the way. Or they may delegate the task to someone else without preparing that person to do the job effectively. This can result in the hiring of employees who don't fit in with the company culture and who don't have the skills they need.

With a simple plan of attack, you can increase your chances of hiring good employees.

1. *Start with a good job description.* It should contain the educational and work experience "desired," not "required" so you leave yourself room to hire someone who would be great for a position with a little training. It should also contain the duties and responsibilities of the position and the person to whom the candidate will report. A statement regarding personal characteristics such as good communication skills will also help screen potential candidates.

2. *Develop an application form.* This will be a self-report measure that the candidate fills in to supply you with basic information. It should also request a résumé from the applicant.

3. *Determine if any tests will be required for the position.* Tests might include aptitude tests, skill tests, and drug tests.

4. *Plan for interviewing candidates.* The real test of candidates is how they conduct themselves in an interview situation. It's the interviewer's job to see that the interview process is conducted in a way that puts the candidate in the best light and gives the interviewer the best chance to evaluate. This is also the place that entrepreneurs often cross the line by asking questions that are illegal to ask prior to the point of hire. A good interview takes preparation.

Tip

Use the interview process to find the best employees.

To give yourself the best chance to find and hire good employees by making the interview a worthwhile experience, try doing the following:

1. Choose a location that will put everyone at ease and doesn't suffer from interruptions.

2. Open the interview in a friendly way to make the candidate feel welcome, perhaps a comment about the weather or the candidate's trip getting to the company.

3. Ask open-ended questions rather than yes-no questions to get more information.

4. Ask questions that go beyond what was on the résumé, either to clarify issues or to explore the character of the candidate. For example, ask the candidate what their greatest accomplishment was. That will tell you something about what is important to the candidate and also what they're capable of achieving.

5. Give the candidate a hypothetical situation and see how they respond.

6. Make sure that you don't talk more than 15 percent of the time.

7. Try doing a group interview and include other key people in the organization so that you can better gauge how the candidate fits into the company culture.

8. Take notes during the interview or immediately after.

9. Listen carefully and watch for nonverbal clues from the interviewee.

10. Let the candidate know when the interview is at an end by thanking him or her and rising from your seat to shake hands.

One major mistake entrepreneurs make is not checking references on candidates, but taking what they say at face value. Often candidates will list references on their résumé or application who may or may not give them a good recommendation, so definitely call references and at least verify information given on the application and résumé, but first get written permission from the candidate to do so. Unfortunately, with the laws as they are, many former employers and supervisors are reluctant to say anything about a former employee except the facts of length of service and so forth. As a result, some entrepreneurs have resorted to hiring independent firms to do background checks, especially criminal background checks, on potential employees.

We cannot stress enough the importance of being careful whom you hire. Since wrongful termination suits abound in

today's litigious environment, it's much easier to spend more time and effort on the front end with an effective hiring process than it is to fight lawsuits when you have to terminate an employee.

Trap

Be careful what you ask at the interview.

You must exercise due care in asking questions of candidates both on application forms and in the interview process. Failing to do so could cost you time and money fighting a lawsuit for discrimination. Following are a few of the questions you should never ask.

1. What is your age? Or when did you graduate from high school?
2. What church do you attend?
3. Do you have children or plan to get pregnant?
4. Have you ever been arrested? (You can ask, have you ever been convicted of a crime?)
5. How is your health? (You can ask, do you have any condition that would prevent you from doing your job?)
6. Where are your ancestors from?
7. You may not ask any questions the purpose of which is to get information about race, ethnic group, religion, sexual preference, or age.

Check with the Economic Employment Opportunity Commission (EEOC) for a list of all unacceptable and acceptable preemployment questions.

Is the Résumé Real?

As we said earlier, it's not uncommon for people to embellish their résumés; in fact, it's estimated that about 30 percent of candidates do. It's also not uncommon for candidates to actually lie on their résumés, assuming that the employer will never check on it. How do you know if a person has been less than truthful in a résumé? Here are a few things to look for:

- How long did the applicant stay at previous positions? Watch out for candidates who seem to have a nomadic work career, hopping from one job to the next in a relatively short space of time. Five jobs in five years might warrant scrutiny.

- Check out all degrees and certificates. This is an area that is commonly falsified.

- Look for gaps in time and find out what was going on during that time.

- Does the appearance and quality of the résumé suggest a candidate who is serious about seeking a position?

- Does the résumé show skills and experience that relate to those your company needs?

- Did the candidate leave out anything that a typical candidate would have included?

- Did the job titles seem appropriate for the experience and education levels of the candidate?

Using Temporary Employees

Entrepreneurs are very nervous, and rightfully so, about hiring employees and then having to carry them on the payroll when business is slow. One solution that is growing in popularity is using temporary employees on an as-needed basis. Temporary help agencies are a high-growth industry that has recently begun to specialize in the very specific needs of many types of businesses. Now it is possible to hire a temporary sales staff, temporary management, temporary production workers, and temporary engineers. You can even hire a temporary executive like a CFO or CEO. Hiring temporaries is also helpful if you want to "try out" a potential employee before hiring him or her permanently. For the entrepreneur there is little risk and great return for hiring permanent employees who have been well tested.

Hiring a permanent employee is one of the biggest expenses for most small companies. Using a temp may cost a little more during the temporary period because you pay the agency's fee in addition to the worker's salary, but over the long term it's cheaper because you're not paying for the same kinds of benefits you would ultimately give a regular employee.

Trap

Don't help the other side in a lawsuit.

Even the best of businesses sometimes find themselves involved in a lawsuit regarding an employee or former employee. Knowing the potential problem lawsuit areas when dealing with employees will help you avoid doing certain things that might come back to haunt you later. Here are a few potential problems to avoid:

- Failure to document problems when they occur. It will be difficult to explain why an employee who had consistently good performance reviews was fired.

- Subjective reasons for termination that could suggest an ulterior motive like age, race, or disability.

- Paying employees with comparable skills in comparable jobs differently.

- Memos in the personnel file that recall historical events, rather than memos dated when the event occurred or an action was taken.

- Benefits and training given to younger employees and not to older ones.

Protecting Your Company Against Lawsuits

Any lawsuit is a costly expense for a young and growing company, so avoiding them is a wise strategy, especially where they involve employees, since the courts generally side with the employee. Here are some of the ways you can decrease your chances of being sued:

- Hire carefully from the beginning. Be sure you spell out all your expectations clearly before the employee comes on board, both orally and in writing.

- Keep records on each employee. Be sure to document all events related to the employee including promotions, raises, training, performance appraisals, etc. It's also a good idea to have more than one person evaluating the employee.

- Any communications with the employee regarding performance should be in writing and very specific. Also, be sure to get a written receipt of the communication from the employee.

- Before deciding to terminate an employee, consult your attorney.

- Any termination meeting should have two people besides the employee present.

- Be firm and concise about the termination, and always remain calm and in control of the situation.

Deciding What to Pay Employees

Entrepreneurs have always been cursed with many needs and few resources in their small and growing businesses. They're not usually able to hire the best or pay them what a much larger company would. Still the issue of compensation is critical to employees looking to work for the company, so having a compensation strategy in place before you start hiring can prevent problems and conflicts down the road.

Tip

Bonuses are excellent incentives.

Bonuses are excellent incentives for employees if given properly. Here are some tips:

1. Be flexible about when bonuses are given. Your company's ability to give bonuses will vary with its natural business cycle. Tying a bonus to an event like a sales campaign goal reached is better than establishing an "annual bonus" not pegged to extra cash coming into the business.

2. Give often. Again, rather than once a year, give the bonus when it's earned.

3. Don't give unless the cash is there to cover the bonus. That's called "betting on the come," and it can get you in trouble.

Before you can begin to think in terms of dollar amounts, you need a good deal of information. Some of the key questions you should be asking are:

1. What are other companies in the industry paying for the same position?

2. What is the supply and demand for employees with the types of skills you need?

3. Which outcomes or behaviors are you desiring to reward?

4. What does the company's cost structure look like (don't forget to figure in a reasonable profit)?

5. Can the company provide training for employees?

6. What is the potential for promotion and growth within the company?

7. Which types of rewards are considered most valuable by potential employees?

Answering these questions will allow you to create a compensation strategy that makes sense for the company and its employees and is compatible with what is occurring in the industry.

Pay comes basically in two forms: cash and benefits. Generally cash forms about 70 percent of pay, leaving 30 percent for deferred benefits such as health care, pensions, and paid vacation. So when calculating compensation, make sure you consider total labor cost, not just what appears on the pay check. In many cases you'll need to figure 30 percent or more on top of what you actually pay the employee to cover withholding taxes, benefits, and so forth. So if your employee's paycheck says $1000 in gross pay, the cost to you of that employee is really $1300 or more.

Tip

Mix up your compensation.

You have a number of choices for how pay and promotion are paid out in your company.

- Bring employees in at a low wage, but allow for substantial growth over time. This becomes a form of probationary period.

- Hire employees at an above-average rate coming in, but take longer to give raises and promote.

- Offer a base salary plus an "at risk" portion that is dependent on performance.

- In sales positions, consider paying completely on commission to encourage sales.

Bottom line: have a broad policy that guides your decision making about how to pay your employees.

In addition to base pay, cash bonuses, and benefits, there are other types of compensation that can serve as rewards to employees and give them a feeling of ownership in the company. Among these are a group of rewards known as *stock appreciation grants.* The basis for these rewards is the future appreciation of the company's stock. There are three types of stock appreciation grants. *Stock options* are rights to purchase shares of the company's stock at a fixed price for a specified period of time. *Stock appreciation rights* consist of the right to receive direct payment for the stock's appreciation during a specified term without actually exercising a stock option. *Stock purchases* actually permit the purchase of stock at a discount under either fair market value or full value, sometimes with the financial support of the company.

Don't forget noncash rewards and incentives. Verbal praise, personal notes congratulating an employee, public recognition, award certificates, recognition lunches, special privileges, such as a special parking place or a weekend trip, and celebrations can go a long way toward creating an environment of belonging and a desire to help the company succeed. These types of incentives are most effective when they're unexpected and personalized to the particular employee.

Your employees really are your most important asset. Treat them as such and you'll ensure the success of your business.

Resources

Case, John. (1995). *Open-Book Management: The Coming Business Revolution.* New York: HarperBusiness.

Davis, S. (1984). *Managing Corporate Culture.* Cambridge, Mass.: Ballinger Publishing.

Kotter, J. and Heskett, J. (1992). *Culture and Performance.* New York: Free Press.

Senge, Peter. (1990). *The Fifth Discipline: The Art and Practice of the Learning Organization.* New York: Currency/Doubleday.

Stark, Jack, with Bo Burlingham (1992). *The Great Game of Business.* Doubleday/Currency.

Ulrich, D. and Kale, D. (1990). *Organizational Capability: Competing from the Inside/Out.* New York: Wiley.

11

Creating and Managing the Processes in Your Company

We have purposely used the term *processes* in this chapter to reflect the current blurring of boundaries between product and service companies. In the past, product and service companies were treated as if they existed in totally different worlds and "never the twain shall meet." But the information technology revolution, globalization, and a fast-changing, highly competitive marketplace have turned product companies into service superstars and service companies into product developers. Successful product companies like Pelco, a California-based manufacturer of video surveillance systems, have put the customer at the center of their competitive strategy and made customer service and satisfaction their number one priority. On the other hand, service companies like Capitol Concierge in Washington, D.C., have developed products that help them give their customers better service.

If you consider risk, cost to operate, and commitment time on the part of the owner, retail businesses are at the top of the pyramid. Because retail businesses deal directly with the customer, they require a facility that usually costs more in terms of appearance and location. Inventory, advertising and promotion, labor, and insurance often cost more as well. And the time commitment on the part of the owner is significant.

While the wholesale business is normally one step removed from the customer, today many wholesalers (and manufacturers as well) are selling direct to the consumer. In these situations, the consumer does not expect a fancy storefront location because the perception is that the most important thing for the customer is to save money. So a no-frills approach is expected.

Manufacturing companies typically have the lowest costs in terms of facility, time, and risk relative to retail businesses, because they normally have the least contact with the customer.

This chapter gives you some pointers for making your product or service company effective. By *process,* we mean everything you do to take a product or service from its conception to the customer's hands. In a business where the focus is on making products, that process is somewhat more complex when there is a manufacturing component.

Understand Process by Taking a Walking Tour of the Business

It's amazing how many people start businesses without ever understanding how the business really works. They put all the pieces in place—counters, cash registers, inventory, salespeople—but they never stop to consider how to go from the customer entering the door of the business to paying for an item, let alone considering the path from supplier to retailer to customer.

Business owners can save themselves a lot of wasted time and money correcting mistakes in process by taking a walking tour of the business *before* they go into business. Let's start with a very simple example. Suppose you're going to start a financial services business where people come to you for advice and to learn how to manage their money. You are planning to have a 1000-square-foot office that contains your private office, a reception area, and a large training room. Now, pretend you're the customer walking in the door. What do you see? Perhaps you see a receptionist's desk and seating for customers. That's a start, but you need to see it in greater detail because doing this walking tour is going to help you develop lists of things you need. Now ask yourself, What activities will be taking place in this area? That will help you determine what equipment, supplies, and personnel you'll need.

Using the reception area as a starting example, your list might look like this:

Reception Area Needs

Furniture

Reception desk and chair

File cabinets

Customer seating

Coffee table

Equipment and Supplies

Computer

Telephone

Fax machine

Pens, pencils, paper, notepads, file folders

People

Receptionist

From there you might walk to the training room and repeat the process. Here different equipment, supplies, furniture, and personnel will be required.

In a manufacturing company, you will find similar needs in the office area, but in the plant itself, of course, the needs will vary according to the type of product being manufactured and the production layout. The basic strategy, however, is the same. You are looking to define the activities that will take place and the associated equipment and personnel needs.

Certainly, the walking tour of the proposed business is also essential in coming up with items that will affect start-up costs and your financial statements. Without it, you may miss a critical item that could adversely affect your company's cash flow.

Learn What's New in Manufacturing

Many people have questioned why a discussion of manufacturing should be included in any book related to entrepreneurship since we are now in an "information age" and most new businesses created are in the service industry. While it is true that more businesses are started in the service industry because it's easier and usually costs less, there has been a strong reemergence of manufacturing in the United States due in large part to the technology revolution, which has simplified production processes, increased productivity, and made possible significant gains in quality. Technology has made it possible for start-up product manufacturers to outsource to existing manufacturers work that would be too expensive for them to undertake in the early stages of the company. Small manufacturers are also now doing much of the work for larger companies. For example, huge companies like General Electric are contracting with smaller companies to do their design work and even the manufacturing of some components that don't fall within GE's core competencies.

Tip

Work with overseas manufacturers.

If you intend to have your products manufactured in another country, make sure to do the following:

- Make at least one trip to that country to inspect the facilities and ensure that they understand your needs and those of your customers in terms of quality, delivery, and service.

- Always ask for a sample of the finished product for your inspection before they go ahead and do an entire production run.

- If you do not speak the language, have someone with you who is an expert in the language and culture so there are no miscommunications that could be very costly to your company.

To be an effective manufacturer today you need to:

1. *Build a team of workers, companies, suppliers, and customers.*   Today's manufacturers rely on teams and smaller physical plants to accomplish what manufacturers used to do with assembly lines and huge, capital-intensive plants. You will need to put workers in teams that are responsible for an entire product or an entire component of a product and give them total control and accountability for quality. They will need to understand what they contribute to the satisfaction of the customer. You will also

want to look to outsource capabilities that you don't have to other companies in the industry so you can focus on what you do best. And you will want to keep your vendors involved in the development and manufacturing of your products so that they can suggest new and better ways to do things. Most importantly, customers must be involved in the product from conception to finished product to ensure that they get what they want.

2. *Focus on products based on the same technology.* If your company is using a core technology for its product, it's wise to look at other ways to use that technology to produce additional products. If the technology is proprietary, that is, your company owns the intellectual property rights in the form of patents, you may also be able to license that technology to other companies and receive a royalty income from sales of their products using that technology.

3. *Try to stick with common parts, components, and product features.* In this way you maintain flexibility. If, for example, a vendor fails to deliver on his promises, you can switch to another product line without having to design and manufacture a part yourself.

4. *Use off-the-shelf parts whenever possible.* Why reinvent the wheel? Designing and building parts takes time and money. When designing a new product, see how existing components or parts from other manufacturers can be used to meet the needs of your product design.

5. *Ask your suppliers to design parts for you.* Often suppliers will design new parts or create modifications of parts they currently manufacture as a way of diversifying their product line. Many times there will be no cost to you for this design because the assumption is that you'll purchase these parts from this vendor, eventually in large volumes.

6. *Use computer-integrated manufacturing (CIM) where possible.* CIM is quite simply a way to coordinate a factory environment that contains people, computers, information, networks, and processes. It allows information to be available to the people who need it through a database. A good computer network is important both within your company and between other companies with whom you outsource your needs so that you don't waste time and risk errors in transferring information.

7. *Use just-in-time delivery (JIT) where possible.* JIT helps companies improve their productivity and delivery times by using material only when it's needed. JIT also helps reduce the cost of inventory. This is really the strategy employed by supermarket owners. In a supermarket the employees stock the shelves in such a way that customers get what they need, when they need it, and in the amount needed. The supermarket restocks the shelves when needed. In other words, everything occurs on an as-needed basis. Like CIM, JIT benefits from computer technology. Some entrepreneurial manufacturers who deal with large distributors like Wal-Mart are even required to be on-line so that they know exactly when Wal-Mart will need to replenish its shelves with the manufacturer's product.

8. *Emphasize total quality control.* Customers today are expecting increasing levels of quality in the products they purchase, and fortunately, U.S. levels of quality have increased to the point that in other countries, American products are perceived as being of very high quality. Much of the source of this increased quality can be attributed to technology, but it is also due to new management techniques that empower employees at every level to make decisions that improve quality. In manufacturing, giving employees the power to "stop the line" for a quality issue ensures that the product reaches the end of the production line with no defects. It also reduces the need for costly inspectors who merely examine samples of products.

Trap

Shoot the engineers and start production!

Everyone has their area of expertise, and engineers are no exception. They are indispensable to the design and implementation of new products and processes, but they often don't think in business terms. If they don't understand your need to meet certain deadlines, you may find that they're still tinkering with the design on the day you thought you'd have a production quality prototype of your product to show a distributor.

Unfortunately, entrepreneurs don't usually have the resources to develop products totally in-house, so they have to rely on outsourcing, which slows the process down and makes it more costly in the beginning.

To prevent disappointments and delays when designing and manufacturing new products, be sure that you use a team approach from the beginning. That way everyone involved in the various functions of the business will be heard, and their needs and expectations, discussed. The team should include:

Design engineer	Finance
Production	The Customer
Marketing	Sales

* Tip

Evaluate vendors very carefully.

Vendors can be found by talking to salespeople in the industry and also checking out who is supplying your competitors. Trade shows and trade organizations are two other sources of vendors.

Finding vendors is the easy part; evaluating them is another story entirely. Be sure to answer the following questions:

1. What is the vendor's reputation for quality and service?
2. What is the vendor's credit rating? (Check with Dun and Bradstreet)
3. What does their history look like?
4. Are they able to provide technical assistance?

Strive for Continuous Improvement

The philosophy of continuous improvement is an outgrowth of the Japanese philosophy of *kaizen*, which means "gradual, unending improvement." It applies not only to manufacturing, but to every aspect of the business. Many versions of kaizen exist but one that is often used in the United States is called *PDCA*, which is an acronym for *p*lan, *d*o, *c*heck, *a*ct. To complete this process, employees must first understand the customer completely so that they will know how to solve any problems that may come up. Once information on the customer has been collected, the process can begin. Suppose, for example, that your methods for checking the quality of the products you produce have not been effective—you're finding too many defects. You know from the information you've collected that quality is the most important aspect of the product for the customer, so you need to reevaluate your processes for achieving that quality. The PDCA process will help you do that.

- *Plan.*   The process that needs to be improved has been identified. Now the team needs to plan for the changes that will take place under a new, improved process. Suppose the team decides to give control and accountability to the people on the production line so that they can stop the line at any time for a quality issue. In this way, you are actually inspecting for quality during the entire production process, and you should end up with products that have zero defects.

- *Do.*   The team implements the new plan.

- *Check.*   During implementation, the team checks the new process to see if it's working as projected. If they find problems in the process, they'll go back and reexamine the plan to improve and correct those problems.

- *Act.*   When the process has been found to work, in this case, production runs smoothly and we end up with products that are defect-free, the changes are permanently put into place.

   PDCA is a simple, straightforward plan for solving problems and implementing change in the processes in your business. While on the surface it appears to be nothing more than common sense, the fact is that most small businesses make changes without any plan at all, which can be a very costly and time-consuming mistake.

Manage Your Inventory Processes

Any business that purchases raw materials for manufacture or products for resale needs to consider the timing of those purchases. Since warehouse space does not produce revenue for the company, it's important to keep inventory at a minimum.

Tip
_____
Using one vendor may be an advantage.

Finding vendors is not the problem. Knowing how many to use is more difficult. Obviously, if a single vendor cannot supply all your needs, using more than one is essential. Using one vendor has two advantages:

1. You'll probably get more individual attention and service.
2. They may be able to consolidate orders, which will give you a discount based on quantity purposed.

The rule of thumb is: Use one supplier for about 70 to 80 percent of your needs, and one or more additional vendors for the rest. That way you always have a backup.

To keep inventories down, businesses are beginning to purchase supplies and raw materials on a daily or weekly basis rather than purchasing much larger quantities on a monthly basis. Still, it's important to keep a balance between what is needed as stock on hand to meet demand and what is needed to produce more product. Effective purchasing requires a strategy comprised of three elements:

- *Quality.* Purchase only those products and raw materials that are suitable for the purpose you intend.

- *Service.* Make sure the product will be delivered when you need it and, if defective, replaced immediately without hassle.

- *Price.* Purchase at a competitive price. This doesn't always mean the lowest price, because price is dependent on quality and service as well. You don't want to sacrifice quality to pay a relatively lower price because you'll end up paying the difference in complaints from your customers.

✳ Trap

Watch for the warning signs of inventory problems.

Here are some of them.

1. Are your inventory levels rising faster than sales?
2. Has your inventory mix shifted significantly?
3. Have your back orders and lead times increased?
4. Are you writing off too much obsolete inventory?
5. Do you have frequent customer complaints about back orders and missed deliveries?

It's also important to keep track of inventory through visual inspecting and counting, an electronic point-of-sale system, or a combination of electronic and physical. Often business owners will physically count items that are sold less frequently and use electronic means for the bulk of sales that turn over often. Informal inventory tracking methods work fine in small and start-up businesses. These include:

- *Ordering on an as-needed basis.*   You can divide the inventory into expensive and inexpensive items and track the expensive items more frequently. A larger retailer would probably use a bar code system for tracking a large inventory.

- *Two-bin system.*   This approach is often used by hardware stores and wholesale businesses to track small items like nails and bolts. Two containers of items are carried at all times with the open container on top of the closed one. As soon as the open container is empty, another carton is ordered and the bottom container is opened.

- *Three group price method.*   Divide the inventory into three price groups and then track each group using the method most appropriate for that group. Typically one group will have a higher turnover than another.

Formal inventory tracking systems require computers and specialized software, but they make tracking a painless task. These include:

- *Point-of-purchase* (*POP*) *systems.*   These systems let you track inventory in "real time;" that is, the minute an item is purchased, its code is entered into a computer terminal and the inventory is reduced by that amount.

- *Bar coding.*   Bar coding (labels consisting of black-and-white parallel bars encoded with product information) is compatible with POP systems because it alleviates the need for the salesperson to enter the code. Instead, the salesperson passes an electronic wand over the bar code and it's immediately entered into the system.

- *Electronic data interchange* (*EDI*).   In this more sophisticated system, data entry and tracking are taken one step further by linking the retailer with the wholesaler or manufacturer/supplier so that reordering now becomes an automatic procedure.

Once inventory is reduced to a certain level, the system triggers the reorder of the item from the source.

Trap

Watch those inventory costs!

Did you know that costs associated with maintaining inventory can add as much as 25 percent to the cost of the inventory? Here are some of the costs to watch out for:

- *Financing costs:* The interest you will pay on the money you borrowed to purchase the inventory.
- *Opportunity cost:* The cost associated with the loss of the use of your money that is tied up in inventory.
- *Storage costs:* The cost of warehouse space to store the inventory.
- *Insurance costs:* The cost of insuring the inventory against damage or loss.
- *Shrinkage costs:* The money lost from broken, stolen, or damaged inventory.
- *Obsolescence:* The cost of inventory that is no longer saleable.

Use Inventory Turnover to Stay on Top of Inventory

One of the best ways to learn if you're managing your inventory well is to calculate your inventory turnover rate, which is the average number of times you sell out your inventory during the year. The rate will differ in each industry and within different product lines. For example, men's clothing typically turns over three times a year, while restaurants turn over their inventory 22 times a year. Finding out the turnover rate in your industry will give you a benchmark against which to measure your effectiveness. Obviously, if you're a new company, you probably won't be able to match the benchmark figure, but it gives you a goal to work toward.

Taking the example of the restaurant with a turnover rate of 22, you can calculate how much inventory you will need to keep on hand to meet average demand.

12 months ÷ turnover of 22 = 0.54 month's supply

This means that on average you will need to keep a two-week supply of inventory on hand at all times. Now you can calculate the cost of that inventory by taking the company's forecasted sales for the year, multiply that figure by the cost of goods sold (which in this case is 40 percent of sales) and divide the result by the turnover rate. For example,

($300,000 × 0.40) ÷ 22 = $5454

Therefore, it will cost $5454 to maintain a two-week inventory, not including carrying costs.

To calculate the company's inventory turnover rate so as to compare it with the industry average, you would divide the cost of goods sold by the average cost of inventory.

$120,000 ÷ $5454 = 22 times (turnover rate)

It's also a good idea to look at turnover of some individual items, especially if your product line is diverse. We cannot stress enough the importance of staying on top of inventory turnover. Inventory you don't sell costs you money every day you have it. Carefully analyze the items you carry in inventory so that you are always well stocked on items that turn quickly. Consider carrying only one of an item that doesn't sell well, or doing special orders on items that don't sell for months at a time. You'll save your business a lot of money in the long run.

Know Your Trade Area

Your trade area is that geographical area surrounding your business from which you will draw your primary customers. Businesses that rely on trade-area statistics to determine a suitable location for their businesses include:

- Restaurants
- Small businesses like dry cleaners, packaging stores, and pizza parlors
- Stores that would typically locate in a neighborhood commercial center like a grocery store or video rental store
- Stores that would locate in a regional shopping mall like a department store or athletic supply store

Tip

___

Find your trade area by constructing a trade-area map.

Follow these simple steps to construct the trade area around your retail/service business site:

1. Using a census tract map from your local building department or economic development office, identify a potential site for your business.

2. From research on the industry your business is in, determine how large the trade area is for a business like yours. For example, some restaurants require a population of 200,000 within a 2-mile radius of the site. Regional shopping centers draw from a much greater distance, perhaps 10 to 20 miles.

3. Put a marker on the site you've chosen; then, using a compass, draw a circumference around the site at the distance you've determined to be appropriate for your type of business.

4. Now identify the location of your competitors within the trade area.

5. Identify which census tracts are within the trade area. Using U.S. Government Statistical Abstracts, you can determine the size of the population, demographics, buying power, and other information that will help you understand your customer base.

6. You also plot access streets to determine how easily customers can get to your site.

This map will be useful not only for understanding your customer base but also for learning about the routes people may take to your site, parking, and other issues that will affect whether or not you choose this site for your business and how easy it is for people to find you—part of the overall process of your business.

Shrinkage: The Problem of Losing Things

It's a common fact of life in business that owners experience loss through shoplifting and employee theft on a daily basis. It is a particularly severe problem in retail businesses because of the size of the inventory. Shoplifting actually accounts for 3 percent of the selling price of any item. The items normally stolen range in price from $1 to $5 because they're usually smaller items that are easily slipped into a pocket or purse.

The reality is, however, that 75 to 80 percent of all loss in business is due to employee theft and this adds an additional 15 percent to the cost of consumer goods. Because employees have access to company goods in ways that shoppers don't, here are some hints for minimizing the opportunities that employees have to steal.

1. Keep all interior doors locked when not in use for entry or exit.

2. Have controls for who has keys to the business, and change the locks if you suspect employee theft.

3. Check the trash bins for stolen items. This is a common hiding place.

4. Watch out for a lot of voided or no-sale transactions.

5. Establish controls so that no one person is in charge of a transaction from beginning to end. For example, one person may handle purchasing, another receiving of goods, and another maintaining purchase records. This way each is responsible for what the other does, and it makes it more difficult to steal.

6. First and foremost, be selective about who you hire and be sure to check their references.

7. Instill in your employees a sense of where they fit in the scheme of things. Help them to understand how they contribute to the profit and loss of the business as well as to how they're paid.

8. Provide incentives for productivity, efficiency, and outstanding customer service. Reward those who spot employee or customer theft.

Tip

Reduce the opportunity for shoplifting.

Here are some suggestions for curbing shoplifting in your business.

1. Put alarms on all emergency exits to control where people can leave the business.

2. Get rid of clutter so you can easily spot gaps on shelves denoting things that may have been stolen.

3. Ask your local police to do an evaluation of your business for vulnerable areas.

4. Make sure all your employees are alert and paying attention when someone walks into the business.

5. Make it clear through posted signs that you will prosecute shoplifters to the full extent of the law.

6. Train your employees to recognize shoplifters.

7. If your budget allows, consider video surveillance, an in-store detective, and electronic sales tags.

A few well-considered precautions will go a long way toward saving the business time and money from shrinkage. And don't forget to include an amount for shrinkage in your cash budget for the business. Shrinkage is cash out of your business's pocket. Don't let the amount surprise you. Plan for it.

Even if you've got an existing business, it's never too late to step back and take a look at how your business works. Is there any way you can make it better? More efficient? More satisfying for both customers and employees? A well-operated business is a pleasure to own and will build more value as it grows.

Resources

Anderson, Robert L. and John S. Dunkelberg. (1987). *Managing Growing Firms.* Englewood Cliffs, NJ: Prentice-Hall.

Agility Forum, Bethlehem, Pa. (800-9BE-AGILE, http://absu.amef.lehigh.edu) Consulting, training, and education services from manufacturing experts.

Barr, Vilma and Charles E. Broudy. (1986). *Designing to Sell.* New York: McGraw-Hill.

J. M. Juran. (1988). *Juran on Planning for Quality.* New York: Free Press, pp. 4–5.

Reza A. Maleki. (1991). *Flexible Manufacturing Systems.* New York: Prentice-Hall, p. 8.

Manufacturing Assistance Program, Oak Ridge, Tenn. (800-356-4USA). Technical assistance from U.S. Department of Energy scientists and engineers.

Manufacturing Extension Partnership, Gaithersburg, Md. (800-MEP-4MFG). A nonprofit network of 200 field offices in 42 states providing federal, state, and local services.

S. Mizuno. (1988). *Management for Quality Improvement: The 7 New QC Tools*. Cambridge, Mass.: Productivity Press.

Richard Shores. (1994). *Reengineering the Factory: A Primer for World-Class Manufacturing*. Milwaukee: ASQC Quality Press.

Adrian J. Slywotzky. (1996). *Value Migration.* Boston, Mass.: Harvard Business School Press.

12
Winning the Cash-Flow Game: The Key to Survival

People are always interested in how much profit a business is making, as if profit is the single best indicator of the health and success of the business. The reality is, while profit is certainly something you want in your business, probably the best single indicator of the health of your company is cash flow or cash position. In other words, how much cash do you have left over after all the bills are paid. Does that sound like your personal checking account? Well, it should. Businesses have to carefully manage the inflows and outflows of cash to the business just as you have to manage the cash flows in your checkbook.

Unfortunately, many companies do not regularly do cash planning. They choose, instead, a reactive approach, which means they constantly find themselves short of cash, flailing around with few options to solve the problem. Because they're in a reactive mode, they tend to make quick and consequently poor decisions. For example, how often have you as a business owner stopped or slowed the payment of bills during a cash crunch? You may think this is the only solution, but your actions may have cost your business its reputation with suppliers over the long term. If vendors stop shipments or put your business on an all-cash basis, you will have even more problems in the future. Another quick solution that is often sought is an emergency loan. Here again, you may have solved the problem in the immediate term, but you've sent a message to lenders that you don't know how to do cash planning.

So, what's the bottom line? You must do cash planning on a regular basis or risk being short of cash just when you need it most. In this chapter we'll look at cash planning from the point of view of the entrepreneur who's just starting a business and from the point of view of the entrepreneur in an ongoing business. You'll get some tips and traps for winning the cash-flow game.

How to Figure What You Need to Start a Business

Trying to figure out how much cash you need to start your business can be a daunting task at best. There are so many things to consider. Remember the walking tour of your business you took in Chapter 11? That's a good starting point, because there you collected a laundry list of people, equipment, and supplies you'll need to run the business. Equipment, plant, and office are what are known as *hard costs* or capital investment. That's one category of costs. The *soft costs,* those that vary as needed, will include personnel and supplies. The numbers for both these categories of costs can be found by first doing the walking tour and then talking to people in the industry to get some real figures. It's important to estimate these as accurately as possible because a major mistake here can mean the difference between starting with enough capital and struggling because you don't have any excess cash for contingencies. So

> **Step One:** Do a walking tour of the business and talk to industry experts to get accurate estimates of soft and hard costs.

One of the most important elements of cash flow is how much money is coming into the business. Generally, this will be through sales of products and services, so it's important to accurately estimate sales for the period you're considering. This is certainly not as easy as it sounds because a new company has no track record on which to base its predictions. And since sales growth is rarely linear, you will have to account for the ups and downs of the period. Knowing when those ups and downs occur comes from an understanding of how your industry works. For example, if you're a retailer of lawnmowers, you may experience heavy volume in the spring and summer months and very low volume in the winter.

You'll also want to know how customers in your industry pay; that is, will it be a cash business (few are) or will customers expect you to extend them credit, which means you will have to carry accounts receivable? This is a very important piece of information when you're looking at cash needs, because if your customers are used to having 60 days to pay their bills, it means a sale on July 1, won't be paid for until September 1. So you'd better have enough cash on hand to carry you during that period.

Tip

Forecasting sales is a three-ring circus.

Whether you have a new business with no track record of sales or an existing business with a track record and a market that is changing, to adequately forecast sales for your business requires the use of at least three sources of information.

1. *Industry Experts.*   Consult with vendors, distributors, and others in the industry who are familiar with products or services like yours.
2. *Customers.*   Observe customer buying patterns, talk to customers about what they need, how much, and when.
3. *Capacity.*   Figure your ability to produce and meet demand. How many units can you produce per month?

Step Two: Forecast your cash inflows from cash sales and accounts receivable.

Figuring cash outflows is easier because, in general, they're fixed. If they vary, it's usually relative to the volume of sales. So, for example, if your inventory costs are about 30 percent of sales, you can apply that percentage to your sales volume each month to see how inventory costs rise with an increase in sales volume.

In a manufacturing business, you have a cost of goods sold (COGS) that is a bit more complex because it usually consists of direct labor, cost of materials, and factory overhead. But you can still calculate the percentage of sales that COGS represents and apply it each month. In service businesses, COGS is really the time you spend doing the service, and the rate at which you bill the service is comprised of direct expenses in doing the service, a contribution to overhead, and a reasonable profit. In all cases you need to apply what you learned from talking to people in your industry to get the most reasonable estimate of costs.

Your general and administrative expenses (G&A) are those related to running the business as opposed to producing the product or service. They include things like office staff, office space, supplies, and so forth. Some of these may be fixed, while others vary, so using a percentage of sales for G&A is probably not an appropriate method of figuring these expenses.

Step Three: Forecast your cash outflows, both fixed and variable expenses.

If you just estimated inflows and outflows and made sure you ended up with a positive cash flow, you may run into trouble. Estimating is not an exact science, so you'd better be prepared for contingencies. You can do this by adding an additional balance to take care of unforeseen events and errors in estimation. There are no clear-cut rules on how much to add. You obviously want to provide a sufficient amount, but putting in too much wastes resources. Your money will just be sitting there not working for you. To determine an adequate balance, consider the following.

1. How volatile is your industry? Do changes occur rapidly and often?
2. What kind of business are you in?
3. How stable are your cash flows? What is the level of your accounts receivable?

Step Four: Estimate an amount that will give you a minimum cash balance that will take care of contingencies.

The last item you'll need to forecast is taxes, which are paid at varying times of the year. Many an entrepreneur has forgotten this item in calculating cash position. You may go through the first four steps and determine that you've got plenty of surplus cash for any contingency. Then you apply taxes, based on the profit you make, which can be as much as 40 percent or more, and you now have a significant shortfall. Taxes are, therefore, an important part of cash planning and management.

Step Five: Estimate your tax obligation for the period.

With all this information, you're now ready to calculate how much cash you'll need to start and run the business until you achieve positive cash flow. If you have an existing business, you'll probably be looking at how much of a cash infusion you'll need to grow the business to the desired size.

Trap

Use caution when relying on accounts receivable to manage cash flow.

If you don't generate enough cash to cover a receivable, you're still faced with meeting your own obligations until that receivable is paid. Your business's cash cycle runs from the date you purchase the inventory or manufacture the item to the date it is paid for by credit. It's not cleared until the receivable is paid in cash. That's a long time to go. To remedy the shortfall, many businesses do one of two things:

1. Pledge the accounts receivable as collateral against a loan from a bank. Your customers' payments will go to the bank to repay the loan.
2. Sell your accounts receivable at a discount to a factor (a specific type of finance company) who assumes the bad debt risk of the receivables and collects on them.

Notice that we said *pledge* or *sell accounts receivable at a discount.* These alternatives are costly. Interest rates usually run several points above prime. In addition, you'll pay a fee to the factor for services. These costs must be figured into your cash budget. Also, remember that by doing either of these, you've removed a valuable asset from your balance sheet, which makes your company less attractive to bankers in general. The bottom line: Credit costs money, so manage cash flow well!

Do an Analysis of Cash Needs

Remember that your cash needs generally fall into four categories:

1. Capital expenditures (hard costs such as equipment)

2. Fixed and variable expenses (soft costs such as personnel and supplies)

3. Working capital (cash needed to carry the business until positive cash flow is achieved)

4. Start-up capital (if you have a start-up business, this is the amount you need to get the business ready to "open the doors." It can include deposits on facilities, inventory, and labor costs during training and setup).

The sum of these four items will be the total amount you need to fund the business at start-up or grow the business to the desired size. See Table 12-1 for an example of a cash-need analysis. In this sample cash budget we have determined that we need

Table 12-1. Save More Products—Sample Cash Budget (Six Months)

	Month 1	Month 2	Month 3	Month 4	Month 5	Month 6
Cash Inflows						
Total Inflows	$90,110	$58,500	$28,600	$32,500	$44,226	$55,536
Cash Outflows						
Purchases*	36,044	23,400	11,440	13,000	17,690	22,214
Wages & Salaries	5,000	5,000	5,000	5,000	5,000	5,000
Lease	1,000	1,000	1,000	1,000	1,000	1,000
Utilities	649	649	649	649	649	649
Insurance	1,587	1,587	1,587	1,587	1,587	1,58 7
Advertising	1,802	1,170	572	650	885	1,111
Vehicle	1,500	1,500	1,500	1,500	1,500	1,500
Accounting & Legal	300	300	300	300	300	300
Payroll Taxes	1,000	1,000	1,000	1,000	1,000	1,000
Income Taxes	0	0	6,000	0	0	9,000
Capital Expenditures	25,000	15,000	12,000	0	0	0
Total Outflows	73,882	50,606	41,048	24,686	29,611	43,361
Net Cash Flow	**16,228**	**7,894**	**(12,448)**	**7,814**	**14,615**	**12,175**
Plus Beginning Balance	17,000	33,228	41,122	28,674	36,488	51,103
Total Cash	**33,228**	**41,122**	**28,674**	**36,488**	**51,103**	**63,278**
Minus Minimum Bal.	12,000	12,000	12,000	12,000	12,000	12,000
Required Financing	**0**	**0**	**16,674**	**24,488**	**0**	**0**
Surplus Cash	21,228	29,122	0	0	39,103	51,278

*Purchases (cost of goods sold) are based on 40 percent of sales.

$12,000 each month in contingency or surplus cash. Subtracting that amount from the total cash tells us if we will have a shortfall that month that will require another source of funding. In the case of a start-up company, it will tell us how much additional working capital we'll need to maintain a positive cash flow.

Use Assumptions to Explain Forecasts

As you prepare your cash budget, keep track of the reasoning and calculations you used to arrive at the projections in your cash budget. In other words, where did that number come from? How did you arrive at your financial projections? What were your assumptions? Remember that assumptions come from your experience and the reasoning you do in your industry and market. Footnote the line items in your cash budget so that six months down the road you won't be scratching your head in front of your banker, wondering why you did what you did.

---

* Tip

The cash budget is the business's lifeline.

One of the most important things you can do as a business owner to ensure the health, growth, and survival of your business is to monitor cash flow regularly. Computer technology and software have made this job very easy. If you do a projected cash budget and then lay that alongside an actual cash-flow statement you create at the end of the six-month period, you can quickly see where problems lie. You can also play with changes in your budget and instantly see the ramifications on the rest of the business. Here we see that we'll need to find additional sources of funding in months three and four, where we experience a negative cash flow or shortfall. Notice the example of an assumption footnote.

---

* Trap

International receivables are another game entirely!

Payment terms customarily used and understood in the United States don't necessarily mean the same thing in other countries. For example, in Malaysia COD means you'll get paid—maybe—in 30 days.

Here are some suggestions for avoiding the trap of international limbo on your accounts receivable.

1. Understand the payment patterns and norms in the country you intend to do business in *before* you sign a contract. You can do this by talking to international consultants, the Commerce Department, or one of the four U.S. trade offices.

2. Check out the foreign customer just like you would a domestic customer. Use your banker or accountant for help.

3. Ask for payment up front with a discount for cash until you know them. Alternatively, use an irrevocable letter of credit, but check out the credit worthiness of your customer's bank.

4. To avoid complex currency problems, insist on U.S. dollars for the deal.

Stay on Top of Accounts Receivable

If you extend credit to your customers, you will have accounts receivable and that will affect the cash position of your company. Accounts receivable are considered a noncash asset, but it's as close to cash as you're going to get in your business, since customers typically pay in 30 to 60 days. There are several things you should do to manage your accounts receivable.

1. Make the time between shipping, invoicing, and sending billing notices as short as possible.

2. Review customers' payment records frequently to catch errors before they affect the cash flow of your business.

3. Provide incentives for early payment (i.e., discounts).

4. Develop a system for collecting overdue accounts to minimize wasted time, effort, and expense.

Credit Lines and Other Short-Term Financing

Short-term financing is also called *bridge financing,* and it's used to overcome seasonal fluctuations in cash flow. A good example is the situation where you're expecting increased demand for your product in the next three months so you want to build up your inventory to levels higher than what you would normally have. This means your accounts payable level will rise higher than normal. In this case, you need to finance the purchase of inventory until the cash comes in to pay for it.

Tip

A bridge loan is one way to survive high interest rates.

At some point, most companies need to finance assets like plant and equipment. This is normally done through long-term financing. But in periods where interest rates are high, it doesn't make sense to tie the company down to a long-term financing arrangement. Instead, you can bridge the period of high interest rates with a bridge loan, which is short-term. Then when rates come down, you can refinance the equipment for a longer term. This way you'll only pay the higher interest for a relatively short period of time and free up cash when you refinance.

There are several types of short-term financing available to businesses. Here are a few:

- *Unsecured bank loan.* Since this type of loan does not require collateral, it is based on the borrower having an excellent credit rating. For this reason, unsecured loans are one of the most difficult types of financing to obtain.

- *Line of credit.* When you establish a line of credit with a bank, the bank commits to making available to the company a certain amount of funds upon demand of the company. So that the bank makes money even if you don't use the money, they usually charge a commitment fee of 0.5 to 1.0 percent of the total amount committed.

- *Revolving line of credit.* The difference with a revolving line is that the bank agrees to supply funds *up to* a certain amount. That way you borrow only what you need when you need it, and you're only paying interest on the amount borrowed. It's very similar to consumer credit cards.

- *Secured short-term financing.* Recall that two types of secured financing are pledging and factoring accounts receivable. You can also use your inventory as collateral for a loan. The value of the inventory is based on how quickly the lender can convert it to cash in case you default on the loan. There are various types of inventory loans, and you should check into all types to find the one that best suits your needs and will also be the least costly.

- *SBA CAPLine credit program.* The Small Business Administration offers this program designed for manufacturers and wholesalers that need long-term, asset-based financing. You'll work with a bank and the SBA will guarantee 75 percent of the credit line amount on accounts receivable and 50 percent on inventory up to $750,000 in case you default. This type of loan fluctuates with the level of your accounts receivable and inventory. Even with a 2 percent guarantee fee and local bank charges, it's less costly than factoring and many other types of short-term financing.

- *Commercial paper.* This is short-term debt issued by corporations and is good for 270 days. You agree to pay the holder a fixed amount at a future date that is specified, and the commercial paper sells at a discount from that amount. Typically, you must be a fairly large company to benefit from this form of financing.

Collecting What's Owed to You

Extending credit is another cost to your business that will have an impact on your cash flow. Today, you don't often have a choice whether or not to offer credit. In most businesses, it's expected. And the cost of providing this service includes

- Credit checking
- Keeping records on accounts receivable
- Writing off bad debts
- Interest cost of financing accounts receivable
- The cost of collecting on delinquent accounts

Trap

Be careful that your collection practices don't violate the Fair Debt Collections Practice Act.

There are a lot of things you can do if someone has not complied with your requests to collect money that's owed you. But the Fair Debt Collection Practices Act says there are several things you absolutely *cannot* do or face penalties. They are:

- Threaten the customer by suggesting force, arrest, or criminal prosecution
- Use abusive language
- Call the customer's employer or family
- Imply that a lawsuit has been filed if it hasn't
- Discuss the customer's case with other people who are not party to it
- Send misleading notices
- Harass the customer

To cut down on collection costs, it's important to develop a credit policy for your company that does four things.

1. Determines how and when you'll extend credit
2. Sets standards or conditions customers must meet to receive credit
3. Establishes a credit period (i.e., 30, 60, 90 days)
4. Sets a collection policy for instances where customers don't comply

Tip

Establish appropriate collection procedures.

The best way to collect from a customer or, at least, have the best chance of ultimately collecting is to put in motion a set of procedures that go from mild to severe in stages.

1. Mail a past-due statement when the account is 10 days overdue. Some companies have found success using language that suggests the customer may have inadvertently overlooked the account. Others have found that humor works to catch the customer's attention.
2. Mail another past-due statement when the account is 30 days overdue. The language here should be more serious but still assume the customer wants to pay.
3. Call the customer when the account is 45 days past due. Be friendly but let the customer know this is a serious situation. Help them save face.

4. At 60 days overdue, notify the customer in writing that the account will be turned over to a collection agency if not paid within 15 days.

5. Turn the account over to a collection agency or an attorney.

6. Go over and collect the check in person.

Managing Your Company's Bills

An important aspect of cash-flow management is managing your own company's bills. When and how you pay your bills is affected by the terms you've negotiated with your suppliers. For example, if you've negotiated a 60-day "trade credit" with your supplier—in other words, 60 days to pay for the supplies you ordered—you have created an obligation for your company but released that cash to use as needed for 60 days. If the vendor offers you a discount if you pay by the tenth of the month after purchase, you now have an important decision to make. Which is more valuable to you, the use of the money you've obligated or the discount for paying early? The answer lies in the nature of the cash flow in your business. If it's irregular, you may not have the cash to pay by the tenth. This is an unfortunate fact of life for many entrepreneurs. Because they are typically short of cash, they have to leverage their cash position by paying vendors at varying times during the month. This obviously means more work for the company.

Tip

Use vendor discounts to save money.

Taking advantage of discounts offered by vendors saves a lot of money. Suppose you purchase inventory in the amount of $100,000 with the offer of a 3 percent discount. You now have the choice of paying $97,000 by the tenth day of the month or paying $100,000 on any of days 11 to 30. If you can afford to pay by the tenth, you'll save $3000 (someone's monthly salary, perhaps). Otherwise, you're better off paying as close to the thirtieth day as possible so you at least have the use of the $100,000 for as long as possible to make up for the loss of the discount.

It's funny but entrepreneurs sometimes forget that vendors are business owners with bills they have to pay and cash flow they have to manage. Establishing yourself as a company that pays its bills on time will go a long way toward building a long-term relationship with a vendor that is mutually beneficial. If that relationship is created, when you have times that you're short of cash, you'll be able to work with that vendor to help you get through it without damaging the relationship. Here are a few strategies for dealing with vendors:

1. Take advantage of trade discounts whenever possible.
2. If you are able to take the goods COD, try negotiating an additional discount to reflect payment of cash at delivery.
3. When choosing vendors, look for those that have the quality you're seeking and the longest terms possible. This way you'll have more flexibility.
4. If you can't pay a bill on time, contact the supplier immediately to request an extension and explain the situation. Under no circumstances should you ignore or avoid the vendor.
5. Manage your cash flow daily if necessary to ensure that you always have enough cash to meet your obligations.
6. Ask the vendor for terms when ordering.

Managing the cash flow of your business is vital not only at start-up where your resources are usually quite limited, but particularly critical while the company is growing. It's not a difficult thing to do. Like everything else, it simply requires a plan and a procedure for getting it done. The benefits to you and your company are a healthier organization that is proactive rather than reactive.

Resources

Bangs, David H., Jr. (1992). *Financial Troubleshooting*. Chicago: Upstart Publishing Co.

Graham, Gina, and John Harrison. *Collection Techniques for a Small Business*. (1994). Oasis Press. 800-228-2275.

National Association of Credit Management. Publishes *Credit Manual of Commercial Laws*. 410-740-5560.

Scolo, James. *Credit and Collection Business Kit*. International Wealth Success. 800-323-0548.

Skar, Leonard. *The Check Is Not in the Mail*. (1991). Baroque. 800-348-1355.

13
Harvesting the Wealth

Why would anyone think about leaving when they've just started or are in the throes of growing their business? Why is it important to have an exit plan at the beginning of a business? To answer these questions, you need to understand the nature of entrepreneurs. A few entrepreneurs stay with their businesses for life, but the majority turn them over to family, professional management, or sell them, so they can go on to do perhaps another venture. For most entrepreneurs it's the excitement of start-up and early growth that keeps them going. They're not interested in management.

But whether you decide to stay with your business or leave it to do something else, at some point you're going to want to tap into the wealth that business has created and remove some or all of your investment and appreciation. If you know at start-up how you intend to "harvest" the rewards of your business, you can make the decisions necessary to get you to that point in the most direct manner possible.

To prepare yourself to build personal wealth through your business, take these few steps.

1. Set up a mini advisory board to guide your personal wealth planning. This group should include an accountant, a tax attorney, and an estate planning specialist. They may actually

be a subset of your company advisory board or board of directors.

2. Find a mentor, someone who has created the lifestyle and degree of wealth you're aspiring to achieve. People who have "made it," who are successful entrepreneurs, love to help up-and-coming entrepreneurs build their success.

3. Focus on the things that will create value for your company over the period prior to harvest. Here are just a few:

- Acquire intellectual property.
- Build a loyal customer base.
- Acquire assets that hold their value.
- Build a successful network of infrastructure people: vendors, suppliers, distributors, salespeople, manufacturers, professional advisers.
- Build a system of incentives and a company culture that will encourage employees to stay on even after you're gone.

There are a variety of ways you can tap into the wealth of your business when the time comes. We'll look at a few of the more common ways to do it.

Going Public

In Chapter 8 you learned about the initial public offering (IPO) as a way to find capital to grow the business. It is also a way to recapture some of your investment. You may structure the deal to pay you a portion of your investment from the funds you receive when the offering is sold. It's probably not wise to take too much of your money out at this point because it sends the wrong signal to stockholders if the founders take their money out just when they're asking others to invest so the business can grow.

Selling the Business

If you want to be totally free of the business, selling it to someone else may be the best choice. You do need to recognize that for the entrepreneur, selling the business is not just a financial event but an emotional one as well. You have spent a good deal of your time, money, and effort in giving birth to this company. You've put the start-up team together, gathered the necessary resources, built the business, hired the employees, and spent day and night growing it. Giving it up is a lot like losing a child. If you haven't prepared for the sale, you could suffer significant emotional consequences. Fortunately, there are several ways to leave the business that allow you to transition out.

Getting Your Cash Out but Keeping a Hand In

Maybe you would like to get your cash out of the business, but still stay involved in some way. There are a couple of things you can do.

1. Sell Your Stock.   If your company is privately owned, you may want to sell your stock to the other shareholders at current market rates if the shareholders' agreement you created when you issued stock allows you to do this. If your company is publicly traded, it's much easier because you can simply sell the stock on the open market.

Having a lot of stock in your public company can mean tremendous wealth for you if you're careful about how you handle it. Remember these two points:

- If you own a substantial portion of the issued stock in your company, you must follow the very strict guidelines from the Securities and Exchange Commission when you decide to sell it. Otherwise, you may face stiff penalties.

- Don't forget that if your company does have a successful IPO, your founder's stock will have increased significantly in value which means a serious tax liability for you. For this reason, many entrepreneurs take out only what they need to meet any goals they have and leave the rest in stock.

2. Restructure the Company.   If you'd like to take a significant amount of money out of your private company and put control in the hands of your children, you can do it by splitting the company in two. You will control the company that contains all of the assets of the original company (plant, equipment, etc.), while the children will own and manage the operating portion of the business and lease the assets from you. This puts the children in charge of the original company and gives you an interest plus an income off the leases.

3. Do a Phased Sale.   You may choose to sell the business to a third party in stages so that you don't have to turn over the reins cold turkey. For example, you may agree to sell the business in two stages. In the first stage you sell a portion of the business but remain in control of the operations and continue to grow the company to the point agreed upon in the sale. At that point, you will sell the remaining portion to the buyer. Since this technique is quite complex, it's wise to use a good attorney.

Merging with Another Company

Joining your company with another has some of the characteristics of a sale and certainly many of the characteristics of a partnership. Depending on how the deal is structured, merging your company with another is a way for you to cash out some of your investment and stay on in a management capacity if you choose, or perhaps just sit on the board of directors of the new company.

For a successful merger, it's important to consider the following:

1. The two companies should have similar cultures; otherwise, when they come together, employees and management alike will have trouble working together. For example, if your company has a more casual culture with high levels of employee participation and input into the business and you merge with a more formal bureaucratic company, there are likely to be disagreements and misunderstandings about how things should be done.

2. The two companies should be complementary in what they do, to where joining them produces a company that is better than either one alone. Merging with a company in another industry is often unsatisfactory.

3. The two companies should be located close to each other geographically to facilitate management.

4. The company with which you are merging should be in a growing industry and market.

Tip

For a successful merger, investigate all aspects of the merger candidate.

Here are some questions to ask about a merger candidate:

1. Why do they want to purchase your company?
2. Are they growing and strong in their industry?
3. Do their financial statements show them to be in a healthy cash position?
4. Do they have a CPA for independent accounting review?
5. Do they have audited tax returns and bank statements for the past five years?
6. What is their sales volume trend?
7. What is the trend for their sales versus expenses?
8. Do they have a business plan?
9. What do bankers think of them?
10. How do their suppliers and customers see the company?

Selling to Your Employees

If your business has more than 25 employees, you can consider doing an option that ends up selling the company to the employees. It's called an employee stock ownership plan, or ESOP, and it lets you cash out of the company but still remain in control for as long as you'd like. An estimated 15,000 U.S. corporations have stock ownership plans. About 20% of the 7,000 publicly traded companies have about 15% of their stock owned by their employees. This trend is more prevalent among private corporations, where 20-40% of their stock is employee owned. The goal of ESOPs is to give employees a greater financial and psychological stake in the success of the business. Here's how it works:

1. You set up an ESOP trust fund into which you put new or existing shares of stock. Alternatively, you can take out a bank loan to buy stock and a minority interest in the company of at least 30 percent so that any cash the owners receive from the ESOP is not taxed if they reinvest it in U.S. stocks or bonds.
2. The company then makes tax-deductible contributions up to 25 percent of the payroll to the trust fund to repay the bank debt.

The ESOP Process

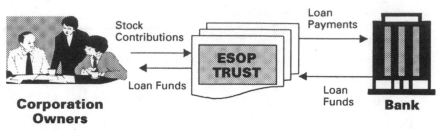

Corporation
Owners

Figure 13-1.

3. The cash-out price for the entrepreneur is the result of the value of the company at the time and negotiation with the ESOP trustee.

4. You should plan for this process to take several years, probably the length of time it takes to repay the bank loan.[1]

The ESOP process is shown graphically in Figure 13-1.

ESOPs are essentially tax-qualified pension plans governed by the Employee Retirement Income Security Act (ERISA) and IRS regulations, and they work if the following is true:

- Your company has revenues of at least $5 million.

- It has an annual payroll of at least $500,000.

- You have assets like inventory, accounts receivable, and equipment that you can use as collateral if you need a bank loan to do the ESOP.

- You have a healthy cash position to repay the ESOP debt and buy back the stock of employees who might leave the company.

Tip

Consider establishing an ESOP.

There are several reasons why ESOPs are popular and should be considered as a way to cash out of the business over time.

---

[1]Allen, Kathleen R. (1995). *Launching New Ventures.* Chicago: Upstart Publishing Co.

1. If you've owned the stock in your company for more than three years, you can reinvest the cash from the sale in other securities and avoid capital gains tax until you sell those securities.

2. If you leave the securities in your estate at death, your heirs will not have to pay a capital gains tax.

3. Your heirs can sell the shares to the ESOP.

4. Your loan interest rates are lower than normal if the ESOP owns 50 percent of the voting stock. This is because the bank can deduct 50 percent of the interest income as an expense under this scenario.

5. The employee shareholders are represented by the ESOP trustee even though they have no voting rights.

ESOPs usually promote a sense of vested interest on the part of employees and so the employees usually perform more productively. Of course, this means that they will also want full disclosure on the operations of the company; so in that sense the company, even if it's private, becomes very much like a public company. An excellent resource from where to learn more about equity-based compensation plans is the Foundation for Entrepreneurial Development in San Diego at 619-551-4981 or in Washington, D.C. at 202-479-2706.

Trap

ESOPs may not be the perfect solution.

On the surface ESOPs appear to be a perfect remedy to the problems entrepreneurs face when they want to cash out of the business. This is because it seems logical to put the company in the hands of the employees and cash out gradually. But the reality is, there are several disadvantages to ESOPs that you should be aware of:

- With an ESOP you can't elect a subchapter S corporation and take advantage of the pass-through option on profits.

- ESOPs are expensive to set up and maintain. Your annual expenses may run over $15,000.

- If you're a private company, you have to repurchase the stock of employees who leave the company.

- When you issue new shares of stock, it dilutes the value of existing shares.

- With an ESOP, you're creating a more open environment and sharing information with a lot more people. As an entrepreneur, you may find this difficult.

Liquidating the Business

Your decision to liquidate your business can come about from a variety of circumstances and for a variety of reasons:

1. You may not choose to sell the business because you don't want anyone else to own it.
2. The business may be a small business in a fragmented industry, so the value is not sufficient to bring a lot of capital beyond the purchase of inventory and equipment.
3. Your business may be in financial trouble and liquidation through a Chapter 7 bankruptcy may be your only option.

Liquidation When There's Little Value

In some industries there's no good way to exit the company and reap the rewards for all your hard work. In these cases, even strong cash flow and good sales don't automatically translate into increased value in the form of a lucrative check to the entrepreneur. Typically what happens is that the buyer purchases just the inventory and assets like equipment and supplies, and the owner is lucky to break even.

One solution to this situation is to do a *reverse merger* where your company ends up being part of a large public shell. A shell is a corporation registered with the SEC but which does no actual business. If you merge with a public shell, you can band with a group of entrepreneurs who have a common goal to eventually gain liquidity by selling stock. After enough small companies are acquired, the shell does a public offering and the small company owners receive proceeds from the sale of their stock. This is a complex solution that requires a good attorney and planning time, but it can result in a much higher valuation for your business at the time of sale.

Liquidation When the Business Can't Survive

Bankruptcy is certainly the last thing that any business owner wants to face. But the reality is that when the business is upside down and there's no conceivable way to save it, bankruptcy may be the only solution to liquidate the assets of the business and discharge most of the debt. Here is the way it works:

- You file a petition under Chapter 7 of the Bankruptcy Code, which constitutes an Order for Relief.

- A trustee is appointed to manage the disposition of the business.

- The goal of the bankruptcy proceedings is to reduce the business to cash and distribute that cash to the creditors in order of priority, first to secured creditors and then to priority claimants. These include (1) administrative expenses related to the bankruptcy; (2) wages, salaries, or commissions; (3) vacation, severance, and sick leave pay up to $2000 per person if earned within 90 days of filing or date of cessation of the business; (4) contributions to employee benefit plans up to $2000 per person and earned within 180 days of filing or cessation, to name just a few.

- Surplus funds remaining after distribution to claimants go to the entrepreneur.

✳ Tip

Plan ahead to avoid bankruptcy.

Here are some things to remember to avoid bankruptcy.

- Don't rely on one major customer or industry for all your revenues.

- Keep your overhead costs to essentials, so that if there's a slump in the market, you're not saddled with high overhead you have to continue to carry.

- Try to keep several months of overhead expense in your account. Liquidity is critical to avoiding bankruptcy.

- Be sure to maintain honest relationships with bankers, creditors, and vendors. Keep them apprised of any cash problems you may encounter and agree to work with them to solve them.

You should know that you have the right to exempt certain property prior to liquidation. If you have a corporation, these exemptions are fairly minimal. You can exempt:

- Interest in any accrued dividends up to $4000
- The right to Social Security benefits, unemployment compensation, public assistance, veterans' benefits, and disability benefits
- The right to stock bonuses, pensions, and profit sharing

Before considering bankruptcy as the final solution to exit a troubled business, seek advice from a specialist in turnarounds in your industry. You should also have your accountant audit your assets and liabilities to see if you can qualify for Chapter 11 reorganization. This would allow you to continue to operate the business while working out a plan to repay creditors. The bottom line is, don't make a quick decision about filing for bankruptcy. The ramifications can stay with you a lifetime.

Trap

Don't try to hide assets when going through bankruptcy court.

If you are in the unfortunate position of having to file Chapter 7 bankruptcy, there are a few things you should *never* do:

- Hide assets or liabilities
- Give preferential treatment to some creditors 90 days prior to filing the bankruptcy petition
- Convey any property fraudulently up to one year prior to the filing of the petition

The court during bankruptcy proceedings may recoup any of the above actions.

Planning for Succession

Succession planning is an important aspect of any business, but it has particular significance in family businesses where it is often assumed that younger generation members of the family will ultimately take over the business some day. It is complicated by complex interrelationships, demands, and expectations that don't challenge a nonfamily business. But considering the fact that 80 percent of all businesses in the United States are family businesses with two or more family members controlling the business, it is clear that this is an issue of some importance.

Problems arise when a family member doesn't have the required expertise or skills to hold the position he or she wants. So, during the first generation of the business it's important to have in place a policy that deals with the potential issues that will arise as new generations enter the business. Some important things to include in this policy would be:

- A fair way of determining that outside talent must be brought into the business to compensate for the lack of skills in a particular area among family members

- A probationary period for new family members that gives them a chance to prove themselves

- Criteria that are the same for family members as for outsiders for compensation and promotion

- All compensation at fair market value

Tip
___
Don't hand the company over to family on a silver platter.

Just because someone's family doesn't mean they're the best choice for the company. Here's some good advice:

- If possible, have family members supervised by a nonfamily person.

- Don't allow a family member to remain at an entry-level position permanently. If they haven't qualified to move up, they need to move out.

- Make it a rule that if a family member wants permanent employment with the company, they need to get five years or more of experience with another company. Working for someone else is quite a different experience from working for family.

Succession Is a Process

Succession planning is not something you do one day and implement the next. Rather, it's a long process that takes place over years, even decades. But it's a process that involves several stages.

Whether the process is described as three or six or seven stages doesn't matter. Essentially a son, daughter, or other family member entering the business will go through a process that generally consists of the following:

1. *Awareness of the business.*   In the beginning of the process the family member becomes aware of the existence of the business, its nature, and his or her potential role in that business. The length of the period of awareness depends on the age of the family member. The younger the person, the longer this period lasts.

2. *Functional awareness.*   As the child reaches the teen years, he or she may be allowed to work part-time in the business to begin to learn more about how it operates and to learn the jargon specific to that business.

3. *Nonmanagerial experience.*   At the appropriate time, usually when schooling is complete and they've had some experience working for someone else, the children may begin work in a full-time position in a nonmanagerial role.

4. *Managerial experience.*   After they have a comprehensive understanding of the functional aspects of the business, they may move into various managerial roles until they have reached the point where they are ready to assume the presidency of the company.

5. *Transition to company leadership.*   In an ideal situation, the transition to the role of president takes about two years, during which time the family member is sharing the role with the president who may be his or her grandfather or grandmother, father or mother, or uncle or aunt.

Succession in Nonfamily Businesses

As the entrepreneur, you need to plan for your own exit from the business by considering whom you want in a successor. Many entrepreneurs leave their companies in the hands of someone else while they go off to start another venture or fulfill another dream. Putting someone in your place who knows the business well and believes in the company's vision will make the transition that much easier on everyone. That's why the most successful companies often promote from within. The advantage of this strategy is the new CEO knows the business inside and out. He or she understands the culture and has bought into the vision. On the other hand, because they've come up through the ranks and are involved deeply in the business, they may not bring a fresh point of view to the situation. You and your board of directors will need to consider the pros and cons carefully.

Transferring Ownership

The succession process culminates with the transfer of ownership of the business. This is not as easy as it sounds in a family business, because typically the owner wants to be fair to all those who stand to inherit. So in the case where, for example, one child is active in the business and the others aren't, giving an equal share to each child immediately makes the active child a minority shareholder against his or her brothers and sisters. This certainly does not benefit the business. A more effective approach may be to give the active child the business and the nonactive children equivalent assets outside the business. Where the nonbusiness assets are less than the business, the nonactive children can be given a promissory note from the active child in an amount that balances the ledger. Involving the heirs in the decision may prevent arguments and lawsuits later that could destroy the business.

Harvesting the wealth of the business is one of the rewards of successful entrepreneurship. Planning for that harvest will help ensure that your company reaches its highest potential.

Resources

ESOP Association, Washington, D.C., 202-293-2971

Foundation for Enterprise Development (1995). *The Entrepreneurs Guide to Equity Compensation:* La Jolla. CA. 619-459-4662.

and The Owners Tool box an Equity Incentives (1997) 1-800-557-4832.

Freidman, Robert. (1993) *Small Business Legal Guide.* Chicago: Dearborn Financial Publishing.

Freiermuth, Edmund P. (1988). *Life After Debt.* Homewood, IL: Dow Jones Irwin.

National Center for Employee Ownership, Oakland, Calif. 510-272-9461.

14
Entrepreneurs and Their Communities

Entrepreneurs Involved in the Community

One need not look any further than the daily newspaper, magazines, or the television news programs to become aware of the great involvement of U.S. entrepreneurs in their communities. However, our government at the local, state, and federal levels regulates how they do business in their communities. All entrepreneurs should address their role in supporting and building their communities, as well as problems inherent in community relationships.

The Social and Political Franchise

First, it's important to realize that America's entrepreneurs exist and are allowed the freedom to do business only by the people and their governments. Many societies prevent and/or discourage entrepreneurial activity. Experience clearly shows that the entrepreneurial activity in a culture is directly related to the attitudes of the people and their governments toward it. Two of the key ingredients are:

1. The Political License
2. The Social Contract

1. The Political License

In some cultures, people are not allowed to have their own businesses. Many governments so stringently regulate and tax private enterprise that entrepreneurship is effectively stifled. Entrepreneurship requires a favorable political climate combined with stable, predictable judicial and financial systems to thrive. Few people care to start a business in a society that has unstable or unpredictable financial or political systems.

Our recent legislative history illustrates the impact of governmental attitudes and legislation upon entrepreneurial activity. Entrepreneurship began flourishing in the early 1980s, partly because of favorable income-tax regulations that stimulated private investment in enterprises through various tax-credit programs and accelerated-depreciation provisions. This situation was suddenly changed in 1986, when Congress changed the tax laws, which greatly discouraged investment in entrepreneurial ventures. No more capital gains. No more tax shelters. No more investment tax credits. Take for example a very successful restaurant that had to close in December of 1996 because Congress prohibited members from accepting expensive meals from lobbyists. The owner struggled for two years to bring the city's powerful expense account crowds back to the wonderful lunches and dinners at Le Mestral, but the customers disappeared and never returned. It is important to realize that an entrepreneur's opportunity to be in business depends on the political climate where they live.

Tip

Entrepreneurs should do everything possible to make their state and community a climate hospitable to starting and growing new ventures.

Do not confuse this with supporting private enterprise. It is quite possible to have a private-enterprise society comprised of huge organizations without any support for entrepreneurs and few incentives to encourage new venture creation.

2. The Social Contract

Underlying the relationship of business with society is an implicit contract between the two. Society grants people the right to do business in exchange for their promise to satisfy society's demands for goods and services. When business fails to satisfy the demands of society, serious conflicts arise. Conversely, when a society restrains entrepreneurial ventures, the supply of needed goods and services is curtailed.

The Entrepreneur's Scope of Concern

The extent of the entrepreneur's interests in social and political affairs is quite broad. It encompasses:

1. Participation in Local Communities
2. Political Activism
3. Economic Well-Being
4. Ethics
5. Personal Life
6. Cultural Success and Religion

Each of these factors is discussed below.

1. Participation in Local Communities

Look around town. Who runs things? Who are the people involved in the multitude of community affairs? The United Way? Little League? Scouting? Churches? Typically, local business people are the backbone of the town. Without their support and involvement, our communities would have an entirely different character. They support by volunteering their time and money to community foundations, nonprofit organizations, and other agencies, often assuming leadership roles. Entrepreneurs share their financial success while helping to strengthen their country. For example, Ted Turner's pledge in September, 1997, of $1 billion—about a third of his current wealth—to the United Nations over the next decade or $100 million a year will be used to clear land mines and support other social causes.

Tip

Become more involved in supporting and contributing your time,

talent, and leadership to your community to share your financial successes and become more socially responsible.

Participation in local communities is a two-way street. It is to the entrepreneur's distinct advantage to do business in a community that is thriving, healthy, and operating smoothly. Sick communities are not good places in which to do business. In the past several years, several business magazines annually list the best communities and support systems for entrepreneurial activity. For example, *Inc. Magazine* features entrepreneurial hot spots (i.e., the best places to do business), which names the best cities with a business-friendly environment to build fast growing companies. *Entrepreneur Magazine,* in conjunction with Dun & Bradstreet Information Services, annually ranks the 30 best cities for small business stating that the key to entrepreneurial success is location, location, location. *Entrepreneur* evaluates the sites on five different categories of risk: business performance, economic growth, quality of life, and state attitude toward small business. Business performance and state attitude toward small business are given extra weight. Below is a chart summarizing *Entrepreneur* magazine's October 1996 ratings of the best cities.

2. Political Activism

The importance of the political climate is shaped by the people who actively participate in the process, which is more than just voting or throwing money into a political campaign. It means spending time in meetings and working on committees, which can be quite frustrating to entrepreneurs who are used to making decisions and taking action.

Trap

If you don't take on an active role in politics, the political system will be taken over by those who, do who may not be your friends, but your enemies.

3. Economic Well-Being

Economic prosperity depends in large part on entrepreneurial activity. The entrepreneur creates jobs, buys things, and makes things happen that provide income, livelihoods, and job stability to many people. Entrepreneurial growth plans directly affect the community and the economy Refer to the chart below from Entrepreneurial Magazine showing the best cities for entrepreneurship. America has and continues to experience the effects of massive corporate restructuring, downsizing, and laying off of staff. The other side of the coin is entrepreneurs creating new jobs and being dedicated to keeping their staff employed. Take the example of worker-exchange programs where entrepreneurs adjust for seasonal fluctuations by placing staff in temporary jobs with other firms for a set period of time during slow periods. This assures job stability for the employee and reduced payroll costs for the owner while keeping trained staff available when needed. This policy creates a climate of trust when staff understands that slow times do not mean job elimination. Keep in mind, if you fail, lay off staff, or close your business, the impact is widely shared. Entrepreneurs are vital cogs in our economy. Without vigorous entrepreneurial activity, the economy lags.

30 BEST CITIES

LARGE CITIES

1. Portland/Vancouver, OR/WA
2. Denver, CO
3. Minneapolis/St.Paul, MN
4. Atlanta, GA
5. Indianapolis, IN
6. Charlotte/Gastonia/ Rock Hill, NC/SC
7. Cincinnati, OH/KY/IN
8. Columbus, OH
9. Pittsburgh, PA
10. St. Louis, MO/IL
11. Chicago, IL
12. Milwaukee/Waukesha, WI
13. Kansas City, MO/KS
14. Cleveland/Lorain/ Elyria, OH
15. Boston, MA

MID-SIZED CITIES

1. Salt Lake City/Ogden, UT
2. Raleigh/Durham/ Chapel Hill, NC
3. Greensboro/Winston-Salem/ High Point, NC
4. Las Vegas, NV/AZ
5. Austin/San Marcos, TX
6. Sarasota/Bradenton, FL
7. Stamford/Norwalk, CT
8. Omaha, NE/IA
9. Richmond/ Petersburg, VA
10. Nashville, TN

SMALL CITIES

1. Reno, NV
2. Colorado Springs, CO
3. Madison, WI
4. Boulder/Longmont, CO
5. Appleton/Oshkosh/ Neenah, WI

4. Ethics

The entrepreneur's ethical code continually affects each and every aspect of the society and business community. Indeed, one of the major reasons our culture has been so economically successful is that, by and large, business people do what they promise to do. They can be trusted. They pay their bills, they perform their contractual obligations, they obey the law, they treat people decently, and they try to behave in ways that result in a better life for everyone. It is difficult to do business in a society in which people do otherwise. Most business is done on trust.

A person without credibility has a difficult time in business. Others don't believe the person and won't do business with him or her. While cynics may snicker at what seems to be our goody-goody attitude, after many years of observation and experience, people who take the short cuts usually end up with disaster. They may look like winners for a short time, but sooner or later an ethical code in conflict with the mores of the culture will catch up with the individual. Most U.S. entrepreneurs believe that high ethical standards and integrity are critical to long-term success.

∗ Tip

Your honor and credibility are reflected in your business decisions. Always be ethical and treat others as you want to be treated and always take the high road.

5. Personal Life

There is much more to life than just business, despite what some dedicated workaholics might have you believe. People do have private lives, activities, and families. The entrepreneur who ignores this reality will pay a price, often a high one, in terms of broken families, unsatisfactory personal relationships, and unhappiness. The old dictum, "All things in moderation!" comes to mind.

Tip

Balance your business life, social life, personal life, and family commitments.

Take the example of Jack Stack, president of Springfield Remanufacturing Center Corp. in Springfield, MO, who turned the company into one of the best performing ventures in America. Stack headed a small group of employees who purchased SRC International Harvester, its parent company in 1983. As a subsidiary of IH, the remanufacturing operation had been losing money. Stack, convinced the numbers could be turned around by involving everyone in the company, turned the entire enterprise into The Great Game of Business and wrote a book, published by Doubleday Currency, about how he turned his company around using open book management techniques. Bonuses, promotions, and contributions to the employee stock ownership plan are the tangible results of a very successful company.

However, after the buyout, the pressures got to Jack who tells the story that he couldn't eat or sleep. He called a doctor who told him he had either Lou Gehrig's disease or multiple sclerosis. He went for a second opinion, and the next doctor said it was stress. He took up bass fishing as a hobby and today is a pro bass fishing professional. He tries hard to balance his hectic life as CEO of SRC, decentralizing his existing business by breaking it into smaller units that can be run as separate companies with spending more time with family, friends, and fishing.

6. Cultural Success and Religion

Entrepreneurs are very much a part of the culture. In the scheme, the American culture is very entrepreneurial. America had to be since it was founded by a variety of people who all had one thing in common. They were fleeing some large institution elsewhere: a displeased king, an oppressive government, an onerous church, prison, pauperism, whatever. One does not come to a wilderness from a relatively prosperous society without forceful reasons. So here they found themselves without any institutions to support them. If the pioneers were to survive, they had to do it themselves. It was up to them. Desperation has and continues to encourage many entrepreneurs. Just look at all the victims of corporate downsizing and layoffs who have become entrepreneurs. It is not surprising that America is the home of the entrepreneurial movement; it's our heritage.

In contrast, some cultures with strong caste systems greatly discourage entrepreneurship in that they remove an extremely important factor from the entrepreneurial equation: the incentive to launch and grow new ventures. If you are not allowed to advance yourself socially through economic skills, then why bother trying?

The Company Culture

Much has been written about corporate cultures, largely in reference to living and working in large organizations. However, working cultures exist everywhere, especially in entrepreneurial enterprises both large and small. Indeed, the culture you create in your venture greatly affects its attractiveness to employees. Many people greatly prefer working for smaller companies, where they can have direct personal relationships with the boss. They often like having to do many things and not having to be a small cog in a big machine. The working environment you create significantly affects everyone's satisfaction in life.

Tip

A strong entrepreneurial climate attracts and encourages entrepreneurial achievers and helps perpetuate the intensity and pace of successful ventures.

Environmental Restraints

Certainly the environmental movement must rank as one of the top forces at work in our society and economy today. It will not abate. Indeed, the next decade will see even more legislation regulating what firms can and cannot do in matters that somehow affect the environment.

Tip

Environmental constraints and regulations are expensive. Factor their costs into your overhead expenses.

Such regulations are expensive and can drive many entrepreneurs out of business who are unable to afford the changes demanded of them by the environmentalists or governmental regulations.

Yet, these same environmental concerns offer alert entrepreneurs opportunities for new ventures. Waste management, toxic cleanup, and asbestos removal are big businesses and will become even more so. The firm that can solve a toxic-waste problem will likely reap big dividends.

More importantly, the alert entrepreneur does not wait until the environmental axe falls to alter operations but anticipates the developments. Many firms have already moved operations from certain areas that are known to be extra sensitive to environmental concerns. One manufacturer of wire shelves sold to retail stores anticipated the regulation of their painting operations and installed a dry-powder process that emits no vapors or toxins.

Economic Constraints

The economy and the firm are obviously closely interrelated. Yet that does not mean that they vary with each other. Many enterprises prosper during times of economic distress and chaos. Nonetheless, the entrepreneur must understand the constraints that the economy is placing on the firm. If money is tight and costly, then the firm's financial planning must recognize that constraint. If costs are rising, close watch must be kept on pricing, and purchasing might want to buy in anticipation of higher prices.

Common Business Problems

Certain business problems are so commonly encountered by entrepreneurs and are so serious that special mention of them needs to be made. The problems, if improperly handled or ignored, can destroy the entrepreneur. The most common problems include:

1. Conflicts of Interest
2. Desperation or Survival
3. Associates and Peer Pressure
4. Legal Roulette

Each of these common problems is discussed below.

1. Conflicts of Interest

One of the most pervasive problems in business and our government is that of conflict of interest. People have vested interests in many things: their careers, the fortunes of the firm for which they work, the welfare of their family, their personal lifestyle, their investments, and their community. It would be nice if all these interests were in harmony, but they aren't.

You are often asked to do things that are in conflict with some of your interests. You may be asked by some sales rep to buy something that would benefit your employer but would jeopardize your career. What do you do? If you buy that new computer system, you may have just put yourself out of a job.

You ask your employees to work at night for the benefit of the firm. They need to be at home for family commitments.

Conflict! It is in the interest of the community's environment that you stop all painting in your plant. If you do so, many people will be out of a job, and your costs will rise.

Conflict! You want to be paid more money as the firm's president. The directors want to receive more dividends.

Conflict! This litany could go on for some time, but the point is that just about every decision you will have to make in some way involves a conflict of interests. Usually, those interests can be easily resolved.

Sometimes they cannot be resolved at all. Often they cost money one way or another. The adept business person learns to recognize the conflicts of interest inherent in any situation and tries to allow for them in some way. It is the hidden conflicts that usually cause the most trouble. You hire an outstanding person as your marketing manager, not knowing that the person is planning to start his or her own firm to compete with yours when ready.

Tip

Recognize inherent business conflicts and weigh each side of the issue and look for creative solutions.

For example, today, employers are being challenged to accommodate the personal and medical leave needs of their staff and to develop new policies to help their employees balance work and family obligations. One way to help employees balance work and non-work demands is by developing alternative schedule arrangements such as part-time work, job-sharing, flexible work schedules, work-at-home arrangements, or compressed work weeks. Develop policies that provide educational support and career development opportunities. Provide initiatives to help employees advance their education and their careers through internships. Assign mentors on your team to work with new staff. Try instituting flexible work policies.

2. Desperation or Survival

Entrepreneurs have been known to do a lot of things they would have preferred not to do just to survive. Desperation fathers many illegitimate offspring. People who would have never considered cheating a creditor out of money may do just that if it seems to be the only way to save the enterprise. It has been observed that one's ethics are unknown until tested. It is easy to be honest if one has no need to be crooked. Starve for a while, and then you'll know your ethical code.

There are times in your entrepreneurial career when you are desperate. You are hurting. You owe money and can't pay it. You may lose your home, your family, your self-respect. This is when the entrepreneur's ethics code needs to be strong and undaunted.

3. Associates and Peer Pressure

You will be subject to many pressures to do things that either you don't want to do or shouldn't do. Your associates want big bonuses; you know the firm needs the cash for expansion. Who gets the money? The firm or your associates? All sorts of players around you are urging you to take your company public, sell stock, and establish a market price for your paper. Your lawyers think it's a good idea. There's an investment banker who is pushing it. Your outside investors want it. Yet down deep you just don't want to operate as a public company. Real conflicts push and pull you every which way.

4. Legal Roulette

In most instances, there are gray areas in the law in which one can operate and probably get away with it. Income-tax-compliance policies are perhaps the most common illustration of trying to walk a line that isn't clearly illegal. However, such legal dilemmas are far more prevalent than just taxes. How do you want to play it? Close or safe? Even if you think you're safe, you may have some surprises coming. Many entrepreneurs don't want to play games with the law. They feel that they have better things to do. Others seem to delight in pushing the law as far as they can, and some of them can push it mighty far.

An editorial observation: experience seems to indicate that the people who push their operations into legal twilight zones, so to speak, sooner or later run into serious trouble and lose their enterprises. The entrepreneurs who play it safe seem to sleep well at night and, in the end, do rather well without all the legal hassles.

However, it must be admitted that there are many entrepreneurs who worked long and hard running their business strictly according to the rules and still, for one reason or another, encountered serious legal difficulties not of their doing. This is mentioned only as a warning to entrepreneurs who feel secure because they know they have not violated any laws that they still should be vigilant of any potential or looming legal difficulties. It may not be enough just to be passively safe, sitting in your office, knowing that you are operating legally. You may have to aggressively protect yourself from legal attacks by people with their own agendas—your competitors, for example.

One large water-meter-repair company that was operating within the law was set up by a competitor in collusion with a newspaper reporter on charges of bribing public officials. It caused no end of trouble and hurt the company severely. Sharp legal counterattacks were necessary.

Social Responsibility

Most entrepreneurs are passionately motivated to share their successes and wealth by giving back and supporting their communities and society as a whole. Most are socially responsible and don't operate their businesses in a vacuum. The rule of social responsibility stems from the value system of the founder and the corporate culture that he or she creates by recognizing the company's socially reflective role in the community.

∗ Trap

Socially responsible business practices will fail if they are just add-ons to established business practices.

They must be fully integrated into the corporate cultures to be accepted and practiced.

Social responsibility blends business practices into a socially reflective and responsive business culture that thrives with the attention and support of the founder and top management. Most all entrepreneurs are socially minded business leaders who try to create an ethically motivated workplace. They are committed to improving their workplace, employee productivity, and retention, thus increasing customer good will while strengthening their community. They use their entrepreneurial creativity to fill market niches while addressing social needs and implementing socially responsible business practices. Take Bob Haas, Chairman of the Board and CEO of Levi-Strauss & Company, who speaks about the importance of corporate social responsibility and community service. He is proud to proclaim that these values have been imbued in the company since its founding by Levi-Strauss himself, and the company is currently recognized as one of the best companies for which to work in America. Bob states that corporations are not separate legal entities, but part of a broader community. He says that unless Levi-Strauss participates actively in nurturing the community and assisting people in it to deal with their problems, which are the same problems of his employees, customers, and suppliers, neither the company nor society can be successful.

Therefore, the entrepreneur has far more to think about than how to make and sell his or her wares. There are a plethora of social, cultural, and legal relationships that require attention. One does not operate a venture in a vacuum. There are all sorts of people, issues, and environmental challenges that require serious consideration. In summary, entrepreneurs are doing more than creating jobs and making profits. Every day their decisions test their moral integrity. Most are concerned about giving something back through a variety of community aid programs, supporting the arts, being responsible about pollution they create in the production process, creating internships, acting as mentors, and a variety of other activities. Take the example of millionaire Scott Oki, who retired at the age of 42 after a 10-year stint at Microsoft, to create his Nanny and Webster baby-blanket business combining entrepreneurship and philanthropy. A local Seattle manufacturer sews the blankets, then uses a sheltered workshop that employs disabled people to assemble and package the blankets. One hundred percent of the gross profits go to children's charities. Oki spends most of his entrepreneurial energies giving back to the community and encouraging other founders to incorporate community giving into their own mission statements.

A number of successful businesses like the Body Shop, Ben & Jerry's, Smith & Hawkins, and Starbucks Coffee don't promote their brand names as much as featuring the philosophies of their business, which are at the core of all their products. This marketing strategy differentiates them from others and creates ways to increase customer and employee loyalty as illustrated by Anima Roddick's Body Shop. Their entrepreneurial spirit and strategy reflects a commitment to social responsibility by establishing trade agreements with underdeveloped countries to bring raw materials to the commercial markets in the form of natural skin care products. She demonstrates the philosophy of her business by using inexpensive, recyclable containers and packages and sells products whose origins lie in nature.

Creative Ways of Giving Back

Many entrepreneurs find creative ways to give back to their communities and satisfy employees by allowing them to continue their social responsibility at work through volunteering. Some firms treat volunteer work as an employee perk. For example, Wild Oats Market, Inc., a health food grocery store based in Boulder, CO, makes sure its employees experience a "charity work benefit." Wild Oats pays 1 hour of charity work time for every hour of company time. In another part of the program, each of the 50 stores provides publicity and 5 percent of one day's sales to a different local charity group each month.

Another approach is using your staff's skills to fill a local need, which is what Abby Margalith, owner of the Starving Students of San Diego moving company did. Over the past 10 years, Starving Students has helped relocate more than 100 women and children from abusive homes. Margalith started small and got help. A local YMCA handles most of the up-front work, while her staff, which varies between 25 and 65 employees, helps coordinate.

Or, take the example of young Colorado billionaire, Kenneth Tuchman, CEO of TeleTech, who built a very successful telemarketing company. TeleTech started with four employees operating out of an abandoned nursery school in Encino, California. Under Tuchman's leadership, he built it to act as a customer-relations phone bank for large corporations that don't have the resources or staff to answer their own customer calls about products. In 1996, the company headquarters in Denver, Colorado occupies three floors of a downtown skyscraper, boasts annual revenues of $150 million and 6400 employees, including 2000 in metro Denver. Tuchman intends for TeleTech to become more philanthropic than it already is by establishing a foundation to give back in big ways to the community. Tuchman feels that it is a corporation's responsibility to be part of the fabric of the community and he plans on doing that with his company.

Tip

Look for innovative ways to build your company and your community, showing you truly care. Lead by example.

Lead by example the way Ewing Marion Kauffman did. A remarkably successful entrepreneur, Mr. Kauffman founded Marion Laboratories. When it merged with Merrell Dow in 1992, the company was valued at about $6.5 billion. His experience with Marion Laboratories as a force and major employer in the Kansas City community convinced him of the importance of entrepreneurship and job creation. Marion Laboratories provided Ewing Kauffman immense wealth; baseball provided him great pleasure; but philanthropy provided him the most joy and the opportunity to give back. So, he created the Ewing Marion Kauffman Foundation to assist others in reaching the goals of self-sufficiency in healthy communities.

Today, the Foundation, with and endowment valued at more than $1 billion, is based in Kansas City, Missouri, and focuses on youth development and entrepreneurship because it was based on the belief that social reform an economic opportunity are inseparable. The Center for Entrepreneurial Leadership Inc., a not-for-profit education institution funded by the Foundation, nurtures and encourages entrepreneurial leadership. The Center was founded on the belief that entrepreneurs are key to job creation and economic growth. [Through entrepreneurship education for adults and young people, an applied research agenda, and assistance to the systems, which support entrepreneurs, the Center encourages entrepreneurs and entrepreneurship in America.] This is one of the major foundations in America that is building on Mr. Kauffman's legacy of entrepreneurial spirit to give back to others in the community and share his wealth.

Other ways new ventures make a difference in their communities is by donating a product or service. James Blackman, Executive

Producer of the Civic Light Opera of South Bay Cities, a very successful non-profit theater company in Southern California,
donates evenings of theater to physically challenged children and
children from the inner city so they can enjoy something they've
never experienced before. Saint Louis Bread Company gives
bread, muffins, and other bakery products to the homeless to the
annual tune of $700,000 retail.

Rhino Records of Santa Monica, California, is teaching their
employees to be more philanthropic by giving employees who contribute 16 hours of personal time per year to community service a
week off at Christmas time with pay. Another example is Just
Desserts in San Francisco, who put a group of 35 businesses together to adopt an elementary school and refurbish the rooms, which
has resulted in an improved learning environment for the students.
And, there are thousands of other socially responsible examples.

Not only are entrepreneurial firms becoming more socially
responsible and making a difference in their communities, but so
are the new leaders of tomorrow's companies. Over the past couple of years, an increasing number of students at top business
schools say they want a career that involves a high level of social
responsibility. The signs of growing campus altruism are increasingly apparent. Take the most active organization at the University
of Chicago business school, The Giving Something Back Club.
This club is involved in everything from tutoring poor students to
collecting toys for tots. A table full of Kellogg (Northwestern
University) students foresees an ideal future that combines running a successful small business half the year and doing good
works, like teaching in a school for the blind, the rest of the year.

Conclusion

There's a new breed of entrepreneurial philanthropy infiltrating
new firms, which will result in a win-win situation for everyone as
entrepreneurs create constructive solutions to critical societal
problems. Entrepreneurs are discovering more ways to launch
and grow new ventures while becoming more socially responsible, thus leading their organizations by example, sharing their
wealth, and teaching others how to do the same.

Index

Accountants, 86, 87
Accounts receivables, 235, 237, 238
Advertising, 191, 192
Advisory board, 90, 91, 245
Agile web, 109, 150
Agility Forum, 229
Alternative schedule arrangements, 268
Amy's Ice Creams, 196
Anchor store, 79
Angel network, 139, 140
Annual Statement Studies, 104
Association of Venture Clubs, 140
Attorneys, 82–86
Autopsy Post Services, 185

Bankruptcy, 252–254
Bar coding, 224
Bean, Leon Leonwood, 42
Beckloff, Mark, 23
Biotechnology, 13, 14
Blackman, James, 274
Blue-sky laws, 175
Board of directors, 88–90
Body Shop, 272
Bonds, 132, 133
Bonuses, 205, 211
Bootstrapping, 112, 113
Brand name, 192
Brand Names: Who Owns What, 76
Bridge financing, 178, 179, 238
Business angels, 139, 140
Business brokers, 101
Business conflicts, 268, 269
Business consultants, 87, 88
Business location, 76–82, 262, 263
Business name, 74–76, 181, 182
Business Opportunity Journal, The, 100
Business Planning Guide, 35

Business plans, 30–37, 53, 54
Business strategy, 46–50
Buy-sell agreements, 62, 63
Buying existing business (*see* Existing business, buying)

C corporation, 59
Campus altruism, 274
Capital Institute, 140
Capitol Concierge, 215
Cash budget, 237
Cash flow, 231–243
    accounts receivables, 235, 237, 238
    cash budget, 237
    collections, 240–242
    forecasting revenues/expenses, 232–235
    resources, 242, 243
    short-term financing, 238–240
    trade payables, 242, 243
Cash-need analysis, 235–237
Center for Creative Leadership, 25
Center for Entrepreneurial Leadership Inc., 273
Certified public accountant (CPA), 86, 87
Charity work, 272–274
Checklists:
    business issues, 49, 50
    buying a business, 106
    personal issues, 44–46
    product/service promotion, 191, 192
Child-care ventures, 18
Children's products/services, 19, 20
Choosing and Using A Consultant, 88
Cities, best, 262, 263
Clawback provision, 177
Clubs/memberships, 187
Collateral, 125, 126
Collections, 240–242

Commerce finance companies, 135
Commercial paper, 240
Commercial real estate company, 79
Common business problems, 267–270
Community involvement, 257–274
  entrepreneurial philanthropy, 272–274
  environmental concerns, 266, 267
  ethics, 264
  participation in local communities, 261,
    262
  political activism, 262
  scope of concern, 261–266
  social responsibility, 270–274
  volunteering, 272
Company effectiveness, 215–230
  continuous improvement, 221, 222
  inventory processes, 222–226
  manufacturing, 217–221
  resources, 229, 230
  shrinkage, 227–229
  trade area, 226, 227
  walking tour of business, 216, 217
Company name, 74–76, 181, 182
Complaint marketing, 187
Complete Book of Corporate Forms, The, 84
Complete Copyright Protection Kit, The, 69
Computer-integrated manufacturing
  (CIM), 219
Conflicts of interest, 267–269
Consultants, 87, 88
Contests, 184
Continuous improvement, 221, 222
Copyrights, 69, 70
Core values, 198, 199
Corporate culture, 196, 197, 266
Corporations, 57–60
Cost of goods sold (COGS), 233
Couponing, 184
Creating Effective Boards for Private Enterprise,
  90
Creative idea sources, 26–30
Credit cards, 138, 139
Credit policy, 241
Credit unions, 135
Customer relationships:
  brand name, 192
  business name, 181, 182
  clubs/memberships, 187
  complaint marketing, 187
  coupons/contests, 184
  database marketing, 182, 183
  frequency programs, 187

Customer relationships (*Cont.*):
  good/bad customers, 188
  just-in-time marketing, 187
  market research, 191
  marketing plan, 188–190
  pricing, 193, 194
  product/service promotion checklist, 191,
    192
  promotional plan, 190, 191
  publicity, 184, 185
  relationship marketing, 185–188
  resources, 194
  yellow pages, 184
Cutuli, Jessica, 182

Database marketing, 182, 183
Dealerships, 154
Debt financing, 125–136
Delaware, 76
Demographic changes, 26, 27
Desperation, 269
Direct loans, 125–127
Disabled entrepreneurs, 11
Do It Yourself Incorporation Kit, 59
Domain names, 163
Double taxation, 59
Due diligence, 102, 103
*Dun & Bradstreet's Reference Book of Corporate
  Management*, 73
Dye, Dan, 23

E-mail, 158
Economic constraints, 267
Elder-care ventures, 18
Electronic data interchange (EDI), 224
Emerson, Ralph Waldo, 53
Employee management company, 116, 117
Employee stock ownership plan (ESOP),
  249–251
Employees, 195–213
  alternative schedule arrangements, 268
  bonuses, 205, 211
  commitment to satisfying customer, 202,
    203
  compensation, 205, 211–213
  empowerment, 203
  human resource policy, 204
  independent contractors, distinguished,
    116
  job interview, 206–208

Employees (*Cont.*):
  lawsuits, 210, 211
  leasing, 116, 117
  noncash rewards/incentives, 213
  open-book management, 204, 205
  recruiting/hiring, 205–209
  references, 207
  resources, 213
  r,sum,s, 208, 209
  selling business to, 249–251
  temporary, 209
  theft by, 228
  worker exchange programs, 263
Engineers, 220
Entrepreneur Magazine, 262
Entrepreneur's Planning Handbook, The, 34
Entrepreneurial opportunities (*see* Venture
  opportunities)
Entrepreneurial philanthropy, 272–274
Entrepreneurial trends, 1–12
Entrepreneurial trends resource guide, 37, 38
Environmental concerns, 266, 267
Equity financing, 136–140
Equity kicker, 177
ESOP, 249–251
ESOP Association, 257
Ethics, 264
  (*See also* Legal roulette, Social responsi-
    bility)
Ethnic products, 20, 21
Ewing Marion Kauffman Foundation, 273
Existing business, buying, 93–106
  advantages, 94–97
  buying vs. start-up venture, 93, 94
  checklist, 106
  disadvantages, 97–99
  due diligence, 102, 103
  evaluating the business, 103–105
  finding right business, 99–102
  growth strategy, as, 157, 158
  negotiating the deal, 106
  pitfalls to avoid, 106
Exit plans (*see* Harvesting the wealth)
Export readiness, 6

Factor, 130
Factoring, 130–132
Factoring accounts receivable, 235
Failure, 54
Fair Debt Collection Practices Act, 240, 241
Family balancing strategies, 50, 51

Family business, succession planning, 247,
  248, 254–257
Family members, hiring, 51, 52
Family money, 137
Feasibility plan, 31, 32
Financing, 123–146
  angels (private investors), 139, 140
  bonds, 132, 133
  bridge, 178, 179, 238
  commerce finance companies, 135
  credit cards, 138, 139
  credit unions, 135
  debt, 125–136
  debt vs. equity, 123
  direct loans, 125–127
  equity, 136–140
  factoring, 130–132
  factors to consider, 141–146
  family money, 137
  government programs, 127–129
  hard-asset lenders, 135, 136
  ideal capital structure, 124
  IPOs, 171–174
  leasing, 130
  mezzanine, 176–178
  money lenders, 133, 134
  private placements, 174–176
  retained earnings, 179
  S&L associations, 134, 135
  SCOR, 176
  short-term, 238–240
  suppliers, 129, 130
  venture capitalists, 167–171
Finding Private Venture Capital for Your Firm,
  140
First National Bank of Maryland, 100
Fitness and health venture opportunities,
  16, 17
Flash Facts, 164
Forecasting revenues/expenses, 232–235
Form of organization, 55–62
Francese, Peter, 27
Franchising, 7–9, 154–157
*Free Money From the Federal Government For
  Small
  Businesses and Entrepreneurs*, 129
Frellick, Von, 44
Frequency programs, 187

General and administrative expenses
  (G&A), 234

General Electric, 218
General Information Concerning Patents, 64
General Information Concerning Trademarks,
    69
General partnership, 57
Giving Something Back Club, 274
Globalization, 4–7, 158–161
Going public, 171–174, 246
Gorman, Leon, 42
Government financing, 127–129
Great Game of Business, The, 205
Growth strategies, 147–165
    buying existing business, 157
    franchising, 154–157
    globalization, 158–161
    Internet, 159, 161–164
    licensing, 151–154
    networking, 150, 151
    resources, 164, 165
    what not to do, 157, 158
Guerrilla Financing, 140
Guerrilla marketing, 182

Haas, Bob, 271
Hard-asset lenders, 135, 136
Hard costs, 232
Harvesting the wealth, 245–257
    bankruptcy, 252–254
    family businesses, 247, 248, 254–257
    going public, 246
    liquidation, 252
    mergers, 248, 249
    preparation, 245, 246
    selling the business, 246–248
    selling to employees (ESOP), 249–251
    succession planning, 254–257
Hearst, William Randolph, 41
Herrera, Vidal, 185
Hiring family members, 51, 52
Home-based businesses, 2, 11, 119–121
Home health services, 19
Home office products/services, 21
*How to Finance Your Small Business with
    Government
Money*, 127
*How to Leave Your Job & Buy a Business of
    Your Own*, 103
How to Prepare and Present a Business Plan, 35
Hughes, Howard, 41
Huizenga, Wayne, 157
Human resource policy, 204

IBEX, 160, 164
Inc. Magazine, 262
Income-repayment loan, 145
Independent contractors, 114–116
Indulgence goods, 17, 18
Information services, 3
Initial public offerings (IPOs), 171–174, 246
Intellectual property rights, 64–73
*Internal Revenue Service Publication 589 - Tax
    Information
on S Corporations*, 60
International Association of Business
    Brokers, 101
International Business, 5
International Business Exchange (IBEX),
    160, 164
International receivables, 237, 238
*International Statistics Yearbook of the United
    States*, 159
Internet:
    advertising, 192
    growth strategy, 159, 161–164
    venture opportunities, 14, 15
Internet service providers (ISPs), 164
Invention marketing companies, 71–73
Inventions, 64–67
Inventory costs, 225
Inventory processes, 222–226
    (*See also* Shrinkage)
Inventory tracking methods, 224
Inventory turnover, 225, 226

Job interview, 206–208
Just Desserts, 274
Just-in-time delivery (JIT), 220
Just-in-time marketing, 187

Kaiser, Leeland, 13
Kaizen, 221
Kaplan Educational Centers, 163
Kauffman, Ewing Marion, 273
Key-person insurance, 63, 64

L.L. Bean, 42
Launching New Ventures, 35
Lauren, Ralph, 47
Law of the landlord, 80
Lawyers, 82–86
Leasing, 130

Legal roulette, 269, 270
Legal strategy, 48
Legal structure, 55–62
Levinson, Jay Conrad, 185
Licensing, 151–154
Licensing agreement, 73, 74
Lifelong customer relationships, 188
Limited liability company (LLC), 60–62
Limited partnership, 57
Line of credit, 239
Liquidation, 252
Location of business, 76–82, 262, 263
Lockup agreement, 171

Manufacturing, 217–221, 233
Manufacturing Assistance Program, 229
Manufacturing Extension Partnership, 229
Market intelligence, 29
Market research, 191
Marketing plan, 188–190
Markulla, Mike, 40
Mentor, 246
Mergers, 248, 249
MESBICs, 129
Mezzanine financing, 176–178
Miller, Amy, 196
Minority enterprise small business investment companies (MESBICs), 129
Minority-owned firms, 11, 12
Mission, 200
Modular strategy, 150
Money finders, 133, 134

National Association of Credit Management, 243
National Association of State Development agencies, 129
National Center for Employee Ownership, 257
National Factoring Services, Inc., 132
Networked company, 109, 110
Networked databases, 159
Networking, 150, 151

Off-balance-sheet financing, 130
Offering memorandum, 175
Oki, Scott, 271

100 Ways to Cut Legal Fees & Manage Your Lawyer, 84
One-of-a-kind stores, 24
Open-book management (OBM), 204, 205
Open-Book Management: The Coming Business Revolution, 205
Opportunities:
  creative idea sources, 26–30
  recognizing, 25, 26
  venture (see Venture opportunities)
Ordering on an as-needed basis, 224
Outsourcing, 3, 112, 113

Pac Man strategy, 157
Partnership agreement, 119
Partnerships, 56, 57, 118, 119
Patent It Yourself, 64
Patents, 64–67
PDCA, 221, 222
Peer pressure, 269
Pelco, 215
People-watching, 27, 28
Personal attitudes/values, 43, 44
Personal errand and shopping services, 25
Personal guaranty, 126, 127
Personal issues, 39–54
  checklist, 44–46
  effect of business on personal life, 41–44
  family issues, 50–52
  reasons for starting new businesses, 40, 41
  risk tolerance, 52–54
  (See also Community involvement)
Personal selling, 192
Pet pampering, 22–24
Philanthropy, 272–274
Pledging accounts receivable, 235
Point of purchase (POP) systems, 224
Political activism, 262
Political license, 260
Pricing, 193, 194
Private investors, 139, 140
Private placements, 174–176
Product franchises, 154
Promotional plan, 190, 191
Publicity, 184, 185, 192
Purchasing, 223
Purpose, 199, 200

R&D limited partnership, 118
Relationship marketing, 185–188

Renting, 80, 81
R,sum,s, 208, 209
Retail boutiques, 24
Retained earnings, 179
Retirees/seniors, 10, 11
Reverse merger, 252
Revolving line of credit, 239
Rhino Records, 274
Risk tolerance, 52–54
RJR Nabisco, 123
Robert Morris Studies, 35
Rogers, John, 108

S corporations, 59, 60
Safe Harbor Law (Revenue Act of 1978),
    114, 115
Saint Louis Bread Company, 274
Satellite systems, 159
Savings and loan associations, 134, 135
SBA, 88, 101, 128, 240
SBA CAPLine credit program, 240
SBDC, 101
SBIC, 129
SCOR U-7, 176
Secured short-term financing, 239
Selling the business, 246–248
Selling to your employees, 249–251
Seniors/retirees, 10, 11
Service franchises, 154
7 A asset loan program, 128
Sharper Image, 3
Shoot-out clause, 62
Shoplifting, 227–229
Short-term financing, 238–240
Shrinkage, 227–229
SITC codes, 160
Small Business Administration (SBA), 88,
    101, 128, 240
Small Business Development Center
    (SBDC), 101
Small business investment company (SBIC),
    129
Small corporate offering registration
    (SCOR), 176
Smart, Todd, 157
Smart appliances, 21, 22
Social contract, 260, 261
Social responsibility, 270–274
Soft costs, 232
Sole proprietorship, 55, 56
Stack, Jack, 264, 265

Standardized forms, 84
Start-up resources (*see* Financing)
Start-up venture, 93
Starting a Business After 50, 11
State of incorporation, 76
Stock appreciation grants, 213
Stock appreciation rights, 213
Stock options, 213
Stock purchases, 213
Strategic alliances, 3, 4, 117–119
Subcontractors, 111
Success trap, 150
Succession planning, 254–257
Suppliers, 130, 223, 242, 243

Tax strategy, 49
Technology, 158, 159
Telecommuters, 21
Teleconferencing, 159
Temporary employees, 209
Term sheet, 171
Texas Instruments, 43
Thomas Register of American Manufacturers,
    73, 75
Three Dog Bakery, 22–24
Three group price method, 224
TLC, 108
Total quality management (TQM), 201,
    202
Trade area, 78, 226
Trade-area map, 227
Trade discounts, 242
Trade Information Center, 5, 165
Trade Names Dictionary, 75
Trade payables, 242, 243
Trade secrets, 70, 71
Trademarks, 67–69
TradeNet, 165
Trading area, 78, 226
Traffic patterns, 78
Training and development venture oppor-
    tunities, 15, 16
Trend-spotting techniques, 28
Tuchman, Kenneth, 272, 273
Turner, Ted, 41, 261
Two-bin system, 224

Unexpected successes/failures, 27
Unsecured bank (signature) loan, 125,
    239

Vendor discounts, 242
Vendors, 130, 223, 242, 243
Venture capital clubs, 140
Venture Capital Network, 140
Venture capitalists, 167–171
Venture opportunities, 12, 13
  biotechnology, 13, 14
  child/elder care, 18
  children's products/services, 19, 20
  ethnic products, 20, 21
  fitness and health, 16, 17
  home health services, 19
  home office products/services, 21
  indulgence goods, 17, 18
  Internet, 14, 15
  personal shopping/errand service, 25
  pet pampering, 22–24
  retail boutiques, 24
  smart appliances, 21, 22
  training and development, 15, 16
Videoconferencing, 159
Virtual companies:
  bootstrapping, 112, 113
  contract, 113, 114
  home-based businesses, 119–121

Virtual companies (*Cont.*):
  independent contractors, 114–116
  leasing employees, 116, 117
  networked companies, 109, 110
  outsourcing, 112, 113
  strategic alliances, 117–119
  subcontractors, 111
  what are they, 107–109
  when not appropriate, 111, 112
Vision, 197–200
Voice mail, 159
Volunteering, 272

Walking tour of business, 216, 217, 232
Weyerhaeuser, 47, 48
Wild Oats Market, Inc., 272
Women-owned firms, 11, 12
Worker-exchange programs, 263

Yellow Pages, 184

Zimmerman, Wes, 195

About the Authors

COURTNEY PRICE is an internationally recognized entrepreneur, writer, lecturer, and consultant, as well as president of the Entrepreneurial Education Foundation in Denver which disseminates the acclaimed Premier Fast Trac® entrepreneurial training program world-wide. She is the author of *Courtney Price Answers the Most Asked Questions from Entrepreneurs,* and writes her own syndicated column, "Entrepreneurs Ask."

KATHLEEN ALLEN is a noted authority on small business and technology and is the author of *Entrepreneurship and Small Business Management, Launching New Ventures,* and *Growing and Managing Entrepreneurial Businesses,* as well as many articles for popular business magazines and newspapers. As a professor of entrepreneurship at the Entrepreneur Program of the Marshall School of Business at the University of Southern California, she helps hundreds of young entrepreneurs start new ventures. (http:/entrepreneur.use.edu) Dr. Allen is also the co-founder of Gentech Corporation, a manufacturer of intelligent power source machines.